TEACHING SINGING

by

John Carroll Burgin

The Scarecrow Press, Inc.
Metuchen, N. J.   1973

Library of Congress Cataloging in Publication Data

Burgin, John Carroll.
    Teaching singing.

    Bibliography: p.
    1. Singing--Instruction and study. I. Title.
MT820.B94   784.9'32   72-10594
ISBN 0-8108-0565-0

To my wife, Emily

and our sons,

Jackie, Jimmy and Jeffrey

ACKNOWLEDGMENTS

It is a pleasant duty to express gratitude for the help I have received from many persons during the preparation of this book. I extend my sincere thanks to all of them.

Appreciation is especially expressed to Dr. Victor Alexander Fields, whose former investigation provided a basic structure for this document, and who graciously gave his permission for this undertaking, his friendly interest as the work progressed and his encouraging response to the completed manuscript.

To Louis Nicholas, Professor of Music, George Peabody College for Teachers, I owe a very special acknowledgment for providing the initial idea for this work and for generously giving me the benefit of most valuable recommendations during its preparation. Dr. Charles Ball and Dr. Ida Long Rogers, also of George Peabody College, have given helpful advice, support and encouragement.

I gratefully recall the assistance of those many librarians who lightened the task of gathering materials necessary to complete this research.

My wife, who is living proof that you can not learn to sing by reading about it, was a wonderful help. Her sacrifice, assistance and encouragement is lovingly acknowledged.

TABLE OF CONTENTS

I.   Introduction   7

II.   Concepts of Vocal Pedagogy   13

III.   Concepts of Breathing   41

IV.   Concepts of Phonation   60

V.   Concepts of Resonance   80

VI.   Concepts of Range   97

VII.   Concepts of Vocal Dynamics   120

VIII.   Concepts of Ear Training   129

IX.   Concepts of Diction   140

X.   Concepts of Interpretation   158

XI.   Outcomes of This Study   173

        Sources of Bibliographic Information   177

        Annotated Bibliography   179

        Subject Index to the Bibliography   270

        Summary of Books Listed in the
          Bibliography   277

        Index   285

LIST OF TABLES

1. Summary of Concepts of Vocal Pedagogy   14

2. Summary of Concepts of Breathing   42

3. Summary of Orificial Control Concepts   53

4. Summary of Concepts of Phonation   61

5. Summary of Concepts of Resonance   81

6. Summary of Concepts of Range   98

7. Representative Vocal Classifications   99

8. Summary of Register Concepts   107

9. Summary of Concepts of Vocal Dynamics   121

10. Summary of Concepts of Ear Training   130

11. Summary of Concepts of Diction   141

12. Summary of Concepts of Interpretation   159

13. Final Comparative Summary of Concepts Used   174

Chapter I

INTRODUCTION

Singing, as a universal response of man, is reflected in various ways in his culture. It may be a spontaneous, joyous cry or it may evolve from a wail of tragic emotion. It is a coordinate act of the mind and the body, and may be the result of careful deliberate study. Much has been written about this complex, artistic expression. The ability to sing is commonly possessed and is subject to scrutiny and to analysis.

Literature about the singing voice is voluminous, at times exhaustively researched and accurately expressed and at other times subjective and opinionated. Much has been written which is confusing and controversial, as well as much that is valid and useful. Fanciful imagination is often evident rather than fact; imagery is used in place of explicit instruction; conflicting terminologies are frequently present and there is much use of ambiguous verbalization of ideas. There is, consequently, a need for the assembling and disseminating of current information and ideas. Despite the advances in scientific knowledge of the singing act, practical application of these findings has been slow to emerge in the studio. A need also exists for a systematic organization of the literature and for a current bibliography on training the singing voice.

The individuality of each voice presents a challenge, if not a problem, in regard to proper instruction. The intensely personal nature of singing makes systematic instruction difficult and the aesthetic judgment of the teacher-listener contributes to the problem. The vocal process is, of course, not open to direct observation. Finally, singing embraces a number of scientific and artistic disciplines. Physiology, acoustics, psychology, aesthetics and drama are all germane to the vocal process. There is a need to clarify existing information about unfamiliar aspects of vocal theory and practice, and a potential investigator must be cognizant of areas not yet researched.

7

A useful exchange of ideas among members of the profession is needed. Much of the traditional, though fading, hesitancy of the voice pedagogue to share methods and ideas has been due to ignorance and uncertainty. The profession needs the benefit of the thinking of those who have published their ideas. An easy review of the findings of others will make it possible for each individual to eliminate much trial and error in his approach to teaching. Confidence in the validity of one's own teaching may be greatly enhanced through the knowledge that it is in line with the body of reputable opinion. A classification of principal ideologies and methods will serve to give direction to the student, the teacher and the investigator.

In 1947, King's Crown Press published Training the Singing Voice: An Analysis of the Working Concepts Contained in Recent Contributions to Vocal Pedagogy. In this publication, Victor Alexander Fields made an analytical study and comparison of contributions to vocal pedagogy from 1928 through 1942. This volume, based on his doctoral dissertation, collected and correlated information about singing and voice culture with a thoroughness never before attempted. This resulted in a compendium of writing about the singing art that included an annotated bibliography of more than 700 items.

Fields undertook his study for several reasons, one of the principal ones being his perception of a need for a research tool that would facilitate the evaluation of teaching methods in singing.

> Both pedagogy and research would be benefited by the juxtaposition and classification of the principal ideologies and methodologies pursued by the singing profession. The findings of such a study would provide the vocal scientist with a background of useful knowledge against which to formulate and test his own theories. The teacher would enjoy the counsel and caution of his contemporaries through an exchange of ideas gathered from a range of knowledge and experience wider than his own [Fields 1947, p. 1].

Since its publication, Training the Singing Voice has served the profession well. Reference to this book is found in almost all the literature on singing instruction; it has remained a pervading influence on research in the singing voice; many areas of research suggested by Fields have since been fully or partially developed.

There has been no comparable research that covers subsequent literature. Many theories and methods have been added to the writings on vocal pedagogy during this period; scientific findings have reached a higher degree of refinement. More than sufficient time has passed to warrant bringing up to date the analysis of working concepts found in Training the Singing Voice.

The aim of this writer has been to engage in a project such as that accomplished by Fields, using the literature published since that time. The plan is (1) to gather sources of information on methods of training the singing voice; (2) to collect and arrange the data by a survey of the concepts used in training the singing voice, and by classifying and distributing these concepts into general and subordinate areas; and (3) to analyze the data through a critical analysis of each category.

Dr. Fields was receptive to the idea of this project and his approval was solicited before the present research was formally initiated. In a letter to the present writer, dated January 24, 1970, he said:

> It is a much needed project. . . . Yours can be a valuable and lasting contribution to the teaching profession. The continued public acceptance of Training the Singing Voice (7th printing) would seem to indicate that. I applaud your courage and determination.

An effort has been made to establish continuity and to derive an accurate comparison between the findings of the Fields research and that of this investigator. His organizational structure and research procedures, therefore, are used as a point of departure for this study. The definition of concept as used in this study is the same as that employed by Fields:

> The function by which we identify a numerically distinct and permanent subject of discourse is called conception; and the thoughts which are its vehicles are called concepts [William James, quoted by Fields 1947, p. 11].

To enlarge upon this, a concept is considered a thought, an idea, a theory, a supposition, a view, a notion, or an opinion which has direct application to singing instruction. In order that the many conceptual ideas expressed in the literature used may be properly correlated, working definitions

must be available.   Definitions will be taken principally
from Training the Singing Voice (Fields, 1947), The Singer's
Glossary (Fields, 1952) and Terminology in the Field of
Singing (American Academy of Teachers of Singing, 1969).

        The main areas of investigation are indicated by the
chapter headings.   These areas are pedagogy, breathing,
phonation, resonance, range, dynamics, ear training, diction, and interpretation.   Chapter I presents an introductory
discussion.   Chapters II through X report the detailed findings of this research; Chapter XI gives a final summation
and introduces the bibliography.   Near the beginning of each
chapter there are tables that reveal the total number of
statements found in each area of investigation.   These tables
indicate the importance and specific emphasis afforded each
category, according to the opinions of the various authors.
Data from Training the Singing Voice (1947) and Teaching
Singing (the present work) are tabulated together to facilitate
comparisons of emphases in these two works separated by
a quarter century.   In so doing, trends are revealed.   Representative quotations, from the total number correlated,
have been chosen to be included in the text.   The numerical
data, however, are not intended to be definitive in the strict-
est sense of controlled scientific research.   The concluding
part of each chapter includes a discussion of the most significant theories on the subject.

        It is assumed that the material found in a published
document, bearing the author's name, represents his carefully considered conclusions; however, this study is a correlation of ideas or concepts and not of authors.   These
conceptual ideas may or may not be representative of the
opinions and methods used by the most experienced authoritative minds.   For the purposes of this investigation, no
attempt is made to validate either the opinions expressed or
the methodologies proposed.

        The task of placing a concept into a certain category
was not found to be easy--for example, the researcher may
have mis-read the author's intent, or a statement, away
from the complete text, may be misunderstood.   Risks involved in selection of a category for another author's concept were fully realized.   Some categories in this study reflect only a small number of conceptual statements.   An explanation of this may include the facts that: (1) the larger
portion of studies and articles were found to be directed to
specific subject areas; (2) some literature was nebulous to
the degree that few conceptual statements could be derived;

(3) various concepts were discussed and prevalent views were given, but the author did not take a position, and (4) there are 162 possible categories in which statements may be placed.

Reactions to published data will vary from one researcher to another. An attempt has been made to maintain consistency and a clear point of view. However, in a subject area of such extent and complexity as that of singing instruction, no two people are likely to have exactly the same interests, and some differences will occur in the coverage of material. Also, certain dimensions may be added to Training the Singing Voice and this present work Teaching Singing when one understands the societies of the two time periods which provided the data for comparison. Although objectivity has been a major goal throughout the defining, the proceeding, and the presentation of this study, the conclusions and evaluation of the findings of two researchers cannot be the same.

Bibliographic references are numerous. For this reason, they are indicated throughout the text in the manner usually employed for scientific papers. The author's name is given and the particular reference is identified by the date of its publication. The bibliography is annotated. This increases its usefulness to those who wish to research in greater depth a specific category of pedagogical thought.

Because of the many areas of related thought, the subject matter in this book is confined to working concepts of voice pedagogy which have been published in English. Related areas, as listed below, are not included.

Technical exercises and drills
Repertoire and programming
General musicianship and theory
Adolescent or changing voices
Vocal anatomy and physiology (medical)
Vocal pathology
Physical health and hygiene of the vocal organs
Singing as a career
History of singing
Selection and qualifications of singing teachers
Preparation for auditions
Methods related directly to choir and group instruction

For this writer, a new perspective was gained from the reading of the literature from the beginning to the end

of a 28-year span.   It may be observed that tremendous
strides have been made by teachers of singing in regard to
professional standards.   The general knowledge of the average teacher is being raised and there is marked evidence of
more tolerance and understanding in the profession.   There
are fewer teachers today claiming to have "the only method."
These strides have been made to a large extent by the professional organizations embracing the teachers of singing.
Prominent among these are the National Association of
Teachers of Singing and the highly respected American
Academy of Teachers of Singing.

Chapter II

CONCEPTS OF VOCAL PEDAGOGY

"Pedagogy" is defined by Webster as the art, the practice or profession of teaching; especially systematized learning or instruction concerning principles and methods of teaching. Fields (1947, p. 16) says that vocal pedagogy is "the aggregate of principles, rules and procedures pertaining to the development, exercise and practice of the art of singing; and the process of training, by a prescribed course of study or technical discipline. "

THEORIES

Introductory Concepts

The Singing Voice

According to Judson and Weaver (1965, p. xviii), voice is laryngeal vibration plus resonance; it may be involuntary or purposive. Definitions of singing and the singing voice are ventured by a number of writers:

> The voice is of all instruments of music the oldest and the newest with every baby born; the most primitive, yet the most sophisticated; common to birds and beasts and all races of mankind, but unique in every individual; the most intimate both as a ready means of self-expression and for communication between singer and listener; and the easiest to use. The human voice can be the most endearing or the most annoying of instruments [Ashworth 1956, p. 275].

> Good singing means skillful playing on a well-tuned instrument--the human voice [Gardiner 1968, p. 9].

> Singing is actually the transmutation of energy into tone [William E. Jones 1947, p. 3].

> The human voice is the only musical instrument with

13

Table 1. SUMMARY OF CONCEPTS OF VOCAL PEDAGOGY

	Number of Statements in "Teaching Singing"	Number of Statements in "Training the Singing Voice"
I. Theories of vocal pedagogy		
A. Introductory concepts	41	34
B. Preliminary considerations		
1. benefits of vocal study	8	10
2. prerequisites of vocal study	27	20
3. the vocal training period	10	13
C. Objectives of vocal training	36	23
D. Coordination as a primary physiological factor	23	14
E. Standardization of vocal training		
1. vocal training can be standardized	7	13
2. vocal training cannot be standardized	4	18
II. Methods of vocal pedagogy		
A. A psychological approach		
1. importance of the psychological approach	36	63
2. voice training as habit formation	13	14
3. singing as a natural function		
a) the vocal act is unconscious and involuntary	26	58
b) spontaneity and naturalness are characteristics	32	19
4. freeing the vocal mechanism		
a) relaxation a factor in vocal training	22	43
b) economy of effort principle	47	51
c) overcoming inhibitions and fears	18	21
5. singing as self expression and joyous release	19	52
6. singing as compared to speaking	31	53

B. The technical approach
  1. technical principles and
      objectives   29   19
  2. removing muscular inter-
      ferences   39   23
  3. handling beginners
      a) classifying voices   53   30
      b) first lessons   25   15
  4. the song approach
      a) songs are useful as
         technical exercises   9   24
      b) vocalises are preferable
         as technical exercises   16   10
  5. principles and procedures
      used in practicing
      a) principles of vocal practice   26   10
      b) supervision of practice   10   9
      c) silent practicing as a device   4   5
      d) piano accompaniments   14   8
      e) various factors in practicing   15   18

          TOTALS   640   690

---

a heart, a mind and a soul [Cooke 1952, p. 15].

Singing ... is extended speaking in both range and power [Slater 1950, p. 6].

Good singing, from the singer's standpoint, is an act of correctly functioning neuro-muscularly co-ordinated athletic activity [Lindquest 1955, p. 20].

Singing is more mental than physical [Ririe 1960, p. 35].

All artful singing is conceptual. A singer cannot possibly sing a pitch without first conceiving it as sensation [Appelman 1967, p. 9].

Training the Singing Voice

Victor Alexander Fields, in Training the Singing Voice (p. 20), defines voice culture synonymously with the system-atic training of the singing voice. "This may be defined as

a process of administering systematic instruction and exercise to the individual student for the purpose of developing
those mental and physical abilities that enter into the artistic
performance of vocal expression in song. " The multi-faceted
approaches to training the singing voice span the gamut from
"The Method" to "a method for each student. " Within these
polar expressions, certain methods, or approaches, or philosophies of singing instruction have enjoyed varying degrees
of use and popularity.   Some vocal authorities have tried to
label and categorize the most prominent pedagogical approaches.   Representative samplings of these writings are
included:

> Voice teachers can be divided roughly into two
> classes: those who believe that vocal control should
> be conscious, direct, and based upon the detailed
> scientific findings of physiologists, and those who be-
> lieve that vocal control should be indirect, largely
> unconscious, automatic, or reflex and based on tonal
> imagery.   One is physiological, the other a psycho-
> logical-aesthetic approach.   The first group are gen-
> erally known as the 'Mechanists' and the second
> group as the 'Empiricists' [Christy 1961, p. 135].

> First, there is the mechanistic philosophy. Essen-
> tially it implies that if the singer will learn all of the
> physical details of the singing act and discipline him-
> self to coordinate them, he will produce a good tone.
> This is the 'scientific school' of teaching. . . .   A
> second pedagogy is that of imagery.   Its philosophy
> is that while the physical details are either unknown
> or not directly controllable, the experience of good
> tone production can be described in figures of speech
> which will enable the student to grasp it. . . .   Third,
> there is the method of demonstration.   Its philosophy
> is that since the production of good tone cannot be
> described adequately either objectively or subjectively
> the best thing to do is to offer a sample. . . .   A
> fourth philosophy is summed up in the slogan, 'Sing
> as you speak. '   It implies that most students have an
> artificial concept of what is beautiful singing tone, and
> that their speech habits are a better foundation for
> voice production than any superimposed efforts to be
> 'artistic'. . . .   A fifth approach is that of learning by
> singing. . . .   Finally, a sixth philosophy might be
> called that of inspiration.   The phrase 'psychological
> approach' is often used.   Essentially the belief is

that whatever potential a student may possess needs
only a favorable climate for its unfolding, that it will
germinate from within and that efforts to mold it
from without are more than likely to stultify it [Ven-
nard 1958, pp. 4-5, 22-24].

Ross (1959, p. 26) has devised further divisions,
methods, or schools of teaching singing:

1.	Bel Canto	8.	Organic Co-ordination
2.	Emotional	9.	Local Effort (physical)
3.	Interpretative	10.	Modern Scientific
4.	Natural	11.	Phonetic Placement
5.	Psychological	12.	Psycho-physiological
6.	Resonance		Acoustical
7.	Speech	13.	Register
		14.	Respiration

Preliminary Considerations

Benefits of Vocal Study

Some reasons for studying singing, other than a desire for a professional career, are given in the following
statements:

I think voice teachers should emphasize more and
more that boys and girls should study singing as a
cultural asset and that the gaining control of the
mental and physical action of singing is the finest
training which can be given children [Samuel 1948,
p. 297].

By striving to attain what is generally thought to be
impossible in voice, the voice is permitted to rise
from the mediocre into excellence [Collins 1969b,
p. 19].

The most important reasons for studying voice...
should be the ultimate pleasure and satisfaction derived [Christy 1965, p. 1].

The study of singing is thought by many to improve
not only physical health by the practice of deep
breathing, but also mental health by the emotional release and enjoyment singing affords [Ross 1959, p. 24].

Song singing presents an ideal opportunity for social
intercourse; indeed, communication between a singer
and audience can become one of the most potent
means for social maturation [Gilliland 1954, p. 5].

Prerequisites of Vocal Study

Can everyone sing. --Based on the opinions of 27
authors (Table 1), there are many physical, imaginative and
native elements which serve as prerequisites for success in
singing. Nikolaidi (1962, p. 130) insists on some points
which are of equal importance: an active, alert, flexible
body, a very much alive face to express the various emotions, a distinct and natural pronunciation of the words in
whatever language, and a musical mind. Douglas Stanley
(1950, p. 52) lists: "a fine ear, concentration, energy,
dramatic ability and musical feeling, plus physical muscular
skill. "

The possession of a good ear is indispensable. "Advisedly I put the possession of a good musical ear, or the
ability to imagine and reproduce pitches, as the very first
prerequisite" (Kagen 1950, p. 13). "The 'artistic ear' is
the main element on which present vocal instruction is usually based" (Kwartin 1963, p. xii). "The teaching of singing is to a great extent the teaching of ear training" (W.
Rice 1961, p. 10).

Imagination, temperament, and personality are important. "Either one has the sacred fire or one has not"
(Jeritza 1947, p. 185). "The possession of the tempera-
mental qualities necessary to convey faithfully the intentions
of the author and the composer is evidently the basis of
good interpretive singing" (Graves 1954, p. 72). "One of
the cruelest possible practices in teaching is that of even
intimating to the pupil that a great vocal career lies ahead
of him, when the teacher knows ... that the pupil has no
personality which could help make great success as a singer"
(Cooke 1952, p. 15).

The desire to sing is vital. "The biggest single
factor in becoming a singer is wish, desire, urge, want,
and an all encompassing urge to become a singer, no matter
what the odds" ("Vocal Success ... " 1952, p. 31). "The
qualities of the teacher are less important than the student's
desire to learn" (MacNeil 1962, p. 24).

Other prerequisites are stressed.   "Musicianship, languages, stage deportment, personality and all the supplementary items may receive high rating, but it is the voice itself that is the keystone of the arch" (Mowe 1954, p. 3). Durgin (1953, p. 23) comments that many men and women have potentially excellent voices, but they have been denied the other attributes that are requisite for fine singing; these are the students who confront themselves and their teachers with so many problems.   Vrbanich (1960, p. 8) suggests that there are "no bad voices, there are only voices badly trained by poor teachers." Stout (1955a, p. 10) uniquely suggests a knowledge of fundamental vocal physiology should be prerequisite.

The Vocal Training Period

When to begin vocal study. --Opinions are varied concerning commencement of vocal training, but a general emphasis on maturity is noted.   Pinza (1950, p. 11) started at the age of 19; at 16, he feels, the voice is not yet developed. According to Mansion (1952, p. 15), it is never too early, or too late, to begin studying singing.   Fuchs (1964, p. 24) says that there is no fixed rule; boys should never begin until they are 17, but girls may start earlier.   "Girls who are of high school age and have the desire to learn how to sing should begin studying voice.   With the boys it would be better to postpone serious study until approximately sixteen years of age" (Sunderman 1958, p. 7).   "First there must be a matured voice before it can be trained" (H. Shaw 1948, p. 15).

How long to study. --Opinions on the length of time it takes to train the voice vary.   Westerman (1955, p. 60) claims that fully resonant tones can be achieved in a few months through the intelligent use of certain proscribed English syllables in vocalizing exercises.   After vocal classification has been established, according to Eugene Conley (1950, p. 14), it may take several months to place the voice in its proper position.   "Radical improvement should come within twenty to thirty lessons" (Harvey 1955, p. 29).   "A year or two, possibly three or four .... " (Stults 1950, p. 24).   "Not less than two years of daily lessons .... " (Gerry 1948, p. 6).   "At least two or three years .... " (E. Lehman 1945, p. 195 and R. Brown 1946, p. 121).

But the values of the first three years have changed

with the growth of the singer.   The three inseparables
then were vowel, pitch and pulse. ...   Technique was
the beginning and end--all of the pupil's world.   Now
the instrument must be taken more for granted.   One
must sing, but sing <u>something</u>--for a reason [Swing
1953, p. 6].

General Objectives

Without a purposeful direction or specific objectives
on the part of the teacher and the pupil, the accumulation of
knowledge and the advancement of the musical art are often
misguided.   "The purpose is to set him going in the direction of becoming a self-sufficient entity, able to realize a
higher and still yet higher level of artistic self-expression"
(Duey 1959, p. 16).   Stout (1955, p. 10) says that the emphasis should be upon improving performance rather than
allowing the student to bask in the idea that he possesses
something rare, which in itself is going to guarantee success.
To this, Duval (1958, p. 178) adds that it is the foremost
aim of the teacher to develop individuality.   Bollew (1954a,
p. 49) observes a triumvirate of general goals: "Correct
vocal production, a good musical education and wide adherence to dietary, bodily and hygienic rules."   Huls (1947,
p. 199) says that it is of paramount importance that the student become a cultured individual.   Christy (1967, p. 14)
provides a comprehensive list, which he calls the ten greatest principles or objectives in learning to sing:

1.   An attitude of enthusiastic interest, pleasure and
confidence.
2.   Intelligent, regular practice habits.
3.   Vital, upright, expansive posture.
4.   Efficient diaphragmatic-costal breath control.
5.   Freedom, vitality, expressive color, efficiency,
sonority and evenness in tonal production.
6.   Mastery of correct, clear and beautiful diction.
7.   Mastery of legato technic.
8.   Mastery of agility and flexibility technic.
9.   Sensitive, intelligent and movingly expressive interpretation.
10.   Natural, gracious, poised and attractive stage
presence.

Coordination as a Primary Factor

"Physiology" is defined as "the study of animate
functions of the organs and parts of the human body.   Since
voice is a product of the functioning of the vocal tract, the
science of voice training may be considered a specialized
outgrowth of its parent science--physiology" (Fields 1947,
p. 26).   Lindquest (1955, p. 20) says that good singing is
the result of correctly functioning neuro-muscularly coordinated athletic activity.   Appelman (1967, p. 9) adds that
artful singing is the act of coordinating instantaneously the
physical sensations of respiration, phonation, resonation and
articulation.   "Were it not for the capacity of the brain to
coordinate information coming to it from various sensory
pathways, there would be no coordinated adjustments of the
vocal mechanism and no singing" (Simmons 1969, p. 15).
"At no time should the smooth-working coordinated activity
of the singing mechanism be upset by concentration upon its
various parts" (P. Peterson 1966, p. 5).

Is Standardization of Training Possible?

With the diversity of methods and approaches to singing instruction, it is inevitable that the question be ventured
concerning the possibility of standardized vocal training.

There is no reason why vocal methods cannot be
standardized [Ross 1964, p. 31].

A good voice has to be trained individually [Donath
1959, p. 90].

All voices should be trained alike, if possible ... but
there is one ideal of voice production [Vennard 1967,
p. 158].

It may be said that there should be as many 'methods'
as there are pupils [Reid 1950, p. 97].

It is far more in harmony with the laws of Nature to
believe that identically constructed vocal mechanisms
can best be trained by a universal system than by a
dozen or more assorted ones [Lamberti 1954, p. 63].

The method will vary with the teacher.   In any case
such methods constitute a trade secret, and are not

to be committed to writing [Kay 1963, p. 75].

The idea of teaching voice as a standardized system
is abhorrent to all who teach the vocal art [Appel-
man 1967, p. 3].

METHODS OF VOCAL PEDAGOGY

A Psychological Approach

Importance of Psychological Approach

A conceptual mental image of the desired vocal
quality is significant, in the opinion of 36 writers. "Most
singing is done not with the voice but with the ears and the
brain" (DeLuca 1946, p. 435). "It seems to me that the
acquisition of vocal technic should primarily rest on the acquisition of control over the non-muscular factors involved
in singing" (Kagen 1950, p. 92). "Many teachers quite
rightly lay great emphasis on the mental concept as a prerequisite of all technic" (Vennard 1967, p. 49). "When we
teach singing we are working with the human body as it is
controlled by the human mind" (Widoe 1955, p. 12).

Certainly, the mechanical defects in vocal technique
must be corrected. The controls, however, are
psychological and, therefore, the student's psychology
must be corrected as well [Garlinghouse 1955, p. 5].

It may be deduced that there are three separate aspects of the mental concept to be considered during
training: (1) a concept which has been formed through
personal identification of long standing, (2) an automatic pre-forming of this concept at the outset of
Phonation in order to duplicate an experience which,
at best, is merely habitual and familiar, and (3) the
need to re-form this concept so as to provoke changes
in the coordinate response of the laryngeal and
pharyngeal muscles engaged in phonation [Reid 1965,
p. 102].

Voice Training as Habit Formation

"By continually striving to make ideal tones which
thereafter can be released when the vocal organs are

properly conditioned, is the best way to secure the highest
voice results" (Cooke 1952, p. 63).   "The purpose of vocal-
ising is to fix correct singing habits into the voice so that
they remain there as second nature" (Bidu Sayão 1953, p. 12).
"Technique should be so firmly established that it is completely unconscious and automatic" (Fisher 1965, p. 13).
"The whole psychology of habit formation must be understood, for we do not inform students, we do not advise them,
we train them" (DeYoung 1953, p. 8).

> As our newly acquired "singing" nucleus within the
> subconscious mind attains a certain degree of com-
> petence and dexterity, it tends more and more to
> direct and assist every action of the singer, particu-
> larly where the varying adjustments of the vocal
> machinery are concerned. In other words, our nu-
> cleus gradually acquires an intelligent automatism
> [Herbert-Caesari 1965, p. 54].

Singing as a Natural Function

The Harvard Dictionary (1969, p. 918) defines the
"natural singer" as one "untutored vocally, " and observes
that such singers "have instinctively known how to use and
coordinate the proper muscles. " Within the framework of
formal, disciplined song, this condition is much desired.
If it is not possessed, it is to be emulated.

The vocal act is unconscious and involuntary. --"Long
before learning to speak the infant takes pleasure in uttering
melodious sounds, singing sounds, which unlike speech, do
not have to be 'learned' " (Husler and Rodd-Marling 1965,
p. 95).   "The vocal organ is not subject to conscious control" (Zerffi 1957, p. 64),   "How the vocal folds function
is beyond our control except for the suggestions of more or
less force and tension which we may be able to exert upon
them" (Mallett 1963, p. 9).   "The consequent oscillations of
the cords generate sound ... consisting of air waves whose
travelling speed is round about 1, 100 feet to the second.
This speed ... is beyond our muscular control" (Young 1956,
p. 17).   "In order to sing naturally ... they must learn to
perform consciously an act that in its ideal state is unconscious. Given enough time it will become automatic with
them too" (Litante 1959, p. 6).   "The ultimate knowledge
in vocal training is to transfer as much knowledge as possible from the conscious to the unconscious mind" (Herbert-

Caesari 1965, p. 56).

Spontaneity and naturalness are chief characteristics.
--"There can be only one right way to produce the human
voice.   That is the way which completely conforms to the
natural laws which govern the functioning of the physical
organism" (Wilcox 1945, p. 1).   "All beginning vocal training must be corrective in nature through seeking to restore
nature's original adjustment of the speech organs in action"
(Stults 1951, p. 15).   "We shall take a step forward when
we begin to view singing as an integral and natural act instead of as a series of separate and disassociated 'problems' " (Leonard Warren 1949, p. 149).

> Like other activities involving muscular control, sing-
> ing is easiest and most effective when it is spon-
> taneous, or seems to be [Wheeler 1954, p. 8].

> The voice is a natural part of the physical organism
> and hence requires natural rather than artificial
> treatment [Tagliavini 1948, p. 581].

> The more subconscious his technique has become, the
> more spontaneous his singing can be [Freer 1959b,
> p. 21].

> Your whole vocal apparatus is surrounded by nerves
> which spontaneously reflect your most intimate
> thoughts [Cooke 1952, p. 20].

Freeing the Vocal Mechanism

Freedom in vocal emission is a quality that finds
universal acceptance.   This element may be further cate-
gorized (1) relaxation, (2) economy of effort, and (3) overcoming inhibitions and fears.

Relaxation as a factor in voice training. --"A good
way to feel relaxed in the throat and jaw is to speak 'ah'
softly under your breath" (German 1952, p. 32).   "There is
an area which should be relatively relaxed and which should,
under no circumstances, function during phonation, i. e. , the
chest, shoulders, neck and jaw" (Stanley 1950, p. 63).
"Concentration on telling the story leaves the mind free from
worry over matters of voice production which tends to develop both relaxation of the throat and a natural way of sing-

ing" (Manning 1946, p. 135). "The pure Italian vowels are
the best approach to singing because they involve less lip
action and provide more relaxed production" (Hines 1951,
p. 49). "One of the greatest pleasures ... has been to hear
singers observe that the clarification of their diction has
been helpful in effecting vocal relaxation and tonal improvement" (Marshall 1953, p. 2).

The physiological accuracy of partial or full relaxation in singing is subject to many questions.   Rose (1962,
p. 44) comments that "every physical training instructor
knows that muscles are developed by placing them under
certain tensions, " but some teachers would have us believe
"that the voice is different in some mysterious way and can
only be developed by relaxation. " "To urge complete relaxation of the body as a general principle in singing is both
physiologically and psychologically unsound" (Christy 1961,
p. 26). "I used the phrase 'relaxation of all unnecessary
tensions. ' These are the areas where we can, by careful
study, disassociate all muscular activity which is not essential to a natural tone production" (O. Brown 1953, p. 16).

Economy of effort as a principle; letting versus striving. --Key words in this category are: ease, allow, and
effortless.

Singing requires great mental and physical exertion--
but we must give the illusion of effortless singing
[Gardini 1950, p. 2].

Whatever he sings, he should feel (a) he can sing
higher; (b) he can sing louder; (c) he can hold the
note longer [Fuchs 1964, p. 85].

The greatest amount of sonorous tonal volume for the
least amount of effort is always the ideal tone containing the maximum of overtones [Christy 1965, p. 49].

Most singers remember certain days in their vocal
lives when it was no trouble to sing, marked by complete freedom from restraint and an insatiable desire
to express oneself in song [Rosewall 1961, p. 41].

Vocal performance should be an enjoyable and satisfying experience when the voice is allowed to sing
[P. Peterson 1966, p. vii].

A flexible tone is elastic--it gives the impression of
flowing easily, of being released without losing the
basic vitality of quality [DeYoung 1958, p. 89].

Overcoming inhibitions and fears. --"Proper techniques,
poise, and self-confidence overcome the problems of fear
and the resulting danger of vocal tension" (P. Peterson 1966,
p. 73). "Most of us have a mortal fear of actually 'letting
go' and throwing ourselves whole-heartedly into interpreting
the sentiments which we should freely express in our singing. We have a fear that our friends will think that we are
affected, trying to show off, or exaggerating the emotions of
the song" (Westerman 1955, p. 137). "Above all, don't be
afraid of making a fool of yourself. You cannot be shy and
a singer at one and the same moment" (Bairstow and Greene
1945, p. 34).

This brings up the question of honesty in praise of
students. It is a delicate point, and one to be
weighed by different standards with each student. In
dealing with an inferiority complex, we have somewhat the same situation as the doctor whose patient
is critically ill. At such a time any fiction that will
enable him to pull through is justified. As is often
the case, the ethics of an act depend upon the motive
[Vennard 1953c, p. 6].

Fear is the most common unhealthy mental attitude
[Lester 1950, p. 178].

Singing as Self-Expression/Joyous Release

Artistic singing is motivated by a desire to express
a mood, an emotion, an idea. "It is the desire to share
yourself and your emotions, combined with a sincere and
kindly dominance that generated a great personality" (Whitlock 1960, p. 32). "Your best tones are simply the means
of getting musical significance out of yourself and into the
selves of your hearers" (G. London 1953, p. 18). " 'Sell'
yourself to your audience as a sincere, likable person.
Speak and sing to your entire audience, and never look at
any particular person" (F. Lawson 1944, p. 67).

Many of us have witnessed miraculous growth in students who have effectively communed with an audience
[Gilliland 1954, p. 5].

According to her nature, her wealth of comprehension, will she express the inner meaning of the phrases she sings and communicate them to her audience [Duval 1958, p. 111].

The first objective in singing is to convey meaning and its attendant feeling [DeYoung 1958, p. 63].

The vocal student, if he desires the most efficient functioning of his vocal organism, must establish a mood of buoyancy. How may that mood be evoked? Through use of the imagination! [Wilcox 1945, p. 14].

Singing is, after all, a simple, spontaneous, and mental process. Joy is perhaps the greatest aid among mental attitudes. A happy frame of mind does much toward arranging the organs of phonation in the best relations and positions [Gould 1949, p. 6].

Singing as Compared to Speaking

Analogies are often used relating singing to speech. The theoretical positions of "sing as you speak" advocates are expressed in 20 statements. Opposing the concept are 11 statements.

Singing is usually sustained speech, or is made up of sustained sounds that could become component parts of speech [Treash 1947, p. 3].

Speak and let the breath do the singing [Puritz 1954, p. 23].

Singing is merely speech at a high emotional level [Levinson 1962, p. 1].

Speech under emotional stress is where singing begins [Bollew 1951, p. 58].

Singing is an extension and elevation of speaking [Cates 1959, p. 7].

I sing as I speak, and I speak as I sing--all on a strong diaphragmatic breath [Mary Garden, as quoted by Fellowes 1952, p. 50].

All of the singer's gifts, all his perfection of technique, all observance of rules go for little or nothing,
if his singing is not speech in song [Eberhart 1962,
p. 8].

Believing as I do that it is possible to sing as you
speak, and mark, with all the subtle inflexions of
speech, it behooves us to pronounce our language in
the right way; that is, with pure vowel sounds [Baker
1963, p. 9].

Those who reject the "sing as you speak" concept are
reflected in these statements: "Singing is not merely sustained speech" (Vail 1953, p. 22). "There is a difference
between the use of the voice as an instrument of speaking
and the use of the voice as a musical instrument.... The
majority of a singer's mistakes come from the speaking
movements and habits" (Vrbanich 1960, p. 8). "Another
difference between singing and speaking is that audibility
of words proceeds from different causes" (Middleton
1951, p. 50).

Studying singing does not have direct correlation to
speech adequacy [Bakkegard 1953, p. 25].

To 'sing as you speak' is in fact just as idiotic as to
suggest that you can learn ballet dancing by going for
long walks! [Gardiner 1968, p. 31].

The Technical Approach

Technical Principles and Objectives

According to the Dictionary of Education, specific
ways of presenting instructional materials embodying skills
constitute technical approaches in teaching. Reid (1950,
p. 108) indicates that the immediate objective sought in
working out a theory of tone production necessarily demands
the use of scales and exercises. As outlined by Vennard
(1967, p. 119), it should be the objective of every singer
"to get as much brilliance as possible and as much depth in
the tone at the same time." Fields (1957, p. 6) says that
the ability to idealize tone is an indispensable part of singing.

Ross (1959, p. 11) provides a comprehensive tech-

nical goal: "A pharyngeal control of the vowel sounds,
balanced by lip action when necessary, with a clear and
accurate articulation of the consonants, supported by a variable pressure flow of the breath, in a nasal-pharyngeal
(normal) quality. "

> Upon these the whole structure of singing technique is
> built, and all faults of voice-production are traceable
> to infringements of one or more of them. In prac-
> tical singing they are demonstrated by: (1) the easy
> emission of all notes within the compass of the voice,
> (2) the sustained intensity of the tone and facility in
> increasing and diminishing its volume, (3) flexibility
> of voice in pitch change, (4) vowel and tone quality,
> and (5) good diction [Judd 1951, p. 65].

> The art of music makes upon the singer five ele-
> mentary technical demands: (a) The sound must be
> sonorous, i. e. , it must be clear and ringing, being
> neither breathy (except for occasional effects), nor
> dull, nor strident nor hollow. (b) The singer must
> be able to produce at will a sound of the finest
> quality of which the individual instrument is capable.
> (c) The intonation must be perfect and the tone per-
> fectly steady. (d) The singer must be able to keep
> the flow of sound continuous and unbroken over the
> full compass of the voice, whether singing either very
> slowly or at the fastest tempo. (e) The singer must
> be able to swell or diminish the sound at will, keep-
> ing the rate of increase or decrease under perfect
> control [Kelsey, Grove's, p. 44].

Removing Muscular Interferences

"Much of our work as vocal teachers is directed
toward the elimination of various sorts of interferences"
(Garlinghouse 1951, p. 2). Directly opposed to vocal problems inherent in muscular interference is the much desired
vocal attribute--freeness of tone. "Vocal freedom is attained when the entire vocal channel continues in total pas-
sivity and when one dimension is fully equal throughout the
scale" (Montell 1950, p. 80). "Freedom from tension and
rigidity in the vocal area is necessary to the singing tone"
(Rosewall 1961, p. 32). " 'Freedom' is an attribute, strictly
speaking, of the technique or of the instrument, but the term
is applied to tone because the ear of a qualified listener

senses empathetically that the singer is free from undesirable tensions or 'interference' " (van den Berg and Vennard 1959, p. 12).

Forcing of the tone is often associated with the problems of muscular interference.   "We should never try to hurl or project the voice if we wish to sing freely" (Christy 1967, p. 62).   "Tones cannot be of any quality if they are produced by propulsion. This is the most usual mistake of singers" (Vrbanich 1960, p. 8).   "Anything that feels strained, forced, hard, or uncomfortable indicates clearly that a wrong system of emission is being used" (Svanholm 1948, p. 540).   "Most forcing and straining stems from anticipatory tension, before we even start singing" (Koppel 1956, p. 19).

Corrective helps for lessening of muscular interference are provided by a number of writers.   Resnik (1948, p. 281) says to keep "a loose tongue"; she speaks in terms of the tongue because "it is simpler, somehow, than a loose jaw. "   Robert Merrill (1947, p. 315) says, "The moment you begin doing conscious things to yourself you tighten yourself up, and constrictions result. "   Bachner (1947, p. 79) urges the daily use of staccati exercises as a help to gradually overcome interferences.   James F. Cooke (1952, p. 63) provides an interesting quote from Enrico Caruso: "When I sing I forget all about my body, my throat, technic, breathing, everything but the words, the music and the drama involved.   As the melody ascends I try to make my voice bloom out like a flower.   The tones always float out.   They are never pushed out. "

Handling Beginners

Principles and instructional guidelines for beginning students are treated throughout this study.   Many concepts are equally applicable to the beginner and to the intermediate and advanced vocal student.   There are, however, specific areas of vocal approach which are generally directed to the beginning student.

Classifying voices. --Varieties in vocal timbre and the compass of the human voice result in certain classifications of voice types.   Traditional classifications have evolved, for which the larger portion of vocal literature is expressly written.   The processes of vocal classification are reflected

In 59 statements.

Silvia Bagley (1947, p. 2) says that a good principle
to follow is: "First FREE a voice, then 'it' will tell you
where it ought to go. " A similar statement is from Christy
(1961, p. 149): "There should be no worry over the matter,
for if the voice is allowed to settle into its own level, as it
will if practice is in a moderate range, the voice will
classify itself. " Whitlock (1967, p. 12) finds it of value to
listen to the speaking voice, especially during animated conversation. Oren Brown (1953, p. 16) implies that too much
emphasis is given vocal classification. He would prefer that
each voice do what is best suited to its natural range and
not worry about classification of the voice into the conventional patterns.

There is frequent reference in the literature to early
or hasty voice classifications. "Voice classification in
young, beginning students is difficult and even ridiculous"
(Best 1957, p. 24). Stignani (1949, p. 350) expresses re-
gret that the young singer's voice is classified at the very
beginning of her work, when she is least able to come to
her own assistance through personal experience. Paul
Peterson (1966, p. 7) says that a common fault is the tendency to classify voices too soon. Appelman (1953, p. 36)
is of the opinion that the voice of a man or woman of college
age is "a voice of transition, and the vocal problems confronted are numerous and varied. " "Vocal range in a beginner can be determined only as training progresses" (Punt
1967, p. 57). "A teacher should never classify a voice at
the commencement of training. Ease within a certain range
is no guide. . . . When tonal imperfections are eradicated and
there is correct attack and emission, the question of classification ceases to be a problem" (Bollew 1953, p. 59). "I
never feel any urgency about classifying a beginning student"
(Vennard 1967, p. 78).

The two factors most frequently seen as determinants
of vocal classification are vocal timbre and range. The relative importance of these factors is frequently discussed:

Voices should be classified rather by quality or
texture than by range [Graves 1954, p. 17].

The possession of low tones does not make a contralto, and the possession of high tones does not make
a soprano; it is the color, the quality of the voice

that determines these things [Rise Stevens 1947,
p. 248].

If there is any single deciding factor, I suppose most
of us would settle for quality [Wheeler 1950, p. 10].

It is both the range and most importantly, the quality
of the voice which count [Jean Madeira 1963, p. 22].

The difference in voices is judged not by range but
by timbre.   Range has actually nothing to do with it
[Robert Merrill 1950, p. 19].

All classifications depend on quality and tessitura as
well as range.   It sometimes takes several years of
voice study before the voice can be classified [Trusler
and Ehret 1960, p. 17].

Vocal range alone is a most unreliable and deceiving
factor in determining voice type [AATS 1956].

Physiological proportions of the neck and the face are
considered by some to be factors in voice classification:

The general physical appearance of the singer gives
additional clues.   As a rule, high voices are found in
persons with round faces, short necks, round or
quadratic chests, high palates with delicate soft
palates.   Long faces, long and narrow necks, long
and flat chests, broad palates with massive soft
palates, are frequent in singers with deep voices
[Brodnitz 1961, p. 23].

An individual who possesses large resonant cavities
will have naturally a sonorous timbre.   The examination of the bucco-pharyngeal cavity in a person of
whom we know the classification through other factors
will then allow us to determine the sub-classification
[Landeau 1963, p. 7].

More specifically, the length and shape of the vocal
folds is theoretically important:

People with low voices have long and relatively narrow vocal cords, while in those with high voices the
cords are short and relatively broad [Brodnitz 1961,
p. 23].

The contralto has long, thick vocal cords very much like those of the male tenor, and the true contralto is usually a big woman, tall, as well as big around [Moe 1950, p. 11].

Baritones and contraltos usually have heavier and more rounded vocal folds than tenors and sopranos, with an associated mellowness of quality [Negus 1962, p. 145].

The prevalently accepted position in regard to voice classification and the dimensions of the larynx is represented in this statement: "It is an elementary fact that the dimensions of the larynx, particularly of the vocal cords, determine the vocal range of each individual" (Luchsinger and Arnold 1965, p. 99). Conclusions of experimentation by the French scientist, Raoul Husson (1957a), reject the anatomical and physiological classification of voices. "In accordance with his own controversial theory, he proposed instead that 'excitability' of the vocal cords and the properties of the recurrent nerve become the basis for classification" (Heaton 1968, p. 1). In an English translation of the original study, Husson (1957a, p. 6) says: "No significant correlation exists between the vocal type on one hand and the length of the vocal cords on the other. Caruso possessed immeasurably long vocal cords. J. Darla, a young, very high soprano possesses very long wide and thick cords." Siegle (1964) made further research employing facets of the Husson theory.

The voice classification problem rests in the anatomic and fundamental evaluation of the vocal apparatus. The anatomic evaluation will take into account the aspect of the larynx, the length and thickness of the vocal cords, the conforming of the bucco-pharyngeal cavity, the development of the respiratory apparatus. To be noted then are the secondary sources: the general morphology, the size of a body-form, the countenance aspect, etc. The functional evaluation will be worked out by determining the actual tessitura and timbre, through the scientific means of investigation at our disposal [Landeau 1963, p. 31].

First lessons. --The 25 statements concerning first lessons reveal a variety of interests and approaches. These inclusions are representative:

The student who comes to me merely listens at first.
I explain to him that any training of the voice automatically will be corrective (Winsel 1966, p. 22).

In the first lesson, the student is made aware of
constantly shifting sensation, and of the importance
of letting them shift (Newton 1957, p. 21).

I have reached a policy of never teaching breath
management in the first lesson.   The student has
come to learn to sing, and so we begin immediately
making tone.   By the end of the first lesson, if the
student's breath control is inadequate, I call attention
to it, and promise to give him specific help in the
next lesson.   By then he will have what the progressive educator calls 'readiness' [Vennard 1967, p. 18].

At the beginning of the study of the voice never sing
pianissimo because you squeeze (clutch) your throat
[W. Brown 1957, p. 133].

Correct postural conditions, and jaw and lip opening
for various dynamics, vowels, and tone colors are
factors that will respond most rapidly at times to
direct attention and control by the beginning student
[Christy 1961, p. 138].

When beginners choose to study the art of singing the
teacher usually finds himself confronted with FIVE
MAJOR PROBLEMS.   They are as follows: (1) un-
educated hearing, (2) undisciplined and uncoordinated
muscles, (3) incorrect breathing, (4) the singer cannot hear himself as others hear him, and (5) the in-
ability of the student to recognize that voice is not a
material thing [McLean 1951b, p. 8].

From the beginning, the teacher must develop the internal sensitivity of the pupil for mastering the instrument [Vrbanich 1960, p. 8].

The Song Approach

Opinions vary greatly concerning the advisability of
developing vocal technique through technical needs found in a
particular work being studied.   The more traditional approach
stresses the extended use of technical vocal exercises to

prepare the student for the singing of songs   Nine statements advocate the song approach to technical proficiency;
16 statements advocate the extended use of vocal exercises.
Listed alternately, are selected opinions concerning this
subject:

> You need to master hundreds of exercises, involving
> every manner of approach to all intervals, in every
> key and in every rhythm [Maurice-Jacquet 1941,
> p. 141].

> The best way to learn to sing is to practice singing
> songs [Christy 1961, p. 5].

> During the first year, the practicing must be limited
> solely to intensive vocalizing [Martinelli 1954, p. 57].

> The student must learn to sing, not just vocalize, and
> it is two hundred years too late to expect him to wait
> like Caffarelli doing a single page of exercises for
> six years [Vennard 1958, p. 23].

> The biggest mistake of the young singer is that, in-
> stead of having patience to practice scales and tech-
> niques, he wants to sing songs [Freeman 1949, p. 10].

> Modern psychological studies have given strong evi-
> dence that long years spent in formalized drill are no
> longer necessary for the acquiring of advanced mus-
> cular techniques, and a great saving in time may
> result when technical problems are taken from the
> music itself [Ducy 1951, p. 156].

> I insist upon an almost complete mastery of the tech-
> nique of the voice before we allow any serious ap-
> proach to repertoire [M. Craig 1950, p. 16].

> Technique, for technique's sake, is of no value.   It
> must be transferred, as soon as it is acquired into
> actual repertoire [Whitlock 1969, p. 12].

> Surely, the singer must have a source of inspiration.
> One student may be able to sing songs far better than
> he vocalizes.   To me this means that he depends
> upon the beauty of the accompaniment, the poem and
> the melody line for his inspiration.   This student
> should not be made to vocalize.   For him to spend

time singing musically trivial vocalises can only result in throaty, dull, harmful singing.   Another student may vocalize beautifully.   He may be enamored
of the sound of his own voice or his teacher's voice
. . . .   This student should vocalize [Foote 1963, p. 22].

Principles of Practicing

A regular and systematic approach to vocal practice
is essential to attaining the desired vocal prowess.   Field-
Hyde (1950, p. 51) says that upon nothing does the progress
of students so much depend as the nature and quality of their
practicing.   Vocal practice relies heavily on the student's
initiative and tenacity.   According to Frisell (1964, p. 84),
in no other art form is a performer so bound by personal
responsibility, and, after allowing for the part played by
others in gaining vocal technique, in the final analysis the
singer himself must be held responsible.

Principles of vocal practice. --"Start the first practice
period by limbering up the body with a few stretching exercises which will tend to relax the body and render it more
alive" (Treash 1948, p. 4).   "It is very important to spend
fifteen or twenty minutes limbering up the muscles of articulation" (Waters 1943b, p. 571).   "Many beginners will not
understand the importance of short but frequent practice
sessions at the beginning of vocal training" (Rosewall 1961,
p. 74).   In order to provide the proper motivation for practice, Field-Hyde (1950, p. 38) and Simpson (1965, p. 2)
stress the need of the student knowing the reason behind
assigning a specific vocalise.

Supervision of practice. --Many teachers prefer no
practicing by beginning students, except under their supervision.   "This is often advisable until one begins to understand what is desired, and the way to go about achieving it"
(Rose Bampton 1949, p. 52 and Astrid Varnay 1943, p. 689).
Douglas Stanley (1950, p. 155) says that technical practice
by the pupil outside the studio is harmful at all times and at
all stages of development; when practising alone, he will inevitably listen to his own voice rather than concentrate on
the teacher's directions.   Fuchs (1964, p. 33) offers a solution to the problem; he suggests letting the student sing un-
corrected at a lesson, and telling him to try and correct
himself.   Only when a teacher is sure that the student can
do this should he be allowed to practice on his own.

Very little vocal practice should in fact be done in
the first months. These first months of the student's
training should be aimed primarily at developing the
muscles, giving him an understanding of the vocal
mechanism and instilling correct mental concepts of
tone and control [Rose 1962, p. 240].

Silent practice as a device. --"On an instrument, one
can practice a group of notes for an hour, but the voice is
not so constituted and one must learn to think more and use
the voice less" (Rosalie Miller 1957, p. 18). "Not all practice need be VOCAL; much of it must be MENTAL, for the
mind can be made to SAVE the voice" (Whitlock 1968a,
p. 17). "A rest period of the length of the practice period
should be inserted between it and the next" (Treash 1948,
p. 4). " 'Silent practice' or tonal contemplation is the practice of listening to tones in one's own mind--tonal imagery.
Lengthy periods can be spent in this manner with beneficial
results" (T. Williams 1953, p. 17).

The use of piano accompaniment. --Cranmer (1957,
p. 23) cautions the teacher about playing accompaniments;
he cannot give full attention to his pupil. Diercks (1963,
p. 23) says that it is well to allow the singer to experience
the accompaniment early in the presentation of the song.
Charles (1953, p. 6) seems to agree: "Without a comprehension of the harmonic structure of a song the singer cannot competently interpret." Whitlock (1967, p. 60) indicates
that a song without an accompaniment is only half a song,
and little more than a vocalise. Neilson (1954, p. 11) adds
that it is often helpful to use such aids as tape, wire, or
disc recording of accompaniments to vocalises and songs.

Various factors in practicing. --The following are
selected from 15 statements offering miscellaneous suggestions for vocal practice:

Take the different cadenzas in your repertoire apart
from the rest of the airs or phrases in which they
occur. Sing them a semitone below the key in which
they are written, then in the original key. When
they go well in the original key, take them up a half
tone higher ... [then] they can be sung in the original
key with more ease [Duval 1958, p. 97].

Work constantly before a mirror [Eberhart 1962,
p. 33].

The daily use of staccato exercises is a most important factor in voice conditioning [McLean 1951b, p. 8].

I exercise my voice every day, never for too long at a time, of course, but with regularity [Eleanor Steber 1946, p. 365].

Do not continue to practice tones you know are incorrect [Christy 1967, p. 24].

SUMMARY, ANALYSIS AND INTERPRETATION

From the literature used in this study, 640 concepts relating to vocal pedagogy were culled.   Over the 26 categories devised for this chapter, a divergence of opinion was expressed on each item.   Trends and prevalent opinions, derived from a comparative study of Table 1 are enumerated below:

1. The benefits of vocal study seem to be assumed by most writers.   Comments were sparse and rather generalized on this subject.
2. Definitive goals and objectives, as a factor in learning to sing, are very important.   Thirty-six statements were gathered on this subject.   Fields gathered 20.
3. Statements concerning the standardization of vocal training found by this researcher are significantly fewer in number than those found by Fields.   Eleven statements were gathered which expressed any opinion on this question in contrast to the 31 statements found by Fields.   Since this facet of instruction does not seem to be of primary concern, it would appear that recent writers are more mature in outlook and more tolerant than those of the immediate past.
4. Approximately half as many statements were gathered in this study as were found by Fields in regard to the importance of the psychological approach.   On the basis of this one item, it may be assumed the empirical approach to singing instruction is less prevalent than during the span of the former research.   Two other factors are pertinent at this point.   The personal interest of the researcher is directed toward the psychological approach and a subconscious

effort to find such concepts would have resulted in a
larger figure, if they were present; however, the
psychological concepts are not as precisely stated
as those of the mechanistic approach.

This trend is further substantiated in two other categories under the general heading of the psychological
approach. The category the vocal act is unconscious
and involuntary tabulates less than half the number
of concepts found by Fields. Relaxation a factor in
vocal training is reflected in the same proportion.
Only one category, spontaneity and naturalness are
characteristics, finds increased acceptance in the
writings of vocal authorities.

5. Fifty-three concepts were gathered on classifying
voices. Fields listed 30. It is conjectured that the
Husson (1957a) experiments have prompted additional
comments on this facet of singing.

Throughout this chapter and subsequent ones as well,
it has been assumed that little agreement exists as to the
best approach to vocal instruction. Divergencies of opinion
come from the difficulties inherent in studying a personal,
artistic activity. These opinions are not only based on the
experimental evidence, as it is seen by experimenters, but
on empirical knowledge gathered from many sources and
compiled at times in disarray. The empiricists generally
found their belief in the personal, traditional approach, in
one degree or another, gained from a succession of teachers
going back to Porpora and his contemporaries. Bernard
Taylor (1951b, p. 6) writes:

> Since the human vocal instrument is the only instru-
> ment that is entirely subject to the laws of anatomy,
> physiology, psychology and acoustics, and because so
> much scientific research has been undertaken during
> the past fifty years, it is only natural and inevitable
> that every new discovery of a scientific nature even
> remotely related to the human vocal mechanism,
> should bring forth opinions that would lay claim to
> this or that idea, and designed to 'settle' once and
> for all, the problem about how to sing.

To accuse the vocal scientist of stirring up controversies for the sake of gaining publicity or personal aggran-
dizement or to charge them with gross overemphasis of physiological factors, in no way settles the various questions.
It is not sufficient to effect a mere review of opposing points

of view.   A position more tenable is that no one school of
thought need necessarily have a monopoly on right answers
in voice instruction.   The facts, as they evolve, reveal that
some part of each opposing point of view becomes vital in
the total and correct picture.

To conclude, statements of Vennard and Gilliland are
helpful in understanding the appropriate position:

> The teacher finds that the mechanistic, which is the
> most physical of all the pedagogies, and the inspira-
> tional, which is the most metaphysical, are intimately
> interrelated.   In this life, at least, what is the mind
> without the body, or the body without the mind?
> [Vennard 1958, p. 25].

> Let us reconstruct our philosophy and teaching pro-
> cedures to the end that our voice and choral students
> will be more desirous of and able to improve the
> quality of their experiences, the stuff of which educa-
> tion consists.   Our profession has a great field of
> subject matter and presents the opportunity to affect
> the lives of countless students.   Why don't we learn
> to use our opportunities to the greatest advantage?
> [Gilliland 1967, p. 57].

Chapter III

CONCEPTS OF BREATHING

"Breathing, " as defined by Fields (1947, p. 43) is
"the act or process of drawing air into the lungs for oxy-
genating and purifying the blood, and its subsequent exhalation. "

In a study of the vocal process, it is helpful to understand the organs and their functions in phonation. The
breathing process is closely connected with the action of the
vocal mechanism. "For over two centuries it has been cus-
tomary in vocal physiology to divide the vocal organs into
three principal parts: (1) the respiratory organ, which
serves as the activator of voice production; (2) the laryngeal
voice generator with the immediately surrounding parts of the
pharynx; (3) the structures of vocal modulation and articulation within the resonance tube" (Luchsinger and Arnold 1965,
p. 3).

THEORIES

The Importance and Nature of Breathing

Breathing Is a Primary Consideration

The respiratory process, being vital to sustain life,
is frequently referred to as "the motive power" of the voice.
Twenty-four authors provided statements which give attention
to the primary function of breathing in the singing art.

> Breathing should be very carefully studied. The
> beauty of singing will depend on how the forces of
> the breathing mechanism are coordinated with phona-
> tion [Lester 1957, p. 26].

> The difference between those who have gained the
> heights and those who have not is all in a confident
> way of breathing. The successful ones learned to
> breathe the breath of life. Those who depended on

41

Table 2. SUMMARY OF CONCEPTS OF BREATHING

	Number of Statements in "Teaching Singing"	Number of Statements in "Training the Singing Voice"
I. Theories of breathing		
A. The importance and nature of breathing		
1. breathing a primary consideration	24	20
2. pre-vocal training advised	8	13
B. Physiological factors		
1. action of ribs and diaphragm	35	17
2. other coordinating factors	25	8
II. Methods of cultivating breath control		
A. A psychological approach		
1. natural breathing advised	30	48
2. singing develops breathing	13	23
3. interpretational controls		
a) by correct phrasing	12	8
b) by synchronization with the music	4	2
c) expressional intent regulates breathing	11	9
d) other devices for improving breathing	8	5
B. The technical approach		
1. postural controls		
a) through physical culture	64	46
b) through maintaining a correct chest position	42	33
2. voluntary control of breathing		
a) direct control of breathing organs advised	14	24
b) direct control of breathing organs not advised	19	11
3. diaphragmatic control		
a) diaphragmatic control is essential	39	27
b) diaphragmatic control is not essential	18	9

4. orificial controls
   a) breathing through
      mouth advised   17   8
   b) breathing through
      nose advised   5   5
   c) breathing through mouth
      and nose advised   11   12
5. quantitative factors
   a) breath economy   42   56
   b) breath pressure and
      support   30   27
   c) breath renewal, fre-
      quency and speed   26   17

              TOTALS   497   428

voice alone, breathed the breath of exhaustion [Kester 1953, p. 13].

My feeling is that the entire basis of good singing is proper breathing [Rosalie Miller 1951, p. 15].

The vital act of respiration is the physiological basis of our life. It is also of fundamental value in the production of the voice [Meano 1967, p. 43].

It is that as the breath is used, so will the voice appear to behave [Kelsey 1952, p. 448].

The respiration for the singer is positively unique, and on this count alone voice culture should be as universal a branch of education as reading and writing [Armstrong 1945b, p. 375].

So important is correct breathing that should the singer's method be wrong, the singing method will not be right [McLean 1964, p. 2].

One thing is certain. The breath is the source of tonal energy and correct breathing is the source of tonal beauty [DeYoung 1958, p. 43].

A great many persons have good voices and plenty of talent, but one thing that almost none have is singing breathing [Protheroe 1945, p. 124].

The breath is not only the motive power of the voice
--it is also the connecting link between his mind and
his body [Freer 1959b, p. 23].

Correct breathing is really the touchstone of beautiful
tone [Sister M. Laudesia 1965, p. 10].

Tone can be no better than the breathing habits that
give it life [Jan Peerce 1944, p. 206].

Pre-Vocal Training in Breathing

According to eight writers, a prerequisite of good
singing control is the development of the breathing mechanism
beyond the needs of normal activity.   The breathing system
must then be trained or re-trained for the singing process.
"It is a mistake to allow a singer to begin training with
vocal exercises.   The young singers should begin work by
keeping silent while learning the mechanics of breathing ...
then assign exercises in the technique of drawing and supporting breath" (Welitsch 1950, p. 18).   "One would not ex-
pect to become championship material in tennis or golf ...
without faithful practice over a period of years, yet many
people who aspire to be singers think that it is not necessary
for them to do any consistent practicing of exercises to increase breath support and agility" (Wyckoff 1955, p. 17).
"The muscles which are usually the weakest, particularly in
the case of female students are the abdominal muscles.
These must be strengthened by suitable exercises" (Rose
1962, p. 115).   "Breathing exercises should be done daily to
attain elasticity and increase the capacity to take as much
breath as needed in singing without forcing" (Koppel 1956,
p. 19).   Slater (1950, p. 25) indicates that his teachers and
every artist with whom he discussed breathing, emphasized
the same deep, diaphragmatic breathing exercises apart from
singing, so that breathing could become an automatic process.

Physiological Factors

Diaphragm and Ribs

The physiological function of the diaphragm is that of
a muscle of inhalation.   This precept is supported in statements by Weer (1948, p. 37), Vennard (1967, p. 24), and
Judson and Weaver (1965, p. 10).   According to Hardy (1958,

p. 12), the diaphragm does not push the air out. When the
singer exhales, the set of muscles opposing the diaphragm
does the work. Consequently, he adds, the diaphragm does
not support breath or tone; what it does is to hold against
the muscles of exhalation so that they will act steadily as
they lift the breath out. Meano (1967, p. 27), an Italian
physician, gives a more technical description of the process:
"The diaphragm has an important function in vocal physiology
for ... it constitutes a true and proper 'mortise' during respiratory muscular contractions, as it creates a partial
vacuum for the expansion of the lung tissues. "

   Baker (1963, p. 14) says the moment the breath enters
the body the diaphragm flattens, the upper abdomen protrudes
slightly. Kelsey, in Grove's Dictionary (p. 55), adds that
this protrusion must not be allowed to become too pronounced,
or the power to contract the muscles inward at the moment
of attack will be lost. Rosewall (1961, p. 17) calls this
function a "falling away" of the abdominal wall and he stresses it should relax completely and instantaneously. James
Lawson (1955, p. 15) states that this bulge or "falling away"
is not the diaphragm, but it is caused by the diaphragm
dropping during deep inspiration; to all intents and purposes,
he feels, if you consider this as being the actual diaphragm
you will not go wrong.

   "Expansive rib action surrounds the entire chest, especially toward the lower and middle back ribs" (NATS 1957).
The function of the ribs, as a controlling factor in breathing, is further stressed in these statements:

   Inhale by lifting the lowest ribs, under the arms, and
   by expanding the waistline [Waters 1943a, p. 91].

   The muscular expansion at the base of the ribs must,
   of course, be full [Rosalie Miller 1050, p. 15].

   Keep the lower ribs unremittingly extended while we
   are actually singing [Young 1956, p. 42].

   If the singer wishes to have fullest control over the
   tension of the abdominal muscles as well as fine control over breath volume, he must first 'set' the ribs
   and then think only of controlling the abdominal muscles and diaphragm [Rose 1962, p. 83].

   The ribs must never fall from your first breath until

your last note [Cranmer 1957, p. 24].

Other Coordinating Factors

Other factors in achieving constant equilibrium and harmonious functioning of the breathing mechanism for singing, are mentioned.   Alberti (1947, p. 6) simply states: "Feel the breath resting securely on the chest and keep it there.   Send out the breath as fast as possible. "   Charles K. Scott (1954, p. 411) describes the action this way:

> Popular sayings nearly always 'hit the nail on the head' and when we are told that a man 'puts no stomach' into his work we are given exactly the right reason for it being of poor quality.   It applies to singing most thoroughly.   If a singer does not use his stomach or, more correctly, belly muscles, he will never have good tone or good rhythm.

Ida Franca (1951b, p. 1) urges the singer to draw in the part of the abdomen below the navel as well as the navel itself. Sharnova (1964, p. 14) seems to agree with this: "Support the breath through firmness in the lower abdomen. "   Weer (1948, p. 23) advocates lifting the breastbone before the lungs are filled with air; the singer should never inhale the breath until after the breastbone has been lifted to its proper position.   Sabin (1953, p. 19), in an interview with Samuel Margolis, quotes the noted New York teacher: "I do not believe that one should breathe only from the diaphragm.   Breathing from the diaphragm is not enough, for if the singer pushes he will not have his breath long.   He should also use the chest. "   The universally accepted precept of "quiet shoulders" is represented in Reid's (1950, p. 147) statement: "Once the student has been made to breathe without raising his chest or shoulders the taking of a breath will automatically cause the diaphragm to do the work for which it was intended by nature.   By keeping the chest and shoulders quiet they are unable to come into tension and interfere with the neck muscles. "

CULTIVATING BREATH CONTROL

A Psychological Approach

Natural Breathing Advised

The Singer's Glossary (Fields 1952, p. 38) defines
"natural breathing" as "broathing that has not been influenced
by direct technical training or localized effort of any kind."
In the opinion of 30 writers, this instinctive manner of
breathing is desirable. The following statements represent
this point of view:

> Despite the elaborate theories advanced by many
> people, no thinking and no muscular control are re-
> quired for breathing [Williamson 1951a, p. 49].

> The art of taking in the breath, must be as uncon-
> scious as it is when we speak [Duval 1958, p. 89].

> Avoid, at first, any 'systems of breathing' ... that
> require mechanical or methodical practising; most of
> them run contrary to nature [Husler and Rodd-Marling
> 1965, p. 50].

> Basically, one does not learn to breathe correctly--
> one only relearns the natural breathing that was un-
> conscious in childhood [Varnay 1943, p. 689].

> The breath takes care of itself; it resents your help
> [Montell 1950, p. 85].

> Of all the methods advocated, there can be no doubt
> that the method of 'natural' breathing is the best
> [Bollew 1952a, p. 22].

> When we try to bring in unnatural breathing and sup-
> port ideas we merely get in nature's way [Mallet 1963,
> p. 8].

Singing Develops Breathing

The basic tenet of this topic is that the requirements
of singing in itself, in practice and performance, will tend to
develop proficiency of breath. This concept is not unrelated
to the idea of natural breathing. "Nothing brings a more
free flow of breath than the thought of spontaneously telling
or imparting something to an audience; it affords the most
perfect release of breath, tone, and words--as well as breaking down self-consciousness" (MacDonald 1960, p. 57).
"Breathing for singing is best taught when it is coordinated
with the sung sound" (Appelman 1967, p. 16).

Interpretational Controls

By correct phrasing. --"The breath, which is supplied
automatically to the singer desiring to express the words,
thus becomes a natural part of the interpretation and phrasing" (P. Peterson 1966, p. 19).   This concept suggests that
breathing habits are governed by the phrase to be sung.
"Breath control is accomplished 'indirectly' through mental
concentration on tone and phrasing desired" (Christy 1961,
p. 26).   "You can sing the average length phrase with no
breath at all" (Dengler 1944, p. 35).   "For a conception of
correct inhalation simply follow one careful and perfect release by a careful and perfect attack" (Theman 1948, p. 5).
"How often does phrasing today sound 'gaspy' because of the
intrusion of too many breaths!   Let me state unequivocally
that when the majority of singers 'need' to take a breath,
they really need to RELEASE TENSION, rather than replenish
the breath supply" (Whitlock 1968a, p. 32).

Synchronization with the music and expressional intent. --Breathing requirements may be governed by the expressional demands of a song.   "One of the chief aims in
learning to breath consciously is to replenish our breath
quickly and effortlessly without disturbing the flow of our
spoken or musical meaning and then to propel our breath
gradually and under complete but relaxed control, and to
finish each phrase in the most telling manner" (McClosky
1959, p. 11).   According to Stanley (1950, p. 127), "timing"
is fundamentally important in singing; the singer must gradu-
ate the degrees of tension for the pitches and dynamics of
the tones with great precision, never relaxing between tones,
only when he takes a breath and then he must relax as completely as possible.

Other devices for improving breathing. --Klein and
Schjeide (1967, p. 28) say a helpful device to activate the reflexes that close the glottis is fast panting, breathing out
until only little air remains.   Levinson (1962, p. 17) suggests
opening the mouth in a relaxed position, and taking a surprise
breath.   Each phrase should begin with this surprise or sus-
pended breath.   In contrast to this, William Jones (1947,
p. 3) urges the singer to guard against jerky gaspings, which
he feels are largely responsible for poor interpretation.

Vennard (1967, p. 34) credits Frans Hoffman for a
helpful device in breath management of long phrases.   He had
his pupils learn long phrases backwards.   That is, the last

two measures are practiced first several times, then the
last three, and gradually adding to the length of the phrase
until finally the student can begin at the beginning and accomplish the phrase without any sense of breath difficulty.

The Technical Approach

Postural Controls

A basic document of laws and precepts upon which
vocal pedagogy may be based has been prepared by the National Association of Teachers of Singing. This pronounce-
ment, Training the Vocal Instrument (1957), defines posture:

> This means a free and graceful body carriage in
> which each part of the vocal instrument is perfectly
> balanced and is in proper relationship to every other
> part. The head is erect, without stiffness; the spine
> straight, not slumped; the chest moderately elevated
> and the feet firmly and squarely placed so that the
> entire body is buoyantly supported.

Bachner (1947, p. 39) places great importance on correct posture for good singing; he says that, in time, correct
posture will actually compel freedom of voice production.
Westerman (1950, p. 7) details a chain of closely allied
actions in singing: poor articulation is the result of poor
muscle actions of resonation; poor resonation is the result
of poor muscle actions of phonation; poor phonation lies in
poor respiration habits; and that poor respiration is caused
by poor posture.   Trusler and Ehret (1960, p. 1) add to this:
"Good posture is the foundation of controlled breathing, and
controlled breathing is the foundation of singing. "   Lester
(1957, p. 26) makes this observation in regard to posture:
"My objections to using the formal posture with all students
are that it requires concentration that might be better applied
otherwise, and it may cause the student to get a fixation on
that one position. "

Ferguson (1955, p. 329), in a study of organic lesions
of the larynx produced by mis-use of the voice, gives suggestions for posture positions; he theorizes that the straight-
ness of the spine and the position of the head, are important
to sound production.   When the spine is straight, there is a
straight pathway out from the larynx, and if the head is
slightly flexed, the anterior cervical muscles are relaxed,

preventing constriction.   Bernard Taylor (1950, p. 10), respected New York voice teacher, similarly urges the singer
to become spine conscious; to do this, we must feel that the
spine, which is the main supporting structure, carries the
entire weight of the body.

Other opinions on the correct mode of posture for
singing are representative of the 106 statements listed in
this category:

He must remember to keep his neck long, his head
slightly raised, his jaw dropped [Winsel 1966, p. 54].

An erect posture, using combined diaphragmatic and
intercostal expansion for inspiration with the use of
the abdominal muscles for the act of expiration is the
Singer's Breath [Ragatz 1952, p. 6].

The head, chest, and pelvis should be supported by
the spine in such a way that they align themselves
one under the other--head erect, chest high, pelvis
tipped so that the 'tail is tucked in' [Vennard 1967,
p. 19].

An erect bodily position--the chest slightly elevated,
the abdominal muscles flat at the start of taking
breath, and the head on top of the spine, not in front
of it--is the ideal posture [Werrenrath 1951, p. 61].

The chest should never be moved, either in inhalation
or exhalation [Fuchs 1964, p. 75].

Three most basic fundamentals to emphasize in ob-
taining good posture are: (1) the upper chest must
be lifted first BEFORE inhalation starts; (2) the chest
must remain comfortably high and quiet during singing; (3) the spine, through the neck downward, should
be kept flexibly stretched [Christy 1961, p. 21].

Voluntary vs. Involuntary Breathing

The controversial subject of conscious and voluntary
control of breathing versus indirect control of breathing is
discussed in statements from 33 authors.   Indirect control
of breathing is the more generally favored approach to singing artistry.   "In singing, we have no direct control over

the organs involved in breathing" (Beckman 1955, p. 72).
"Breathing is automatic, and all muscles are elastic and
responsive" (MacDonald 1960, p. 18). "Breath becomes voice
through the operation of the will and the instrumentality of
the vocal organ" (MacRae 1948, p. 2). "There should be no
attempt to consciously 'control' the breath in the vocal act"
(Wilcox 1945, p. 4). "It is much more logical to let the
subconscious breathe for you" (Cor 1944, p. 27 and Ririe
1960, p. 18).

Some authors' opinions concerning direct control of
breathing are represented in the following:

One must understand that breathing for singing is
always controlled or stabilized expiration; it is not
passive as is breathing for living [Appelman 1967,
p. 12].

The singing breath, so necessary for the support of
tone and the maintenance of the phrase, is on an altogether larger scale. It is diaphragmatic, it fills
the entire lung cavity, and it must be mastered consciously and voluntarily [Resnik 1948, p. 281].

Considerable voluntary control of breathing exists in
that rate and depth can be altered at will and breathing can be arrested altogether for a limited period of
time [Campbell 1958, p. 69].

The majority opinion, however, is that breathing,
being a form of physical coordination, can be dealt
with directly [Casselman 1951b, p. 21].

Diaphragmatic Control

The opinion is held by some teachers and writers
that the employment of conscious control of the diaphragm
is essential for the technical requirements of singing.
Thirty-nine statements favor diaphragmatic control, while 18
statements reject direct control of the diaphragm. Fracht
and Robinson (1960, p. 58) feel that the diaphragm is important for controlled breathing because it is the projecting
force for deeper tone. According to Uris (1956, p. 7), good
voice production depends on control of the diaphragm and of
the lower muscles supporting it. "Always bear in mind,
that the starting point, or foundation, of breath control is

the diaphragm" (Martino 1953, p. 41).

        DeYoung (1958, p. 43) believes that it is important
that the diaphragm should be left free, so that its action is
functional.   Other opinions rejecting direct control are represented in these statements:

        The diaphragm does not respond to the will of the
        performer. Its spasmodic contraction causes what
        are called hiccoughs, which cannot be shut off at
        will [Briggs 1955, p. 9].

        The diaphragm needs no deliberate handling whatever
        [Husler and Rodd-Marling 1965, p. 36].

        The attempted conscious control of the diaphragm is
        not only wrong but dangerous, because it causes
        muscular rigidity, and that in itself is the enemy of
        flexibility and freedom [Baker 1963, p. 15].

        We allow the diaphragm to create its customary
        vacuum and the air is drawn in automatically, letting
        the sides expand [Golde 1952, p. 12].

Orificial Control

        Whether breathing should be through the mouth, the
nose, or both is a question which often evokes opinions.
Respiration can be accomplished through the orificial opening; however, in respect to the aesthetic sense, some writers
say it is desirable to inhale quietly through the nose. The
concern of the writers is that there be little disturbance of
the resonance or articulatory areas. Table 3 reveals the
large number of writers who have expressed opinions on this
question.

        Breathing through the mouth is advised. --"Nose
breathing, which permits the intake of air at a slower rate
only, becomes insufficient for the needs of speedy inspiration
in speaking and singing" (Brodnitz 1953, p. 41). Vennard
(1967, p. 27) says that the air is taken "in" through the nose
or mouth, preferably the latter. "In most cases it cannot
be taken fast enough through the nose without dilating the
nostrils noticeably, and furthermore, inhaling through the
mouth tends by reflex action to adjust the resonators correctly. " Vennard (p. 93) further stresses that while the

Table 3. SUMMARY OF ORIFICIAL CONTROL CONCEPTS

Breathe Through the Nose	Breathe Through the Mouth	Breathe Through Both
Bairstow & Greene 1946, p. 20	Brodnitz 1953, p. 39	Bachner 1947, p. 121
Gigli 1945, p. 13	R. Brown 1946, p. 68	Beckman 1955, p. 69
Longo 1945, p. 23	Collins 1060a, p. 33	Bullard 1947, p. 75
Maurice-Jacquet 1947, p. 15	Field-Hyde 1950, p. 16	Christy 1967, p. 59
Puritz 1956, p. 15	Frisell, 1964, p. 31	German 1952, p. 32
	J. Lawson, 1955, p. 24	Klein & Schjeide 1967, p. 45
	Liebling 1956, p. 6	F. Lawson, 1944, p. 6
	MacDonald 1960, p. 18	W. Rice 1961, p. 32
	Reid 1950, p. 148	Sharnova 1964, p. 14
	Ross 1959, p. 21	Tkach 1948, p. 6
	C. Scott 1954, p. 9	Westerman 1947, p. 20
	Sharnova 1949, p. 42	
	Sunderman 1958, p. 22	
	Vennard 1967, p. 27	
	Weer 1948, p. 96	
	Wilcox 1945, p. 5	

nasal passage is ideally suited to its function of filtering and warming incoming air, "it is a poor means of taking breath quickly, and it is a poor resonator for either improving or building the tone. For these reasons, most singers both inhale and sing through the mouth." Field-Hyde (1950, p. 16) says the real objection to nasal inspiration is not so much based on the quantity of air that can be inhaled through the mouth in the same length of time, as on the rapid and constant readjustments which have to be effected by the tongue and soft palate, in order to inhale between the musical phrases.

Breathing through the nose is advised. --"Never, never breathe through the mouth. To breathe through the mouth is to court ruin of the tone, the inrush of air dries the throat" (Gigli 1945, p. 13). "Breathing through the nose is in accord with nature. It supplies more oxygen to the lungs in a quicker length of time than breathing through the mouth" (Maurice-Jacquet 1947, p. 15). "Whenever possible, breathe through the nose, as that ensures a deeper breath as well as being kinder to the throat" (Puritz 1956, p. 15).

Breathing through the mouth and the nose is advised. --"Inhale through the nose and mouth" (Sharnova 1964, p. 14). "Take a quick half-breath simultaneously through both the mouth and nose" (Christy 1967, p. 59). "Breathing through the nose as well as the mouth is helpful in maintaining the opening between the soft palate and the back of the throat" (Klein and Schjeide 1967, p. 45).

Quantitative Factors

The relationship between the vital capacity of the lungs and the amount of air needed in singing is discussed by forty-two authors. Economy of breath is a central theme, around which quantitative factors are constructed.

Economy of breath. --A noted laryngologist, Friedrich S. Brodnitz (1953, p. 79) says the goal of good singing can best be reached with the greatest economy of air: "The less air used for a certain sound--whether piano or forte--the better the result will be." Some other statements, represented here, are also concerned with minimal utilization of air for singing:

> Learn to take as little breath as possible. It is not so much the amount, but rather how it is used [Bellows 1963, p. 97].

> If you make a habit of taking in a lot of air, of holding it and hoarding it, you will eventually weaken your breathing organ and, in consequence, your throat as well [Husler and Rodd-Marling 1965, p. 50].

> The faulty idea persists that inspiration should be maximal, and that phonic exhalation should resemble a vigorous exercise [Luchsinger and Arnold 1965, p. 18].

> Breath control, as applied to singing, means economy of the breath while singing [Judd 1951, p. 34].

> In singing, an excessive intake of breath induces tension of the throat, the diaphragm, and other parts of the body [Bollew 1952a, p. 22].

Economy of breath as applied to volume. --"A beginner should never be allowed to fill his lungs to the limit in
taking a breath for singing.   It is unnecessary and even
harmful, since it leads to undue punishment of the larynx"
(Frankfurter-Karnieff 1951, p. 23).   "The abdominal cavities
should not be filled to capacity, otherwise a phrase cannot
be attacked well, with smooth, clear tone" (Fuchs 1964,
p. 75).   "Those who believe in progressively increasing the
intake of breath always remain shallow breathers.   In any
case, it is now considered doubtful whether the capacity of
lungs, as determined by the spirometer, gives any true in-
dication of physical vitality" (Husler and Rodd-Marling 1965,
p. 37).   "To convince the student that little breath is needed
to launch vocal tone ... we require him to 'Take no breath,
attack a high note, sing a series of high notes, or a phrase,
or up and down the scale' " (Herbert-Caesari 1951a, p. 290).

Breath control is intuitive. --There are those who
favor the concept that it is preferable to "leave the breath
alone. " Nelson Eddy (1943, p. 77) has said that he does not
detect a great difference between breathing in ordinary conversation and breathing during singing; he wonders why a
dark mystery is made of breathing.   Another professional
artist-singer seems to agree.   Hertha Glaz (1943, p. 503)
feels that too much preoccupation with artificial techniques
of breathing becomes confusing and may lead to constriction.
Louis Nicholas (1969, p. 6) suggests if a student has no particular problem with breath, it is usually better not to bother
him with any mention of it until he needs help to overcome
some particular difficulty or momentary slump.   Professor
Nicholas goes on to say: "Technical explanations and work
on breathing often confuse the intuitive or natural singer and
make him feel self-conscious and constrained so that his
singing becomes even more effortful. "   Eugene Casselman
(1951b, p. 21) agrees: "The cardinal principle is this: teach
breathing sparingly; the more the student can gain with little
or no mention of the breath, the less inhibited will he be. "

Breath pressure and breath support. --In this concept,
the concern of vocal authorities is the amount of breath
pressure employed to produce a given note during singing.
Kelsey's (1950, p. 78) view on breath pressure is that a
steadily applied pressure of the chest, downwards towards
the surface of the diaphragm, causes the diaphragm to push
upward with equal steadiness against the base of the lungs.
Thus the air is squeezed out, says Kelsey (1951, p. 203),
"as both Caruso and Bonci insisted. "   Collins (1969a, p. 32)

and Charles K. Scott (1954, p. 9) use the term "stored-up
energy" to describe what they consider the secret of proper
breath control.   According to Paul Peterson (1966, p. 82),
added breath pressure is attained by the increased actions
and firmness of the large breathing muscles.

        Brodnitz (1961, p. 21) says that the air flow increases
as a response to dynamic change.   According to Herbert-
Caesari (1951a, p. 97), there is absolutely no need to increase the breath pressure as the pitch rises; it should be
kept constant all the way up the scale.   Finally, Appelman
(1967, p. 11) defines support as "the act of constantly sustaining the vocalized sound with the breath pressure. "

        Breath renewal, frequency and speed. --The advis-
ability of a rhythmic flow of the breath, as opposed to
"breathe, hold, sing, " is reflected in these positions:

>   The object in taking a breath is not to store it up in
>   the chest, but to let it out again in a steady con-
>   trolled flow....   Any attempt to hold the breath back
>   leads inevitably to muscular stiffness, and this is the
>   death-blow to all singing [Baker 1963, p. 13].

>   I never saw any of the great artists breathing with
>   any effort, but watching them carefully, I did notice
>   that they always took a breath in advance and not im-
>   mediately upon singing a note.   In other words, the
>   process is breathing, holding, and singing; a breath
>   taken immediately at the beginning of a phrase
>   hampers clear singing as well as clear thinking
>   [Maurice-Jacquet 1947, p. 14].

>   For what the singer has to do is to appear never to
>   breathe [C. Scott 1954, p. 5].

>   There should never be a static moment in this life
>   activity; we should never 'hold the breath, ' instead,
>   we should make use of what I term 'breath timing'--
>   the precise awareness of when to inhale before be-
>   ginning a phrase [Beckman 1955, p. 73].

>   Time the inflow of breath to avoid holding [Garling-
>   house 1951, p. 5].

SUMMARY, ANALYSIS AND INTERPRETATION

Statements totalling 497 were gathered on the theoretical and methodological concepts of breathing. A consideration of these statements leads to the conclusion that respiration is given primary consideration in the acquisition of singing technique. A comparative analysis of the tabulated data in Fields' Training the Singing Voice and the tabulations of this study reveal the following prevailing positions:

1. The proper mode of breathing for singing is essential for good vocal production.
2. Pre-vocal training in breathing is not extensively employed.
3. The diaphragm, as a muscle of inhalation, does not give direct vocal support. The primary position of the ribs for singing is a high expansive feeling, particularly around the lower and middle back ribs.
4. The chest and shoulders should remain quiet with very little movement during all phases of respiration.
5. Natural breathing, as an unconscious, instinctive act, is a desired objective in vocal technique. During the formative period of vocal study, however, deliberate, conscious emphasis should be afforded the respiratory process.
6. It is not generally accepted that the needs of breathing for singing can be met through a song approach.
7. Correct phrasing, synchronization of breathing with the music and regulation of breathing for expressional intent can be achieved only as breath control is gained, but these factors are not felt to be of strong significance in developing breath control.
8. Continued strong emphasis is afforded postural position as being vital to good singing.
9. Positions are almost equally divided regarding voluntary versus involuntary methods of breathing. Fields found a decided preference for direct control.
10. Conscious diaphragmatic action as a technique in singing is advocated by a majority.
11. Breathing through the mouth is the prevailing method of orificial respiratory control.
12. The vital capacity of the lungs is not a significant factor in breath control.
13. An exaggerated emphasis on the breathing process is harmful rather than beneficial.

Comprehensive statements on the methodology of
breathing for singing are chosen as being representative of
the two most prevalent approaches to singing instruction.
The mechanistic-scientific method is represented in statements by Appelman and M. Greene.   Statements by Tomlins
and Baker are representative of the empirical school.

>The first technique of body control and support re-
>quires a sensation of abdominal pressure being
>countered by thoracic resistance in such a manner
>that the abdominal pressure is always greater than
>the resisting antagonist forces created by the mus-
>cles that comprise the rib-raiser group. . . .   The
>muscular sensation of effort is felt above the belt
>line.   The singer does not need to concentrate upon
>low tensions at the pubic arch.   Such contractions of
>the pelvic diaphragm are automatic. . . .   The second
>technique of body control and support is one in which
>the singer releases the dominating pressure of the
>abdominal and back musculature and employs a bal-
>anced suspension of thoracic and abdominal muscular
>forces that enable him to sustain the quiet vocalized
>sound with apparent ease [Appelman 1967, pp. 13-14].

>The most efficient method of respiration for vocal
>purposes is that known as the intercostal diaphrag-
>matic method, which may be considered as a 'central'
>type of breathing and distinct from other less efficient
>methods. . . .   A modification of the intercostal dia-
>phragmatic method is widely advocated for public
>speakers, actors and singers.   This consists of the
>introduction of the 'rib-reserve.'   The intercostals and
>levators hold the ribs in a position of full elevation
>throughout the repeated cycle of inspiration and ex-
>piration necessary for prolonged and continuous ut-
>terance.   The diaphragm and abdominal muscles are
>entirely responsible for filling and emptying the
>lungs.   Fixation of the ribs provides a thoracic res-
>ervoir of air which may be drawn upon in an emer-
>gency by relaxation of the intercostals to meet,   for
>example, the exigencies of opera or Shakespearean
>drama [M. Greene 1959, pp. 12-13].

>Nature sees to it that breathing is a continuous pro-
>cess; we should see to it that this breathing is equal
>to all demands made upon it and well up to the mea-
>sure of importance that the Creator in the economy

of nature intended. We cannot store up breath in advance of its need in actual use, as we do meat and drink, or replenish it afterward. With breath we live, as it were, from hand to mouth, each moment sufficient unto itself. ... Schools of breathing based solely on one or other of these parts, fail to understand the completeness of breathing, and the proportional interaction of the parts [Tomlins 1945, pp. 21-29].

Before I conclude this chapter on breathing, may I offer these warnings: (1) Let there be no forcing of the breath against the vocal cords. (2) Never stiffen the diaphragm before the act of singing in order to (what is called) 'support the tone.' A stiff diaphragm does not support the tone; it only stiffens it and eventually destroys it. (3) Methods of singing, the aim of which is to control breathing by muscular action or actions, are basically wrong. (4) Do not be misled into thinking that one's ability to juggle with names like Thorax, Trachea, Glottis, Pharynx, or to know that the diaphragm in a state of repose is the shape of a dome, will help one to breathe or sing any better. It is useful knowledge about the anatomy of singing but it has nothing whatever to do with the art of singing [Baker 1963, p. 15].

Chapter IV

CONCEPTS OF PHONATION

"Phonation" is the "act or process of generating
vocal sounds; it is the conception of vocal tone at its point
of production in the larynx. More explicitly, phonation is
the vibratory activity of the vocal cords so as to produce
pulsations sufficiently rapid to cause the sensation of tone"
(Fields 1947, p. 98). Vennard (1967, p. 248) defines this
act as "producing vocal sound. "

There is no disagreement on the point, and we may
accept it as a fact, that voice is initiated in that
part of the air tract known as the larynx. At least
as far back as the time of Galen (175 A. D.), it was
recognized that the edges of the glottis were an
essential factor in the production of voice. Views
concerning the manner in which the vocal folds
function have progressed through three stages: First,
the vocal 'cord' was thought of (Rayleigh, 1894) as
a string having its mass concentrated at its center
between its two points of attachment. Such a conception makes it easy to explain the production of
fundamentals and partials. In the second place, the
vocal 'bands' have been considered as membranous
bands stretched across the air channel. Finally,
the vocal 'lips' may be treated as elastic cushions
(Ewald, 1897; Scripture, 1901) which yield under
compression [Judson and Weaver 1965, p. 53].

The term "vocal cord" is in itself misleading.
"Vocal folds, " for instance, more accurately describes
that structure of the larynx having to do with primary tone
production. Vocal bands, lips, cushions, ledges, ligaments,
shelves, muscles, processes, and edges are other names
given to the voice-producing mechanism.

Table 4   SUMMARY OF CONCEPTS OF PHONATION

	Number of Statements in "Teaching Singing"	Number of Statements in "Training the Singing Voice"
I. Theories of phonation		
General description and physiological factors	171	137
II. Methods of controlling phonation		
A. A psychological approach to phonation		
1. total coordination is required	34	23
2. mental concept of tone and pitch		
a) anticipation controls phonation	31	43
b) anticipation controls pitch	27	19
B. The technical approach to phonation		
1. control of the oral cavity		
a) mouth opening is important	24	29
b) mouth opening is not important	17	9
2. lingual controls		
a) low tongue advised	34	31
b) free tongue advised	26	19
3. palatal controls		
a) palate should be raised	19	2
b) palate should be free	4	4
4. open throat concept		
a) control of throat advised	26	22
b) control of throat not advised	22	17
c) yawning as a device	32	20
5. position of the larynx		
a) larynx should move	14	9
b) larynx should not move	11	9
6. the attack	34	19
7. the vocal vibrato	32	51
TOTALS	558	463

THEORIES

General Description/Physiological Factors

There is yet no complete agreement as to how voice is produced in the larynx.   Several theories have been formulated.   (1) The voice is initiated as eddies of air current in the glottis, the shape and width of which are adjusted by the vocal folds; this is the "reed theory."   (2) The "vibrating string theory" presents the view that the voice is initiated by vibration of the vocal folds.   This vibration has been attributed to an air current which acts as a violin bow.   (3) More recently, the French scientist, Raoul Husson (1956, 1960) formulated a theory which suggests that the vibration of the vocal folds is an active process controlled by motor impulses from the central nervous system.   This is known as the "neurochronaxic theory."   (4) The "myoelastic theory" advances the idea that the interruption of an air current into puffs by the vocal cords results in variations of air pressure. "The subglottic pressure causes abduction when the arytenoid cartilages are immobile.   Adduction is caused by the elastic resistance of the vocal folds" (Sonninen 1956, p. 9).

The Husson findings have not been widely accepted (Brodnitz 1961, p. 17).   In a number of publications, van den Berg (1958) has attracted renewed attention to the classic myoelastic theory, giving particular emphasis to the aerodynamic aspects of the theory.

From various sources, authorities have contributed views concerning the act of phonation and the functional characteristics of the related musculature.

The Vocal Instrument is an Adjustable Vibrator

"The vibrator is in the larynx or voice-box.   It has been neglected by teachers until recently because it lies below the level of consciousness.   Since it could not be directly controlled, it was not trained, except by imagery and suggestion" (Vennard 1967, p. 16).   "The cords become thinner and again widen during vibration.   When the cords close, their edges not only meet, but actually overlap one another" (Tarnóczy 1951, p. 42).   "But the cords do not merely vibrate as a whole; they also vibrate in segments, and these segmental vibrations add harmonics (overtones) to the fundamental cord tone" (Punt 1967, p. 17).   "The laryn-

geal vibrator is adjustable in length, thickness, and tension
at the will of the singer" (Herbert-Caesari 1951a, p. 74).

Phonation Results from Inter-Play of Parts

Lateral to the vocal fold lies the thyro-arytenoid
muscle, divided arbitrarily into internal and external
portions. The vocal fold, extending from the thyroid
alae to the glottic process of the arytenoid, forms an
elastic boundary to the anterior two-thirds of the
glottis, and with the faculty of vibrating for purposes
of phonation; the posterior third of the glottic margin
is bounded by the arytenoid [Negus 1962, p. 165].

But--and it cannot be repeated too frequently--a properly functioning singing organ consists of one vast
interplay, widespread cyclical process, in which all
parts co-operate to support and help each other.   In
short, each muscle, as antagonist, regulates the action
of another [Husler and Rodd-Marling 1965, p. 23].

It is so little known and appreciated how the mouth-
pharynx cavity plays a really vital part in the adjustment
of the vocal cord mechanism; for weal or woe, its influence on it is enormous [Herbert-Caesari 1951a, p. 167].

Essentially, the sound-producing medium itself consists of two bands of flesh and muscle positioned on
each side of the larynx and extending parallel from
front to back.   They are anchored in cartilages that
are muscularly controlled, and when they are silent
they form a V, the point of which is fastened at the
front.   When we sing, the front is fixed, and the
arytenoid muscles at the rear tense them and make
them approximate; this together with the pressure of
the breath on the edges of these bands produces pho
nation [Cates 1959, p. 5].

Just as a small boy can change the shape of his arm
merely by tensing and relaxing his biceps, so the
vocal lips can change their shape by the action of the
fibers of the thyroarytenoids, but obviously change
may also result from any movement of the arytenoid
cartilages.   These odd-shaped little levers to which
the posterior ends of the vocal folds attach are operated
by the cricoarytenoid muscles [Vennard 1967, p. 57].

Phonation Results from Motive Power

The control of the flow of air over the vocal cords to
produce sound must be given to the powerful muscles
of breathing. It should never be accomplished by
using the vocal cords like a valve to pinch off the air
partially at the throat [J. Lawson 1955, p. 20].

In phonation, the false vocal cords relax, and only the
true vocal lips are brought together. The resistance
they offer to the breath causes it to vibrate as it is
forced through the valve by the action of the intercostal muscles plus the abdominals, controlled or
steadied by the diaphragm. The objective here is a
maintenance of pressure by a flow of breath. ... It
is the elasticity of air that determines this speed, not
the flow of breath. That which travels is not air,
but energy from released air pressure [Vennard 1967,
p. 38].

Compared with the sounding of musical instruments,
production of the voice in the larynx is rather unusual.
Its main principle may be defined by the aerodynamic
theory of passive vocal-cord vibration in the following
manner. When the vocal cords are closed, the subglottic air becomes compressed to such an extent that
its mounting pressure explodes the glottal closure.
At this moment the condensation of air is propagated
through the oral cavity into the surrounding air.
Following this explosive reduction of air pressure, the
vocal cords are driven back into closed position
through the elasticity of their contracted musculature.
Subglottic pressure increases again and the process is
repeated [Luchsinger and Arnold 1965, p. 25].

Phonation Results from Total Coordination

Although the singer has no direct control over a particular organ of the laryngeal anatomy, it is an hypothesis of this experimenter that the movements of
these specific parts are the result and not the cause
of a complex gestalt [Appelman 1953, p. 3].

To accomplish the complex act of phonation, the singer
has to bring under control the proper functioning and
coordination of all the organs which are active during

the production of vocal sound [Simmons 1969, p. 17].

The study of phonation cannot be expected to limit itself to the larynx--to the action potentials travelling
through the recurrent nerve--because it is proved that
the pneumophonic synergy (coordination of breathing
and phonation) is an essential factor of voice production [Tarneaud 1958, p. 12]

The physiologist, and particularly the modern speech
expert, strive to view the functions of living organ-
isms as global processes--in other words, as indi-
visible Gestalten of holistic psychology.   Whenever we
speak, we call into use all muscles of the organs of
voice and speech, which function in complex coordination.   Nearly all these muscles are part of the
upper respiratory and digestive systems, which have
assumed the secondarily superimposed function of
phonic expression [Luchsinger and Arnold 1965, p. 458].

The Voice Is a Musical Instrument

We have, within our bodies, a musical instrument
(nearest in comparison, to an old fashioned reed
organ) consisting of a bellows (lungs), reeds (vocal
bands) and pipes (resonators) [Lindquest 1955, p. 3].

Although the vocal organs share many characteristics
with the wind driven instruments (wood-winds and
brass), in the regulation of pitch the larynx makes
use of a mechanism similar to the string instruments
[Brodnitz 1961, p. 9].

I have been struck by the similarity between production of tone in the voice and in brass instruments
[Long 1953, p. 16].

The larynx of man as a biosocial organ has no exact
functional counterpart in man-made instruments, and
teaching techniques must be built around conceptual
differences in tonal control but with complete insight
and an awareness of the physiological and the psychological phenomena involved in each vocal act [Appel-
man 1967, p. 67].

True comparison ... of the vocal instrument with any

other musical instrument is impossible because the
living mechanism is incomparably more versatile than
any instrument of human manufacture [M. Greene
1959, p. 7].

The Voice Is a Pitch-Determining Mechanism

Too many singers have the mental concept wherein,
particularly as the voice goes higher, with the vocal
cords stretching tighter, similar to the action of a
rubber band, the air pressure in the trachea must
rise higher and higher to oppose this increased tension. Actually, this rubber band tension does not
exist for still another reason. For successively
higher pitches it is true that the tension is increased
somewhat, but just as meaningful and significant is
the fact that the vocal cords also become more
slender and, in addition, decrease their vibrating
length [R. Taylor 1958, p. 32].

Pitch changes, then, are not directly attributed to a
single act of lengthening, thinning, tightening, or
loosening of the vocal folds. Rather, the pitch
change is caused by the modulation of tracheal air
pressure resulting from the changes in the elasticity
of the glottal margins. It is thus assumed that the
changes in the elasticity are caused by changes in
mass, length, and tension of the thyroarytenoid in a
synchronized act, a most complicated process [Appel-
man 1967, p. 69].

We have seen that the action of the cricothyroid muscles causes the distance from the thyroid notch to the
cricoid plate to increase, thus stretching the vocal
folds longitudinally. The increased tension causes
them to return more promptly to the midline after
breath has separated them, and this obviously raises
the frequency or the pitch [Vennard 1967, p. 60].

Vocal pitch does not rise in response to increased
air flow alone.... The mechanisms of vocal pitch
and intensity are so interrelated that to isolate one
from the other, except for the most elementary considerations, is virtually impossible [Rubin 1963,
p. 1011].

The pitch of the voice is the result of the frequency
of the vibratory cycle of the cords. This, in turn,
is determined by the length, the mass of the cords
and their stiffness. The long cords of a man with
their greater mass produce a deeper sound than the
shorter cords of women [Brodnitz 1961, p. 21].

METHODS OF CONTROLLING PHONATION

A Psychological Approach

Total Coordination Required

The balanced coordination of all the vocal muscles
and their related parts is therefore one of the foundation objectives of any system of vocal training. Voice is a product
of mind and many coordinating muscular movements, each
one governed by a time factor and a dynamic factor" (Fields
1952, p. 17).

It is almost redundant to say that coordination is one
of the most widely accepted vocal precepts. Even those who
are most avid in teaching "local effort" procedures are found
to favor the general concept of total coordination. Representative statements are given below which underscore the
principle of total coordination:

In my opinion the cornerstones of any approach to the
study of vocal technic should be: (1) The strengthening of this natural coordination; (2) The increase of
reliance upon it in the singer; (3) Forming the habit
of guiding his voice primarily by means of his own
inner ear; and (4) Forming the habit of employing
conscious muscular effort only if such effort does not
impede his natural coordination [Kagen 1950, p. 55].

Good singing, from the singer's standpoint, is an act
of correctly functioning neuro-muscularly co-ordinated
athletic activity [Lindquest 1955, p. 20].

Good singing habits can be established when the singer
has acquired three essentials for effective vocal tone:
one--a poised and flexible body for increased physical
power and action; two--an aesthetic appreciation of
beautiful tone that is properly related to accurate
phonetic sounds colored with interpretive sensitivity;

three--a sensation of tonal 'ring' and vocal power
when the correctly formed and expressive language
sounds are allowed to be resonated and projected from
a well-coordinated singing mechanism [P. Peterson
1966, p. 6].

A knowledge of the various processes involved in singing is like a disjointed skeleton until their interrelation is understood. An organism is greater than the
sum of all its parts, and no analytical study discovers
the whole truth until it leads to synthesis [Vennard
1967, p. 191].

Mental Concept of Tone and Pitch

A mental concept of tone and pitch is required for
control of phonation. An anticipation, or a pre-hearing, of
tone and pitch is implied. This is a fundamental precept of
the psychological approach to phonation and it finds wide acceptance.

No singing is acceptable if the singer's imagination or
total concept is faulty.... Let the student think before he sings [McCook 1947, p. 206].

The vocalist will sing no more freely and beautifully
than he thinks [Christy 1961, p. 40].

Singing is a thinking process ... we sing as we think
[Montell 1950, p. 20].

The clear thought of the pitch and word should find
immediate response in both breathing mechanism and
vocal cords [DeYoung 1958, p. 58].

It is an axiom that correct emission of the voice is
dependent only upon right thought governing the pitch
and quality of tone [Field-Hyde 1950, p. 41].

It must be kept in mind that all physiological adjustments are at first mental adjustments [Sunderman
1958, p. 46].

The beautiful and satisfying tone associated with artistic singing must first be heard mentally as a vocal
image [P. Peterson 1966, p. 5].

You must know exactly what you are going to do; you
must plan every note, eveyr tone, every effect, in
your mind before you give it out with your voice
[Tucker 1954, p. 13].

The Technical Approach to Phonation

Control of Oral Cavity

"The oral cavity (the mouth) is that part of the vocal
tract or tone channel through which voice is conveyed from
the larynx to the outer atmosphere.   The oral cavity includes
the tongue, teeth, cheeks, lips, chin, and jaw ... " (Fields
1952, p. 40).   Christy (1961, p. 59) says that the degree of
mouth opening is not determined by vowel formation, but is
controlled by the range and dynamics.   Fuchs (1964, p. 46)
says the mouth should never be opened to its fullest extent.
Behnke (1945, p. 61) suggests that all we need do is to stop
holding the jaw; it will drop on its own accord.

According to Whitlock (1969, p. 12), the great arch-
foe of singing is tension; we should then look first for faults
in the jaw.   "The longer I teach, the more I become convinced that eighty percent of vocal problems are to be found
in the jaw" (1968a, p. 32).   Others have urged a loose, free
jaw.

The student must be encouraged to allow the jaw to
drop loosely [Judd 1951, p. 69].

Much has been said about the position of the jaw, but
its freedom is of greater importance.   A tight jaw is
a symptom of a tight throat [Vennard 1967, p. 117].

It is desirable to keep the lower jaw as loose and
limber as possible [Graves 1954, p. 51].

The condition of the jaw (freedom from tension) is
more important than its position [Klein and Schjeide
1967, p. 39].

While comparing the x-rays, we noticed that the jaw
seemed to hang looser for vocal efficiency [Perkins,
Sawyer and Harrison 1958, p. 4].

I insist always on that relaxed feeling of the lips [Lam-
son 1963, p. 12].

To imagine relaxation in the cheek muscles under the
eyes is the best method yet devised to eliminate jaw
rigidity [Christy 1965, p. 62].

Some writers have suggested a more defined forming
of the jaw and lips.   The recommended formation of the
mouth often determines the position of the jaw.

I think the old Italian method of the mouth in the
position of a suppressed smile is probably as good
as any I know [Swarthout 1950, p. 49].

The open square position is suggested as the basic
position from which deviations can be made [Ross
1959, p. 63].

Drop your jaw and tongue when you sing and round
the corners of your mouth so that it makes an oval
shape like an egg [German 1952, p. 32].

You open your mouth horizontally not vertically. Sing
horizontally--by opening your mouth across--and the
tip of your tongue, your teeth and your lips never
leave their economic stations [Bairstow and Greene
1945, p. 23].

Elisabeth Schumann was convinced that the more one
could make oneself feel and look like a bird, the
better one would be able to sing, and she said that
one must form one's upper jaw into a beak which
protruded over the lower jaw.   This cannot be done
by just pushing the lower jaw in; one must definitely
feel as though one were sticking the upper jaw out,
as if, for example, to bite into an apple [Puritz
1954, p. 25].

For quite ninety per cent of the singer's work his
jaws need not be further than one finger's width apart.
If he can arrive at that with easy production he can
be trusted with the remaining ten per cent [Judd
1951, p. 69].

Lingual Controls

"The tongue is a freely movable and protrusive muscular organ in the mouth.   Its base or root is attached to

the hyoid bone and therefore, indirectly to the larynx"
(Fields 1947, p. 116). The position of the tongue receives
a great amount of attention. Puritz (1954, p. 26), writing on
the teaching of Elisabeth Schumann, says that it is in error
to flatten the tongue, it is far better left to itself. Husler
and Rodd-Marling (1965, p. 53) believe that it is of no value
to practice tongue exercises. Eleanor McLellan is quoted by
Collins (1969b, p. 13) as saying: "The tongue must go up for
high notes, but it must remain flexible and do it of its own
volition. " Resnik (1948, p. 281), Bachner (1944, p. 61), and
William Rice (1961, p. 36) are among those who favor an
agile, free tongue. Rosewall (1961, p. 107) and Graves (1954,
p. 29) advocate a dropped, low-lying tongue.

> Whereas the tongue may change its shape in endless
> variations, its volume remains approximately the
> same. During protrusion its base appears elevated.
> When the tonguetip is reflected backward, the tongue
> base is flattened. A strong anatomic coupling exists
> between tongue and larynx. When the tongue is drawn
> backward, the pharynx becomes narrower, the epi-
> glottis is lowered, and the laryngeal vestibule is
> constricted. In functional contrast, forward position-
> ing of the tongue widens the pharynx and the laryngeal
> vestibule [Luchsinger and Arnold 1965, p. 81].

Palatal Controls

Vennard (1967, p. 254) defines the soft palate as a
"muscular and tendonous extension of the roof of the mouth.
Its lower edge is the velum. In the center is the uvula, and
at each side, extending into the sides of the throat, are the
pillars of the fauces. " Nineteen statements (Table 4) were
found which generally support the use of an arched soft
palate; four statements were read which indicated the re-
verse. Statements reflecting the two positions are indicated
as follows:

> One of the essentials of good singing is the necessity
> for raising the uvula away from the base of the
> tongue, as the latter widens the opening above the
> larynx by arching toward the soft palate for the higher
> tones [Reid 1950, p. 52].

> The greater the elasticity, strength, and control by
> the singer of his soft palate that terminates in the

uvula, the greater will be the mastery of his voice.
It was said of Patti that she had a 'uvula of gold'
[Franca 1959, p. 23].

The arching and lowering of the soft palate in ascending and descending scales, with the nasal port open
throughout the range, is the secret of uniform resonation, tone quality and the blending of pitch mechanism
changes [Westerman 1955, p. 36].

The mouth opens--and only to a minimum degree--
because we sing; we do not open the mouth to sing.
The normal, correct position of the soft palate in
singing is low and forward. It should not be consciously raised, distended, or contracted [Bachner
1947, p. 61].

Waengler (1968, p. 32), in a review of research relevant to the use of the soft palate in speech and song, says
it is unreasonable to assume complete nasopharyngeal closure
is constantly present in normal speaking and singing. He
supports the theory that the soft palate seems to practice a
fine control of nasopharyngeal constriction in order to avoid
unwanted nasalization; singers and actors who assert that
their soft palate does not completely close off the nasal
passage are not as mistaken as certain scientific research
has indicated. Waengler found that the velar flap valve can
take unusual liberties in preventing audible and undesired
nasalization.

Open Throat Concept

A tight or constricted throat is anathema in the production of clear, resonant quality. The expression "open
throat" is used to describe the desired expansion of the
pharynx. The expression is a misnomer, but it has less
misleading connotations than other traditional terms. The
concept is widely accepted but the approach to the desired
goal varies. Twenty-six statements were gathered which
suggested conscious "opening" of the throat; 22 statements
implied an indirect approach.

DeYoung (1958, p. 70) reminds us that opening the
throat does not require the front of the mouth be spread; he
adds further: "When you open the throat it feels as though
the ball-socket joint just in front of the ear releases the

jaw so that it can drop slightly back and down. " "Singing
with a free throat means to me that a beautiful, coordinated
tone is emitted without any muscular interference" (Sharnova
1964, p. 14). "In a general way, the open throat is sympto-
matic of the best singing" (C. Scott 1954, p. 169). Appelman
(1967, p. 80) provides this description: "The open throat
used in singing is the result of increasing the anterior-pos-
terior, transverse, and vertical dimension of the oral and
pharyngeal cavities from their normal positions used in the
production of speech sounds. " "In general, the bucco-
pharyngeal resonator should be tuned to encourage low partials in the tone. It should be enlarged.... The factors in
this tuning are all more or less subject to conscious control
and may be trained locally" (Vennard 1962, p. 511). On the
other hand, Duval (1958, p. 14) suggests: "We must never
be conscious of the bow in the violinist nor the throat in the
singer. "

        Yawning as an aid to "opening the throat" finds wide
approval from the empirical and the mechanistic schools.
Vennard (1967, p. 109), Ririe (1960, p. 30), Bachner (1947,
p. 73), Appelman (1967, p. 15) and Wyckoff (1955, p. 20) are
among 32 writers who recommend this device. One guarded
comment, made by Rosalie Miller (1951, p. 15) indicates she
finds students tighten and depress the tongue too far in the
yawn and she suggests a better model is the sensation felt
at the beginning of a sneeze.

Position of the Larynx

        Should the larynx move during phonation? Fourteen
statements indicate this is desirable; 11 statements urge a
low but unmoving larynx (Table 4). Fields found the authors
evenly divided on this question. Herbert-Caesari (1951c,
p. 64) urges a normal position of the larynx in the throat--
not too high nor too low. He calls this position a "floating
level. " Mack Harrell (1949, p. 479) believes: "Whether you
sing up or down, high or low, the position of the vocal
mechanism should remain the same"; interestingly enough,
this same concept is suggested by two other basses, Jerome
Hines (1951, p. 49) and Cesare Siepi (1952, p. 26). Other
opinions are:

        The larynx--in a slightly lower position than that of
        silence ... [Kelsey, Grove's, p. 52].

Always, for any pitch, the larynx must remain in the
low-lying position where Nature has placed it ...
[Pescia 1948, p. 737].

A strongly rising larynx is found by all singers with
unsatisfactory performances or in the early stage of
training.   As was said before, the demand on the
vocal cords is much stronger when the larynx rises
[Ruth 1963, p. 3]. ...   The ideal, most perfect function of the vocal-organ can be achieved only if the
larynx drops with the rising pitch of tones [p. 5].

For colour, the larynx certainly changes its position.
For lugubrious tones it will be low; for happy, high.
But not only the larynx, the whole vocal mechanism
seems to be lifted up for the latter, depressed for
the former, though such depression should never be
the result of forcing down the larynx from above; it
should always be drawn or sucked down from below
[C. Scott 1954, p. 39].

Sonninen (1956), in an important research effort related to the external laryngeal muscles, observed certain
phenomena which provide some insight into the position of
the larynx.   In ten professional singers, the larynx tended
to draw further away from the spine when the pitch was
raised.   In a review of the literature, Sonninen reflected
that Garcia found there need be no upward movement of the
larynx as the pitch is raised; also, that Barth demonstrated
the best voice habit is that in which the larynx very lightly
drops with increased pitch of the voice.

The Attack

The "attack" is defined as "the beginning of the
tone. ...   Upon the mental conception of the intended or desired sound, the breath comes in contact with the resisting
vocal bands, which are immediately set into vibration"
(AATS 1969, p. 8).   Kelsey (Grove's p. 56) grapples with the
semantic implication of the word when he says: "A vocal
sound is never attacked: it is launched; and the gesture of
the instrument which brings it into being always partakes of
the nature of a caress.   The art of the singer lies in making
the laryngeal caress quite firm and clean. "

Some suggestions for improving the attack are:

No method of attack takes cognizance of the fact that
only purity of tone is the essence of correct attack
and emission and good vocal production [Bollew 1953,
p. 59].

In attacks, especially in the higher register, the
mouth must be well open with the lips relaxed before
the note is struck, and loosely and gently the mouth
must continue to open and the lips continue to relax
during the whole duration of the note [Lamson 1963,
p. 10].

For a good attack, stroke or caress the tone out with
the delicate touch of the artist's brush, pencil or pen.
To stroke is to caress, denoting gentle action. First
'point in' the vowelled tone and then 'talk' it in, glide
it in [Herbert-Caesari 1951a, p. 289].

Beginners, as well as those who have not studied
properly should remember that the first rule must
be: do not gasp immediately before the attack
[Longo 1945, p. 27].

Christy (1961, p. 50) provides a detailed statement on
the attack; it is included here in its entirety because of its
comprehensive nature.

Proper attack occurs: (1) When there is, first of
all, proper concept of pitch, vowel and dynamics desired.   (2) When the vocal bands and pharynx are
properly 'opened' and relaxed previously through a
deep, gentle inhalation with a 'sigh-like' feeling. (3)
When the tongue is allowed to lie loosely in the mouth
with the tip barely touching the base of the lower
teeth.   (4) When the vocal bands resist breath pressure properly.   (5) When application of the breath and
adjustment of the vocal bands on phonation are simultaneous.   (6) When breath support is applied immediately to sustaining tone and continued. . . .   (7) When
the vowel is preceded by a tonal 'uh' attack as a
common denominator.   (8) When diction is confident,
natural, and 'neat' or precise.

The "glottal stroke" is an attack which begins with the
vocal bands closed.   The sudden release, particularly on a
beginning vowel causes a sharp click.   This type of attack
is also called the "stroke of the glottis, " "glottal stop, " and,

a term made familiar by Manuel Garcia, the "coup de glotte."
"Garcia and his followers always insisted that a tone should
be preceded by what he described as a 'very slight cough'"
(Fields 1952, p. 17).   This type of attack is vigorously opposed by the majority of vocal authorities, yet others claim
it has been misunderstood.   Christy (1961, p. 32) cautions
against the stroke of the glottis as well as urging the complete avoidance of a more harsh form--the shock of the glottis.   Kelsey, writing in Grove's Dictionary (p. 57), indicates
the "coup de glotte" is not essential to a correct attack but
(p. 48) "since so many great singers have both practised and
recommended the 'coup de glotte,' the answer must surely
be that all depends on how it is done."

The Vibrato

        "The 'vibrato' is a periodic pulsation in pitch frequen-
cies, the average of which is approximately 6.2 to 6.6 per
second, varying with the emotional impulse involved.... Vibrato is an integral part of good quality, and should not be
confused with 'tremolo'" (AATS 1969, p. 23).   Christy (1961,
p. 43) adds: "The vibrato is caused by an intermittent supply
of nerve energy, resulting in regular fluctuation of muscular
energy in the vocal bands....   Vibrato is an essential concomitant for beauty and freedom of vocal tone."   Appelman
(1967, p. 23) writes "the vocal vibrato is a vocal ornament
that is directly related to the sensation of support.   It is
physiologically controlled by the muscles of respiration, and
is thereby, basically, a respiratory function assisted by coordinated laryngeal controls."   Mason and Zemlin (1966) indicate the breathing musculature and laryngeal depressor
mechanism do not appear to be causally linked to vibrato
production.   Ethel Smith (1970), however, found evidence to
support Appelman's position cited above.

        The vibrato is not unrelated to the vocal "tremolo."
"This is an abnormal pulsation of the voice, marked by a
perceptible variation in pitch; is due to a lack of proper coordination of the vocal mechanism, because of incorrect use
of the breath or unnatural physical tension" (AATS 1969,
p. 22).

        The vocal tremolo, therefore, is a nervous tonal
        flutter caused by unrelieved tension [Reid 1965, p.175].

        Tremolo is caused by the combination of any number

of elements such as general fatigue, bad posture,
poor breathing habits, muscular straining for power,
poor phonation, emotional instability, lack of awareness of the tremolo, and singing by imitation [P.
Peterson 1966, p. 63].

The tremolo is due either to weakness of some muscles involved in the vocal act or to interfering muscle
tension. It will automatically disappear when the weak
muscles are strengthened through proper exercise or
the interfering muscles are inhibited from interfering
[Wilcox 1945, p. 45].

If the wavering becomes excessive--up to twelve times
per second--it is called tremolo, a greatly feared
symptom of poor or deteriorating voices. It happens
frequently in "throaty" voices and may be due to over-
tenseness of the muscles which creates a vibrating
trembling in the throat, the tongue and sometimes
even the jaw [Brodnitz 1953, p. 85].

SUMMARY, ANALYSIS AND INTERPRETATION

The interrelationship of singing as a technique, as an
art, as an acoustical phenomenon, and as a physical process
is found in each major area of discussion in this study.
This total response is especially apparent in factors related
to phonation. The working concepts in this chapter that do
not make some reference, directly or indirectly to another
category of singing are in the minority. Allusions and direct references to breathing, range, resonance, vocal dynamics, diction and interpretation are prevalent.

Culled from the literature used in this study were
558 concepts relating to phonation. A wide divergence of
opinion was found, with no categories receiving complete
approval. A possible exception to this is the general acceptance of a raised soft palate: 19 statements advocated a
raised palate; four statements suggested the soft palate
should be free. In almost all technical categories, there are
sufficient statements to indicate marked acceptance. Most
authorities consider the "yawn" an acceptable device for
attaining an "open throat." This device appears to be among
the most popularly accepted in the broad scope of training
the singing voice.

The numerical listings of the teaching concepts, as reflected in Table 4, show a general proportionate increase over those of the earlier study by Fields. Two categories should be mentioned. In the present study, a larger proportion than Fields found indicated the mouth opening is not important. As mentioned earlier, the most distinct difference is found in the category concerned with palatal controls.

No agreement has been reached regarding the best technique for generating acceptable vocal sounds. The subject of phonation is filled with conflicting theories, techniques and methods. In The Science of Vocal Pedagogy, Appelman (1967, p. 62) summarizes that contemporary vocal theorists accept as facts:

1. That all vocalized sound is the result of expiration of air through the cone-shaped narrowing of the phonatory tube at the apex of the trachea.
2. That further constriction is applied by the vocal folds which are capable of completely or partially interrupting the expired air.
3. That both the vocal folds and walls of the airway are elastic and yield under pressure.
4. That the vocal folds are capable of varying in length, tension, and contour--thereby regulating the size, shape, and the position of the glottic aperture --as well as undergoing vibrating movements.
5. That the laryngeal muscles do not produce the vocal sound. Rather, phonation is an aerodynamic phenomenon in which the muscles merely adjust and hold the folds in a certain position, tension, and shape. The modulation of the expired air stream, caused by the movement of the vibrating vocal folds, makes the sound. The resulting pressure variations create the multiple sine waves which comprise the complex vocal spectrum.

The complexity of elements that mold the human voice makes an analysis extremely difficult. The individuality and uniqueness of each human instrument, capable of a multiplicity of sounds, musical and otherwise, have also made the analysis difficult. The teacher of voice, the speech pathologist, the laryngologist and the phoniatrist have contributed to a compartmentalization of the voice. "Today, poets are better judges of the elusive products of the larynx than many of us who claim the scientific approach. The intuition of poets is keen, their responses sensitive, and they grasp the meaning of the totality, the 'Gestalt,' expressed by the voice" (Moses 1954, p. 7).

Chapter V

CONCEPTS OF RESONANCE

"Resonance is the transmission of vibrations from a vibrating body to another body" (Apel 1969, p. 726). A definition of resonance, which applies more directly to singing, is provided by the American Academy of Teachers of Singing (1969, p. 19): "In singing, [resonance] refers to carrying power of voice. Singers include quality in the employment of this term. " Vennard (1967, p. 239) adds that resonance is the reinforcement of sound by synchronous vibration.

THEORIES

General Description

Resonance largely determines the ultimate character of a speech sound. Since singing tone is an elongation of vowel sounds on a predetermined pitch, resonance is vital to the quality of the tone. "The resonators of the human voice are those air-filled cavities situated above and below the vocal cords to which the sound waves have access and from which they receive sympathetic reinforcement in their passage to the external air" (M. Greene 1959, p. 40). "Amplification and modification of the mixed tones produced at the larynx and passed through the resonators result in the production of vowel sounds; the character of these varies according to the shape of the resonator" (Negus 1962, p.150). "The tone is produced under exact same conditions; it is the resonance areas that change. Therefore, assume no preconceived notion as to what feeling you should have for the production of any specific tone on any specific word. Simply produce the tone demanded, and allow the word to direct the tone into the available resonators" (Waight 1962, p. 17).

Muscular action is necessarily included in most discussions of resonance. "Every single 'focal point' is identified with different muscles and groups of muscles in the vocal organ, all of which are component parts of a large mechanism; it follows, therefore, that to train the voice

80

Table 5. SUMMARY OF CONCEPTS OF RESONANCE

	Number of Statements in "Teaching Singing"	Number of Statements in "Training the Singing Voice"
I. Theories of resonance		
A. General descriptions	34	19
B. Acoustical factors	20	44
C. Physiological factors		
1. head resonance		
a) head cavities are important	27	7
b) head cavities are not important	11	3
2. function of sinuses		
a) sinuses are used	see	9
b) sinuses are not used	above	4
3. nasal resonance		
a) nasal cavities are consciously employed	17	14
b) nasal cavities are not consciously employed	5	3
4. importance of mouth and throat cavities	45	11
5. importance of chest cavity	4	7
6. the entire body as a resonator	6	16
II. Methods of controlling vocal resonance		
A. A psychological approach		
1. expressional intent controls resonance	14	6
2. is direct control possible		
a) resonance is directly controllable	7	5
b) resonance is not directly controllable	9	8
B. The technical approach		
1. quality as a guide	19	16
2. acquiring a vocal focus		
a) the voice should be consciously focused	10	41
b) the voice should not be consciously focused	18	19
3. the value of humming		
a) humming is a useful device	27	25
b) humming is not a useful device	1	5
TOTALS	274	262

properly each 'position' must be practised in turn, until the
various muscles are so well-innervated that they require no
special attention to function freely" (Husler and Rodd-Marling
1965, p. 73). Sonninen (1956), in an earlier study, gives
support to the theory that muscles which adjust the resonators
are even more basically involved in the primary vibration of
the vocal mechanism.

Coordination of the singing process is essential in
order to achieve ideal resonance. Nelson (1951, p. 20) suggests that correct posture assists breathing; correct breathing, in turn, assists perfect phonation. Perfect phonation
assists full resonation, and then full resonation assists
articulation.

Acoustical Factors

Resonance occurs when a vibrator is in tune with its
generator. An understanding of this acoustical phenomenon
is considered helpful to the singer; within the literature of
singing pedagogy, many writers attempt to define resonance:

> Scientific evidence suggests that there is a vocal po-
> sition of each pitch and vowel where the phonatory
> tube is in complete accord with the laryngeal tone.
> When such a position is assumed by a singer the
> resonators become stable and greater resonance is
> realized [Appelman 1959, p. 44].

> If the response of the body being set into vibration
> is maximal, the tuning is said to be sharp. If the
> generator and vibrating body are greatly out of tune,
> there can be but little resonance [Judson and Weaver
> 1965, p. 89].

> Any cavity coupled with or in close proximity with a
> vibrator may act as a resonator if its natural fre-
> quency is the same or approximately the same as the
> fundamental of the tone or one of its overtones; in
> other words, if the cavity is in tune with the tone
> initiated by the vibrator (Stout 1955b, p. 6).

> When cavities are connected their pitches are not the
> same as they would be separately [Vennard 1967,
> p. 83].

The respiratory mechanism and the resonating cavities
rank equally with the vocal cords in determining the
acoustics of the voice.   All three parts belong and
act together.   They constitute, to use the acoustic
term, a coupled mechanism of three parts that constantly act on and influence each other [Brodnitz 1961,
p. 9].

Sound cannot be 'thrown' or 'projected' and the palate
or teeth cannot act as a 'sounding board' to reflect
sound waves from their surface [Punt 1967, p. 88].

Tone Quality or Timbre

An acoustical definition of "quality," quoted from the
dictionary, is helpful: "In singing, that property of a tone,
apart from pitch and intensity which distinguishes it from
another tone. " Fields (1947, p. 141) describes quality as the
identifying character of a vocal tone determined chiefly by
the resonance of the vocal chambers in uttering it.

Scientists say: 'The quality of a sound depends upon
the number of overtones associated with the fundamental, and their relative intensity'; and 'quality refers to the harmonic composition of a complex tone--
the arrangement, points of concentration, and general
distribution of overtones with relation to the fundamental' [Mowe 1955, p. 8].

The quality of the tone produced depends on the manner in which the vocal cords vibrate, the varying
shapes of the resonator air cavities in the mouth and
nose and the condition of the accessory airfilled
sinuses [Carp 1956, p. 10].

Many factors influence the quality of tone.   Paul
Peterson (1966, p. 27) has written: "The correct production
of the vowel induces a healthier vibration of the vocal cords,
which in turn improves the quality of a tone. " James F.
Cooke (1952, p. 63) relates another factor, expressed by
Enrico Caruso; the great tenor remarked that he "learned
instinctively that the beauty of tone did not depend upon the
vocal organs alone, but upon the concept of tone beauty in
the mind. " Graves (1954, p. 45), relating tone quality to
breathing, suggests that the quality of the sound is better
when superfluous air is not inhaled.

Christy (1967, p. 62) describes the requisite to a beautiful tone: "Conditions are right for good tone when the throat feels free, relaxed and open; if you are conscious of any feeling of discomfort, strain or 'gripping,' you may be sure the tone is poor."

"Fritz Kreisler, in answer to the question, 'What is a beautiful tone?' is said to have replied that he did not know, but that when he heard one he felt it up and down his spine.   This standard of measurement is not scientific but it indicates the basis on which the quality of tone is generally judged--the way in which it affects us" (Mowe 1955, p. 8).   This remark is illustrative of a viewpoint of quality of tone taken by many musicians.

Physiological Factors

Head Resonance

The part head cavities play as chambers of resonance during singing has been scientifically established.   There is sufficient evidence that neither the sinuses nor the nasal cavities contribute appreciably to resonance.   Contrary to the scientific findings, in this study 27 statements were found which supported theories that resonance occurs in the cavities of the head; 11 statements indicated head cavities were not important as resonators.

"Head cavities" are defined in The Singer's Glossary (Fields 1952, p. 27) as "chambers ... lying above the level of the mouth."   These are principally the six sinuses and the nasal passages.   Many writers refer specifically to one or the other of these; other writers refer only to "head cavities."   For accuracy in this study, some statements will be listed which refer to "head cavities," with no conjecture made as to the specific cavity.

This resonance of the skull and its cavities is called head resonance and singers who are able to sing with the use of it enjoy fundamental advantage over others who do not know the secret or are not able to acquire it [Fuchs 1965, p. 12].

There is a true and infallible method, and it can be mastered by anyone.   To 'focus the tone in the head cavities' may sound like an empty phrase, yet it is one of the two most fundamental and vitally important of all the principles of good singing [Samoiloff 1943, p. 2].

We may liken the head cavities and bony parts which make for resonance to the sounding board of a piano or the box of a stringed instrument [McClosky 1959, p. 26].

Send the breath high and forward into the facial chambers of resonance [Siepi 1952, p. 26].

One should take the sound from without and carry it into the focus of the resonances, which is located in the head, then attack it at the very focus [Franca 1959, p. 12].

Always the one true gage when in doubt, is the vibration felt in the masque [McLellan, as quoted by Collins 1969a, p. 34].

It is necessary to concentrate completely on directing the vibrations of the vocal cords up as high as possible into the mask of the face [Bollew 1952a, p. 50].

The second vital point in basic production is resonance. The problem here is to get the tone into the mask and to guard against any guttural intonation [John Charles Thomas 1943, p. 701].

Function of Sinuses

The word "sinus" means cavity, according to R. M. Brown (1946, p. 74), "for singers those resonant openings, the sinuses, are of the utmost importance. To sing correctly they must be employed constantly. Considering this, they are too little understood. " Giving support to this concept, is Lisa Roma (1956, p. 11): "Singing is the controlled flow of breath through the vocal cords, hitting resonating chambers of the eyes, nose and sinuses, like hammers hitting on bells or mallets on a xylophone. " "They [vibrations] also influence the air-filled paranasal cavities, which together with the bone-vibrations create the sensation of the head resonance" (Ruth 1966, p. 20).

Statements which reject the concept of physiological

occurrence of nasal resonance are in the minority, although
they frequently bear the weight of scientific research:

> Our conclusion was that neither 'nasal resonance' nor
> 'sinus resonance' has validity [Vennard 1967, p. 96].

> In contrast to popular assumption and to the tenets of
> many books on singing, the sinuses play no part in
> the resonance of the voice [Brodnitz 1961, p. 32].

> In comparing the resonating values of sinuses by
> applying the formula of the Helmholtz resonator, we
> find that the contribution could be very small even
> under the most optimum conditions and only at very
> high frequencies. Actually, in many cases the open-
> ings into the sinuses are so filled with mucous or the
> sinus itself is filled with fluid, so that in actual prac-
> tice their contribution amounts to practically nothing
> [R. Taylor 1955, p. 23].

> But the resonance afforded by the naso-pharynx is so
> obvious and definite as to leave little, if indeed any,
> material influence to be ascribed to the sinuses with
> their tiny openings.... Sensations are certainly often
> felt in the head, but they are no proof whatever of
> sinus resonance [Field-Hyde 1950, p. 90].

Nasal Resonance

        Two theories should first be considered in a discus-
sion of the nose as a resonator: (1) "the naso-pharynx, and
thereby the whole nasal resonator, can be shut off by a
sphincter action of the soft palate and the superior constrictor
muscle of the pharynx" and (2) "the cavity itself is not adjustable, so the control consists entirely of shunting it in or out
of the resonance system" (Vennard 1967, p. 93).

        Within the framework of traditional empirical vocal
terminology, "nasal resonance" is a desired quality, "nasality" is not. "The term 'nasal' is used to denote an unfavorable aspect of vocal sound. There is a so-called post-nasal
resonance that contributes to the over-all balance of sound.
A 'nasal' tone is not to be confused with normal coordinated
post-nasal resonance, which is desirable and essential"
(AATS 1969, p. 16). From the literature used in this study,
17 statements were found indicating that the nasal cavities

are consciously employed as resonators; five statements re-
puted this concept (Table 5). Representative statements are
given, reflecting the extreme positions pertaining to this
controversial area:

> The nasal cavity is one of the main resonators in
> singing--a fact established long ago by the science of
> acoustics [Husler and Rodd-Marling 1965, p. 53].

> In singing open vowel, nasal cavities do not resonate
> nor reinforce the vowel sounds sufficiently to be de-
> tected by the human analyzer.   Therefore: the nasal
> cavities cannot and do not furnish any part of the
> vocal tones.   Nasal resonance ... must be due to
> some other manifestation [Wooldridge 1956, p. 29].

> The nose is the most important organ of voice....
> The production of a clear, well pointed, brilliant yet
> soft tone, demands a channel through which the reso-
> nance of the head and of the skull itself, can reach
> the outer air, and the nasal cavity and passages form
> the only such channel [Armstrong 1945c, p. 679].

> The quality of tone as resonated by the nose is well
> known even to the layman.   It is a 'honky' muffled
> sound, which should not be confused with what is
> sometimes called 'nasal twang'....   How much of this
> quality is admissible to singing?   I lean toward the
> opinion that it should be eliminated entirely [Vennard
> 1967, p. 93].

> Some degree of nasal resonance is essential, but as
> soon as it is heard, a singer may be sure he is using
> too much.   It is like salt in scrambled eggs; it is
> obvious if there is not enough, but if it can be tasted,
> then there is too much [Fuchs 1964, p. 60].

> In nasal tone, the voice passes, either entirely or
> partially through the nose; in nasal resonance it
> passes out of the mouth, and only co-vibrations take
> place in the nasal cavity [Behnke 1945, p. 71].

Mouth and Throat Cavities

Forty-five statements were found which give importance to the throat and mouth cavities as resonators of vocal

tone.   Rosewall (1961, p. 27) says that the greatest resonant
cavity over which the singer has control is the opening of
the throat, the back of the mouth.   Franklin D. Lawson
(1944, p. 45) adds that additional resonance may also be obtained by creating a feeling of extreme width in the back
part of the mouth.   In regard to deliberate alterations, Rose
(1962, p. 166) comments that the size and shape of any of
the adjustable cavities may affect the size and shape of the
adjacent cavities and their respective openings; in this manner, the position of the base of the tongue affects the size
and shape of both the throat and mouth cavities.

   The boundary lines between the oral and pharyngeal
cavities are not easily distinguished.   The relative importance of each of these cavities as a resonator is often discussed.   Klein and Schjeide (1967, p. 45) indicate that the
mouth is not a good resonator because its walls are too
flexible and too changeable for consistent reinforcement.
However, James T. Lawson (1955, p. 24) disagrees: "All
singing should come easily out of the front of the mouth. . . .
Try to develop this consciousness of the sound resonating
against your hard palate at the front of the mouth. " Stanley
(1950, p. 60) theorizes that only in incorrect technic is the
mouth used as a resonator.

   The degree of mouth opening, as a factor in resonance, is a subject of much interest.   Punt (1967, p. 36)
says for maximum volume of mouth resonance, the larger it
is, and the larger its front orifice is, the better.   Robert
M. Taylor (1958, p. 31) says that this is a fallacy: "Many
voice teachers encourage the student to open the mouth and
throat as large as possible"; he adds that "any effort beyond
a certain optimum is futile. "   Collins (1969a, p. 36) quotes
Sidney Dietch concerning the degree of mouth opening: "It
depends on the individual.   The width of the mouth is not
the primary cause of resonance and vibration.   If the throat
is right, the mouth will adjust and take care of itself. "   On
the other hand, Longo (1945, p. 20) says the correct opening
of the mouth is the only determining factor in the quality of
sounds.

   The pharynx, as part of the throat, is prevalently
considered a principal resonator of the voice.   "We have
ample proof that the primary resonator of the voice is the
pharynx" (Cates 1959, p. 5 and Werrenrath 1951, p. 61).

   The pharynx has assumed the secondary, specialized

function (primary function is the transport of food) as resonator for laryngeal voice ... widening of the pharynx increases resonance, making the vocal sound full, dark, strong, and resonant. In polar contrast, narrowing of the pharynx is associated with a thin, sharp, dampened, and throaty (guttural) timbre of the voice [Luchsinger and Arnold 1965, p. 454].

The real mouth of the singer is not the lip-aperture, as so many conceive it to be, but the internal cavity, of which the back half, or pharynx, is the most important [Herbert-Caesari 1951a, p. 47].

Chest Cavity

The term "chest resonance" is a relic of a former day of pedagogy, according to Vennard (1967, p. 85). He adds that it may be tolerated, but the chest must not be seriously included in a list of vocal resonators. "The resonators are cavities of air, and while there is air in the lungs it certainly is not free to vibrate as an integral mass. The chest is not a resonator because it is not a cavity!" Kwartin (1963, p. 36) is diametrically opposed to this: "One of the main factors for development of the male voice is chest resonance. ... If the chest resonance is not sufficiently used, the tone invariably will lack virility." Luchsinger and Arnold (1965, p. 81) dismiss the chest as a resonator: "Vocal resonance occurs in the resonating cavities above the vocal-cord level."

Entire Body as Resonator

Six statements were found which accredit the entire body as a resonance factor; psychological and physiological implications are here. Psychologically, the human body as a resonator is imagery; physiologically, direct resonance of the body is suggested. "Every part of the human body is in rapport with the phonating apparatus" (Meano 1967, p. 142). "It can be said that nearly every bone in the body vibrates during singing" (Mansion 1952, p. 35). "The entire self is the vocal instrument. The body carries the tone" (Ririe 1960, p. 10). "The voice, of course, starts in the head, but the entire body is an integral part of the instrument. When the sound goes through the mouth, it vibrates all the muscles and nerves of the body without exception. This has

been proved through scientific experiments" (Maurice-Jacquet
1947, p. 11).

METHODS OF CONTROLLING VOCAL RESONANCE

A Psychological Approach

Expressional Intent Controls Resonance

Fourteen writers claim all resonance controls are
psychological, that mental imagery and emotion govern resonance.   The following represent opinions gathered on this
subject:

> The singer must have the mental conception of keep-
> ing the low resonance or overtones in the top; the
> conception of keeping the high resonance and over-
> tones in the bottom [Sidney Dietch, as quoted by
> Collins 1969b, p. 32].

> The mind must take over to direct the stream of
> tone through an open throat, and decisively into the
> nose and upon the hard palate, above the teeth [Wyck-
> off 1955, p. 23].

> Sometimes the control comes only by 'ear.'   That is,
> instead of giving attention to the tongue, the student
> concentrates on getting better tone, and the [tongue]
> groove appears at the same time the tone improves,
> and to the same extent [Vennard 1967, p. 113].

> Tone is not a physical thing.   It is the expression of
> a mental concept, and a feeling for expression.   To
> result in good resonance, the mental concept must
> first be clear as to pitch and vowel, which should
> result in level and form [DeYoung 1958, p. 61].

> To sing artistically one must know how to keep from
> interfering with this guiding emotion and what it does.
> Your greatest problem in voice will be to avoid re-
> straint.   Method creates restraint.   When you allow
> yourself to sing as your emotion directs you to, then
> you sing artistically [Cor 1944, p. 11].

> Control over the resonators is gained first by correct
> thinking, and then by correct practice [Reid 1950, p.
> 56].

He must always remember that a happier mood makes for clearer and more beautiful tones, tones which are free to express the emotions of the text [Levinson 1962, p. 26].

The three basic moods are often expressed by children in emotional exclamations which take different vowel forms, ah as an utterance of joy or surprise, ee as aggression or distaste and oo as fear or terror, and the expression of these moods in singing seems to call for different actions within the larynx, actions which can be associated with the production of these three vowels, though not with the mere articulation of them [Fry and Manén 1957, p. 691].

Is Direct Control Possible?

Sixteen opinions were expressed on the subject of direct control of resonance. These are almost evenly divided, with seven statements indicating resonance can be directly determined by voluntarily creating the best possible resonance conditions, and nine statements indicating that it cannot. The latter present the opinion that favorable vocal resonance will automatically occur as a result of a free voice production. "Your use of your resonance cavities is determined by movement of the pharynx, tongue, jaw, lips and soft palate. These are your means of conscious control" (Fracht and Robinson 1960, p. 52). "The resonators can be controlled consciously, by careful training" (Vennard 1967, p. 80). "The singer must be able to use nasal or neck resonance at will, to the extent almost of excluding one or the other. When he can do so he has practically full command of all the possibilities of vocal colouring" (C. Scott 1954, p. 176).

Natural resonance is a result over which we have not direct control [Beckman 1955, p. 146].

Resonance will come of its own accord when the relaxation, right breathing and support allow the voice to emerge easily and in a free-flowing manner [McClosky 1959, p. 30].

Any attempt to increase the resonance by direct control actually defeats its own purpose by producing

tension of the throat, confining the tone, and distort-
ing the diction [P. Peterson 1966, p. 42].

I feel that resonance is the result rather than the
cause of a complete tone [Werrenrath 1951, p. 61].

The Technical Approach

Quality as a Guide

"Vocal quality or timbre is objectively determined by
the form of the sound wave issuing from the singer's lips
and the relative frequencies and intensities of its harmonic
constituents or overtones.   Quality is also the aesthetic
effect or beauty of a tone" (Fields 1952, p. 46).   Dr. William
Ross (1959, p. 42) adds to this: "A ringing resonant tone
with a cover of beauty and a point or metal that projects.
A physical description may be stated as follows: a singing
tone that has a vibrato of 6 to 7 cycles per second; a low
formant centering around 600 to 700 cycles per second for
mellowness and beauty of tone; a high formant centering
around 2800 cycles, a little higher for female voices, for
metal or ring; and intensity. " Klein and Schjeide (1967,
p. 80) lend much credit to the vibrato as an essential element
in vocal quality; they say that no voice can be really beautiful without a ringing vibrato.   Christy (1961, p. 44) is of the
opinion that tone quality and variations in tone color are
more important factors in evaluating a beginning student's
potentialities than extensive range, great volume or perfect
pitch.   Schiǿtz (1970, p. 4) comments upon the diverse
opinions of what constitutes a good and beautiful tone.   There
is general agreement, he states, that it must contain certain
aesthetic qualities besides the technical ones.   A beautiful
tone must flow freely and uninhibitedly on its way from the
singer to the listener.

Acquiring Vocal Focus

The term "vocal focus" is in that category of expressions which are similarly confusing and contradictory.
"Focus" is often considered synonymous with "placement. "
Placement has two meanings: (1) to "place," or to localize
the tone in a particular part of the human anatomy, and (2)
to "find," to enhance, or to achieve a good vocal coordination.
Focus is also used to describe a tone with "point, " or

"ring"; in this context, the term finds its most favorable re-
ception and empirical use.

The American Academy of Teachers of Singing (1969)
has adopted a position on these commonly used terms.
"Focus" is "a concentrated point of tonal vibration: the
opposite of a 'spread' tone" (p. 13). "Placement" is "a term
of imagery: voice cannot be placed. In reality, refers to
integration and coordinated production of the voice as it
applies to the particular individual." (p. 17).

Twenty-eight comments concerned with vocal focus
were found; of these, 18 statements reject the concept.

After a time, when correctly placed and focused, the
singer's voice sounds to him as if it were detached,
outside of his body. Only then can he be his own
critic [Roma 1956, p. 26].

When the physical action is correct, one feels nothing
but an exhilarating thrill. There is no 'placing' of
tones; you let them flow out, and they 'place' themselves [Freemantel 1946, p. 30].

I align myself with the many pedagogs who believe
that 'focus' or 'ping' is the sine qua non of good singing. One should not strive at first for a beautiful,
'rich, ' or even big voice. Rather one should work
for complete freedom of the mechanism [Vennard
1967, p. 156].

When I first heard of 'tone placement' I tried that.
But not for long! Having only one voice to lose, I
decided that such things were not for me. Nowadays
when students are told by a teacher that he wants to
'place' their voices, these aspirants should know
enough to stay away from him [Galli-Curci, as quoted
by Seward 1964, p. 52].

One should realize that a big voice (one large in
volume) is harder to place than a small one. ...
One's facial structure, too, has much to do with the
placement of his tone. ... The one whose face is
heart-shaped, however will find it easiest [Levinson
1962, p. 26].

Negatively, it may be added that the direct placing of

resonance is a snare and a delusion. The nature of
sound is such as to make it impossible [Judd 1951,
p. 50].

Of all the words used by singers to describe the
process of voice teaching, 'focus' and 'placement' are
perhaps the more common. The teaching of voice
placement (or focus) consists of inducing the student
to adjust unconsciously the cavities of the head and
throat in such a way that their interaction creates,
through increased resonance, a richer spectrum of
overtones [R. Taylor 1958, p. 240].

Value of Humming

Statements of 27 authors give support to the concept
that humming benefits vocal development. Bachner (1947,
p. 65) rejects the value of humming. DeYoung (1958, p.60)
says the vowel that maintains its "line" focus or impinge-
ment seems to be that which is based on humming regardless of whether the hum is used as a teaching device or not.
Simmons (1969, p. 17) defends humming as an excellent way
of developing an understanding of resonance. James Melton
(1953, p. 15) accedes the use of the hum to begin the attack,
but cautions against likely tensions. Some exaggerated
claims are made for humming; for example: "Humming will
not only clear a head cold but will also relieve sinus con-
gestion, and eliminate many afflictions that have their origins
in the sinus" (Lamberti 1954, p. 35).

SUMMARY, ANALYSIS AND INTERPRETATION

An analysis of 274 concepts of resonance offers evidence that there are few areas of vocal theory or practice
in which authorities totally agree.   In Training the Singing
Voice, Fields listed 262 concepts (Table 5).   While these
totals are similar in number, within some individual categories there are significant differences.

During the period of this research, the category the
head as resonator (including both sinuses and nasals) was
discussed in 60 statements; in the former study, 40 statements were listed. This appears to indicate that, despite
scientific evidence to the contrary, singing instructors, professional singers and others still employ the term carelessly

and evidently without knowledge of the physiological inac-
curacy of their statements.

This researcher found 45 concepts relating to the importance of the mouth and throat cavities; Fields lists 11.
This tabulation appears to indicate increased pedagogical
attention to this resonance area. The psychological concept
which considers the entire body as a resonator appears to
be of waning importance. Training the Singing Voice records
16 statements suggesting the entire body as a resonator;
this study lists only six.

In the category the voice should be focused, the current study lists ten statements that hold basic agreement to
the concept; Dr. Fields, however, catalogued 41 statements
in this area. It may be conjectured that the writers on
singing instruction are purposely avoiding this terminology
because of the controversy surrounding its use. The value
of humming continues to be mentioned as a useful device for
enhancing resonance factors.

Scientific theory, concerning the factors of resonance,
indicates that resonators alone do not create sounds. Resonators are limited to the function of taking sound that already has been produced by some form of generator and
amplifying certain frequencies. The generators of sound for
the vocal mechanism are the vocal folds. From these, there
are produced fundamental tones and overtones of relatively
weak carrying power. The resonators within the vocal tract
amplify certain phonative tones, dependent upon the volume,
the aperture and structural material of the resonating cavity.

In order to achieve the greatest amount of resonance,
as well as ease of production, the generator and resonator
should be in tune with each other. Vocally, this can be
accomplished largely through mental concept and control.
The exact pitch as well as the vowel and the tonal timbre,
or color, should be mentally conceived before producing a
tone. In so doing, the mind has an opportunity to present
the proper psychological impulse for the best physical condition and response. This is called by some writers "natural
production."

The teacher of singing must thoroughly understand the
principles and effects of vowel resonance to achieve the best
results in singing. Vowels resonate and, because of their
individual resonance characteristics, they are produced

easier at certain pitches than at others.   This factor of
vowel resonance makes certain songs more effective in certain voices than in others, and it also accounts for loss in
ease of production and in acoustical factors in some English
translations of Lieder, chanson and arias.

The confusion centering about head resonance, or the
"head voice, " bears comment.   It should be remembered
that "head voice" is a term of imagery and does not represent a reality.   "It seems to indicate that the tone is produced in the head, but it is an established fact that all vocal
vibrations originate in the larynx.   What undoubtedly originally led to the use of the term is the sensation of vibration
in the head area" (AATS 1969, p. 13).

Head voice is prevalently seen as the desired result
or outgrowth of the falsetto, and as such is a correlate to
the lower mechanism.   It is misleading to call one of the
vocal registers the "head voice, " for this leads many to
associate and to confuse head voice and head resonance.
"The 'head voice' is not 'head resonance. '   What resonance
is to be found in the nasal passages is so negligible as to
add almost nothing to the vitality of the tone" (Reid 1965,
p. 40).   Wilhelm Ruth (1966, p. 20) only partially agrees
with this; he says that vibrations influence the air-filled
paranasal cavities which, together with the bone vibrations,
create the sensation of head resonance.   Wooldridge (1956)
clearly refutes the theory of nasal resonance as a physiological occurrence.   Christy's (1961, p. 47) viewpoint is:

> In this respect it is well to point out to those who
> argue that the actual scientific presence of resonation
> in an area, and the feeling for proper resonation to
> control tone, may not coincide, since we do not al-
> ways feel stimuli where they actually occur.

A discussion of resonance is complicated by numerous
interrelated parts of the vocal mechanism.   An analysis of
tonal properties is an acoustical subject.   A study of structures of resonating cavities is concerned with physiology.
Self expression in singing has psychological aspects.   The
general study of resonance, as it relates to the vocal art,
validates and encourages a Gestalt approach to the study of
singing.

Chapter VI

CONCEPTS OF RANGE

"Range" is the compass or gamut of the singing voice. It is also the number of frequency changes possible between the lowest and highest pitches of the voice (Fields 1952, p. 46). Extension of the vocal compass is not a goal in itself, but provides a function whereby the vocal artist can convey the musical and textual elements. "Let us keep in mind this important fact: the successful singer is not conscious of range per se but only of the exhilarating sensation of completely released singing" (W. Rice 1961, p. 39).

THEORIES

Average Compass of Voices

According to the majority of writers in this survey, the human voice has a singing range of approximately two octaves. Culver (1951, p. 160) is among several who suggests a good voice should have a compass of at least two octaves. Franklin D. Lawson (1944, p. 70) is more specific; he says the usual compass of the singing voice is "two octaves of well-placed tones (low C to high C for high voices, low G to high G for medium voices, and low E to high E for low voices)." "A well-trained voice of professional calibre will probably have a compass of two octaves. Wider ranges are not uncommon, but in order to generalize we may hold to the interval of the fifteenth. The bass voice is roughly from F_2 below the bass staff to F_4 above it. The baritone octaves are a third higher, and the tenor should be able to reach C_5 above Middle C. Altos may be thought of as an octave above bass; mezzo, above baritone; soprano, above tenor. Endless embellishments are made upon this outline because no two voices are identical" (Vennard 1967, p. 79).

Christy (1961, p. 72) also agrees that a well-coordinated two octaves is sufficient to cover the compass of all but a very few of the songs and arias sung today. Buckingham (1965, p. 28) and Klein and Schjeide (1967, p. 7), among

Table 6. SUMMARY OF CONCEPTS OF RANGE

	Number of Statements in "Teaching Singing"	Number of Statements in "Training the Singing Voice"
I. Theories of vocal range		
A. Average compass of voices	39	29
B. Theory of registers		
1. general descriptions	39	32
2. number of registers in voice		
a) voice has one	5	11
b) voice has two	15	16
c) voice has three	18	7
3. value of falsetto tones		
a) they are legitimate tones	14	2
b) they are not legitimate tones	2	2
II. Methods of cultivating range		
A. A psychological approach		
1. mental causes affect registers	10	6
2. using the track of the speaking voice	4	8
3. the "high" and "low" fallacy	5	19
B. The technical approach		
1. sectional treatment		
a) practice with entire range	0	2
b) practice with middle range	24	30
2. directional treatment		
a) downward practice advised	8	13
b) approaching high tones	34	16
3. various technical devices		
a) importance of scale work	18	17
b) blending the registers	22	18
TOTALS	257	228

others, believe that a performing range of three octaves is
desirable. Wilcox (1945, p. 12) is more qualitative when he
suggests every normal soprano, mezzo or contralto voice
should "be able in vocalization to comfortably span a range
of approximately three octaves." With proper employment of
the falsetto, Wilcox points out, many male voices may be extended to almost three octaves of vocalizing range in the
true voice.

A compass of the voice classifications (Table 7),
graphically illustrated by Husler and Rodd-Marling (1965,
p. 86), is representative of the writers who supplied voice
ranges.

Table 7. REPRESENTATIVE VOCAL CLASSIFICATIONS

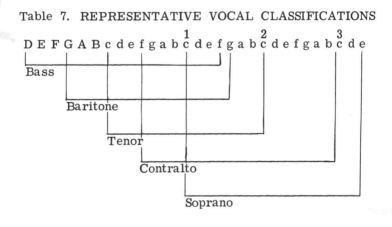

Theories of Vocal Registers

The Harvard Dictionary (1969, p 722) defines "registers":

> The different portions of the range, which are dis-
> tinguished, according to their place of production and
> sound quality, as 'head register,' 'chest register,'
> etc.   There is considerable disagreement among
> singers and voice teachers regarding vocal registers,
> high and low. ...   Formerly the registers played a
> prominent part in teaching and writing about singing,
> but today the whole idea is generally considered of
> little importance.

That registers are of little importance is in sharp contrast
to the 33 statements found in this study, which give unequivocal importance to register definition and function.

        Franca (1959, p. 14) says that registers are sounds
that are akin. She distinguishes the following: (1) chest register, (2) falsetto or mixed register, and (3) head register.
"A register is a series of tones produced in a certain area
of the voice, their functioning produced so as to give them
a chest, mouth (naseo-palatal), or head quality" (Sunderman
1958, p. 33).

        Registers, which could aptly be described as resonat-
        ing platforms, are subtle adjustments of the vocal
        apparatus governed by changes of pitch and which in
        a truly free production take place automatically [Baker
        1962, p. 25].

        We can speak of a chest register, a middle or mixed
        register, and a head register. Above the head reg-
        ister lies, in male voices, the falsetto. The whistle
        register with flute-like sounds that are not produced
        by vibration of the cords but by the whistling escape
        of air is exhibited above the head register by high
        female voices [Brodnitz 1961, p. 23].

        Registers should never be anything more than the
        sounds made by the activity of individual muscles
        temporarily dominant within the whole co-ordinate
        process [Husler and Rodd-Marling 1965, p. 58].

        The words "register" and "registration" have been
suggested for this phenomenon. The terms "heavy mechanism, "light mechanism" and "falsetto mechanism" are
often used. "Witherspoon first used the term 'lift' because
he felt that it most adequately described what should happen
in the individual's thinking at the place in the voice where
the break or change in register seemed to be" (Williamson
1950, p. 23).

Are Registers Natural?

        During the period selected for this study, 33 opinions
were found which stated or inferred the existence of registers
in the voice. There were five statements which questioned
the reality of registers, and these implied that any noticeable

48824

"breaks" were the result of a particular vocal approach. The latter position is represented by the following statements:

> Psychologically, it is wrong and often disastrous to think of three registers, and this may be the cause of the 'breaks' in voices. It is erroneous to assume that there are three ways of placing the voice [Roma 1956, p. 36].

> The wrong interpretation given by the old school to so-called 'registers' is nothing but a treacherous stumbling-block along his road of real progress; that he can happily ignore registers entirely, thanks to his knowledge that there is only one level for his voice: above his mouth [Lamberti 1954, p. 101].

According to a majority of writers, representative of scientific and empirical viewpoints, registers are accepted as natural physiological phenomena which occur in singing.

> It is absolutely impossible for the teacher to make any real improvement whatever in the pupil's voice, unless he thoroughly understands the process of purifying and developing the registers [Stanley 1950, p. 131].

> When one's laryngeal function is so crude as always to be static, with breaks between different adjustments, we hear what are called 'registers' [Vennard 1967, p. 58].

> An individual singer may possess two or three voices! That is, he has two or more separate sets of tonal characteristics in different parts of his voice range .... The individual singer finds that he must shift from voice to voice by adjusting his technique of production [Rosewall 1961, p. 36].

> While I believe there are registers in even a perfectly trained voice, my aim is to see that there are no breaks between the registers [Margolis 1951, p. 34].

Head, Chest and Falsetto Registers

How registers are used and their exact meaning is
not always clear. The terms "head," "chest" and "falsetto"
are most commonly used as names for the vocal registers.

> The various vocal responses of the human larynx are
> most commonly divided into the three main registers:
> chest, head or mid, and falsetto register. ... These
> names are a hodge-podge arising from such divergent
> sources as: secondary clues (resonances in the chest
> with the chest voice), misconceptions (non-existing
> resonances in the head with the head voice), acoustical
> illusions (with the falsetto voice), acoustical resem-
> blance (the rattling sound of trodden straw with the
> Strohbass voice), and similarity of origin, (eddies
> generated in a narrow opening and subsequent cavity
> resonance with the flute or whistle register). How-
> ever, the classification is almost generally accepted
> and, vague as it may be, works practically without
> difficulty, unless experts are asked to classify tones
> in the region where chest, head and falsetto voices
> overlap each other. We then realize how subjective
> the judgements are and must be, as no objective cri-
> teria are used [van den Berg 1963, p. 16].

A clear understanding and distinct knowledge of the
terminology related to vocal registers is important in order
to avoid confusion. This point of confusion is most obvious
in the use of the term "falsetto." Falsetto is most generally defined as the thin, unsupported, feminine-like tones
of the male high voice. Some writers, however, describe
falsetto as that area of the voice, whether male or female,
which lies above the register transitional note around f^1; in
this wise, that part of the male voice more generally called
"head voice," supported or unsupported, is sung in falsetto,
as well as most of the soprano range. These divergencies
of opinion often are a result of semantic difficulties rather
than methodology. The following are statements which attempt to define the falsetto and state its limits:

> This upper register must be developed from the un-
> developed falsetto [Whitlock 1967, p. 30].

> The light, pure falsetto is the basis for developing
> the mixed falsetto, a somewhat more sonorous type
> of production. ... Extensive practice of the falsetto
> is the only way that the strength of the arytenoid
> muscles can be developed sufficiently to balance the

action pull of the thyroid muscles in the larynx, making possible easy top compass production of the true head voice [Christy 1967, p. 144].

On very high pitches the sharpened margins of the vocal folds vibrate and sometimes over a small length only; this is known as the falsetto mechanism [Negus 1962, p. 150].

Reserve the term falsetto for that characteristic quality of high notes produced by some singers (they are nearly always tenors, and usually 'lyric' rather than 'dramatic' ones). This is, in fact, the general use of the term [Punt 1967, p. 30].

The difficulty in singing above E flat so universally experienced by basses and baritones, however, is directly attributable to the unfortunate neglect of the falsetto register [Reid 1950, p. 95].

No danger whatever is attached to exercising the 'elastic scaffolding, ' that is to say, in strengthening the falsetto. On the contrary, practising it strongly enough eliminates the danger of 'cracking' from one register into another, because 'registers' as such will no longer exist [Husler and Rodd-Marling 1965, p. 67].

The criterion of the usefulness of the falsetto must be held to be: First and foremost, a quality which can be so cultivated as to differ but little from that of the register below. Secondly, facility of transmission to and from the falsetto, without an appreciable break. Thirdly, the ability to preserve a homogeneous quality through changes of vowel and the use of consonants [Field-Hyde 1950, p. 97].

With men, the unused register is falsetto.... The development of the 'unused register' produces two good results. It builds muscular strength somewhere in the vocal instrument.... Second, this practice gives the singer a feel of something that he should be doing but which he probably does not when he uses only the other mechanism [Vennard 1967, p. 76].

With men's voices the lesson generally starts with the falsetto [Stanley 1950, p. 232].

The female voices have no real counterpart to the
male falsetto [Brodnitz 1953, p. 82].

Luchsinger and Arnold (1965, p. 95) describe the types
of male head voice: "(1) the thin-sounding natural falsetto
voice of the untrained.   (2) the delicate artistic falsetto as
practised by the countertenor, or as a special decrescendo
(fading) effect, and (3) the loud full tone of the trained head
voice with added resonance.   It is a goal of singing instruction to develop the crude, thin falsetto voice into the pleasing resonance of full head voice."

Reid (1950, p. 32) seems to substantiate this viewpoint when he says that the head voice is an outgrowth of the
falsetto and represents a coordinate relationship between that
mechanism and the chest register.   "Such being the case,
the falsetto must again be made to play an important role in
vocal training."   Fuchs (1964, p. 96) adds that a head tone
can be sung by singers of both sexes.   Rosewall (1961, p.36)
says that the head voice possesses a light quality characterized by a floating or buoyant sound and that it sounds
"alive" to the listening ear.

According to Martino (1953, p. 63) the chest register
is distinguished by its dark quality in the low and lower
medium portions of the vocal range and it is produced by
the lowest position of the larynx.   He adds that the resulting
rich tone "seems to the ear to have originated in and to have
issued directly from the chest."   Pedagogues are often in
conflict as to the advisability of developing the chest register
in high voices.   Wilcox (1945, p. 11) discussed the hesitancy
of some female voices, who have used the light mechanism
voice predominantly in both singing and speaking, to practice
the heavy mechanism tone, which inevitably sounds coarse
and unpleasant to them.   Wilcox urges, however, a period of
consistent practice which will contribute to the power, range
and quality of their voices.   Winsel (1966, p. 85) states that
the male singer always sings in the chest register.   "When
he sings a very soft pianissimo, it is of course falsetto; the
minute he starts to swell on the tone, the chest register
takes control."   "The lower third of the vocal range is called
the heavy mechanism by some and the chest register by
others.   This is because the vibrations seem to find their
major reinforcement in the chest area" (DeYoung 1958, p.
80).   "The chest register is characterized by greater energy
in the higher partials while the middle register has a stronger
fundamental" (Large 1968, p. 15).

The Action of Registration

Greisman (1943, p. 24), by means of planigraph, observed that as the singer ascends the scale, the closely
approximated vocal cords become more and more stretched,
lengthened, thinner and tauter. There finally comes a point
at which any further active contraction of the passively elon-
gated vocal muscle becomes impossible. This is the point
at which one can hear a break in an untrained singer's voice
in going farther up the scale. According to Greisman, it is
at this point the mechanism of voice production changes from
the so-called normal, or chest, mechanism into the mechanism for falsetto tones for further raising of the pitch. This
was corroborated by Hollien and Curtis (1962).

Sonninen (1956) also observed, from lateral roentgenograms of the larynx, that the vocal cords lengthened as the
pitch increased; the elongation took the shape of a typical
curve which was at first steep, becoming almost horizontal
at about the limit between the middle and the upper register.
Vennard (1959b, p. 10), commenting on the Sonninen research, adds that the lengthening of the cords, which was
rapid in "chest" voice, becomes less so in the middle voice,
and while somewhat erratic from there on, nevertheless
shows a definite tendency to remain at maximum length in
"head" voice. In "chest," active function of the intrinsic
muscles occurs and in falsetto, there is passive function.
Vennard goes on to say: "This gives the two-register hypothesis the most satisfactory scientific basis thus far advanced. It makes middle voice the area of overlap, in which
coordination of the extrinsic and intrinsic functions must be
learned. It justifies the expression 'voix mixte'."

Commenting further on the action of registration,
Fuchs (1964, p. 95) observes that in normal singing, the
vocal cords vibrate as a whole, but that in falsetto only the
edges vibrate. Herbert-Caesari (1950, p. 58) says that there
are three distinct vocal membrane mechanisms producing
three individual tonal qualities, the falsetto, the pharyngeal
(his term for head voice) and the basic, or so-called chest
voice. He states that the pharyngeal and the falsetto are
produced with the same thin upper edges of the vocal cords,
but in the pharyngeal, the edges are drawn very close together as they vibrate to leave only a thin-razor edge slit.

Writers often express caution concerning forcing the
heavy mechanism too high in the vocal range. "The student

should avoid 'pushing up the chest,' or carrying the heavy
adjustment too far up the scale" (DeYoung 1958, p. 81). "The
several lower notes just preceding the transition need to be
gradually modified to the unforced head quality, and no notes
above the pitches indicated are sung with the heavy 'chest'
adjustment or forcing and shouting result" (Christy 1961,
p. 74). "Boundaries between registers are not absolute, and
they shift from tone to tone and finally disappear, as the
singer's technique develops" (Vennard 1956, p. 5).

Number of Registers

        Table 8 illustrates the diverse opinions in regard to
the number of registers of the singing voice.   Selected statements advocating several opinions are listed:

    The safest and best teaching, totally ignores registers
    and allows the tessitura (that part of the range in
    which one sings the easiest) to develop in each indi-
    vidual naturally through correct techniques of posture,
    respiration, phonation, resonation, and articulation
    [Westerman 1955, p. 39].

    Such 'true-art singer' shows no different registers,
    with him the 'one-register-voice' became reality.
    The intensity of the head-resonance and the diaphragm
    support is incomparably stronger in this singer than
    in the mediocre one [Ruth 1963, p. 4].

    There are two registers, or mechanism, in all
    voices, one called the 'falsetto,' the other the 'chest'
    [Reid 1950, p. 67].

    Thus we have two extremes of vibration, two 'reg-
    isters' if you wish to call them that.   One covers the
    lower two thirds of the compass and the other applies
    to the upper two thirds [Vennard 1967, p. 63].

    Physiologists explain that there are only two sets of
    muscles in the larynx which control all singing and
    speaking, the thyroid and the arytenoid.   There are,
    therefore, only two registers, the lower controlled by
    the thyroid muscles and the upper (falsetto) controlled
    by the arytenoid [Christy 1961, p. 79].

    Every normal man or woman is capable of using two

Table 8. SUMMARY OF REGISTER CONCEPTS

One Register	Two Registers	Three Registers
Bachner 1947 p. 18	Christy 1961, p. 79	Appelman 1967, p. 91
Björling 1950, p. 21	DeYoung 1958, p. 78	Behnke 1945, p. 106
Lamberti 1954, p. 101	Frisell 1964, p. 16	Brodnitz 1965, p. 22
Roma 1956, p. 31	Kloin & Schjeide 1967, p. 61	R. Brown 1946, p. 11
Westerman 1952, p. 38	Lueders 1968, p. 7	Franca 1950, p. 14
	Martino 1953, p. 62	Fuchs 1964, p. 64
	Punt 1967, p. 30	Herbert-Caesari 1950, p. 58
	Reid 1950, p. 67	Judd 1951, p. 94
	Rosewall 1961, p. 36	Kelsey, Grove's, p. 49
	Stanley 1950, p. 86	Large 1968, p. 15
	Vennard 1967, p. 63	Liebling 1956, p. 13
	Weer 1948, p. 53	Luchsinger & Arnold 1965, p. 94
	Whitlock 1968b, p. 10	Ross 1959, p. 48
	Wilcox 1945, p. 9	Siepi 1956, p. 46
	Winsel 1966, p. 37	Sonninen 1956, p. 95
		Sunderman 1958, p. 33
		van den Berg 1964, p. 16
		Young 1956, p. 55

voices. These two voices, 'head voice' and 'chest voice,' can cooperate but they can never blend [Weer 1948, p. 53].

Every voice, regardless of its quality, has three registers--low, middle, and high--marked off from each other by two definite points of passage [Siepi 1956, p. 46].

The point of practical importance to the voice-trainer is that there are undoubtedly three changes of acoustic sensation perceived by an expert singer when using the voice over its full compass [Kelsey, Grove's, p. 49].

Teachers of singing realize and research verifies that all voices have three registers that may be utilized in singing [Appelman 1967, p. 91].

An uncertainty has continued as to the even higher

sounds emitted by certain sopranos attaining octave
no. 6. It is thought that in these higher tones the
vocal cords no longer vibrate, and that the glottis
then emits a flowing sound whence the name whistle
register.... This uncertainty was lifted, April 28,
1951 by Dr. Garde and myself, by laryngeal strobo-
scopic observation. The vocal cords vibrated always,
with an unchanging vibratory morphology [Husson
1956, p. 12].

There are four distinct registers [Kwartin 1963, p. 65].

Falsetto Tones

The falsetto tone is considered by some writers to be
a natural form of the voice. "Since the falsetto exists in
all voices and is never suppressed but only rendered quies-
cent, it is difficult to understand how it can be considered
anything than a perfectly natural part of the voice" (Bollew
1954b, p. 14).

Comments upon the legitimacy of falsetto quality are
summed up in Gutman's (1959, p. 17) statement: "Many con-
demn and taboo the so-called 'falsetto,' but a study of the
masters of the bel canto period will show that, if properly
used, head tones may be of enormous value." The following
are representative of opinions regarding the falsetto tone:

The 'Falsetto' cannot be developed into a full round
tone [Freemantel 1946, p. 52].

Falsetto can be a help in demonstrating how to strive
for an equal freedom in full-round tones that exploit
all the overtones [Litante 1959, p. 42].

The falsetto quality should be predominantly a
pharyngeal-mouth resonance [Ross 1949, p. 5].

The immediate spanning of such a wide vocalizing
range by male voices is only possible through employment of the falsetto tone at the higher pitches
[Wilcox 1945, p. 12].

METHODS OF CULTIVATING RANGE

A Psychological Approach

Registration Is Mentally Influenced

Ten writers consider register adjustment and the capacity of the vocal range to be influenced by mental concepts:

Mental picturing of 'upper' sound often aids in finding
the head voice [Rosewall 1961, p. 39].

The difficulties associated with high or very low notes
are to a large extent due to a false mental picture
[Puritz 1954, p. 23].

Many persons are positive that they have very limited
range.   When they are shown that they have 'sung
higher than they could sing, ' they begin to be aware
that the problem is as much (or more) mental as it
is vocal [Paul 1967, p. 14].

The singer should never think of the note itself, but
only of how to prepare for it [Fuchs 1964, p. 83].

The emotional stimulation of a well-written phrase
should carry the singer through without worries such
as: 'That F is my "changing note"' [Vennard 1967, p.78].

Keep fear and violence out of the high notes.   Let
them alone.   Think an octave below the high notes.
Let the notes come instead of trying to make them
[Kagen, as quoted by Collins 1969b, p. 15].

Using Speaking Voice Track

"The value of speaking on different pitch levels, as
an aid to developing full and free singing tones has been
recognized by most concert singers" (Manning 1946, p. 135).
"It is from the middle voice that the other extremities of
range proceed.   This is so because the middle voice most
nearly approximates the natural speaking voice" (Gorin 1943,
p. 786).   "There is a basic difference between singing and
speaking in that the latter involves phonation on definite
pitches with a wide variety of qualities.   Furthermore, the
singing range is much more extended than the speaking range"
(Beckett 1958, p. 30).

The "High" and "Low" Fallacy

     "The illusory height and depth of the voice which the
singing student feels when ranging along his entire vocal
compass, comes from an erroneous association of 'upness'
with a direction that is contrary to the pull of gravity"
(Fields 1947, p. 155). "High tones should feel just as easy
and comfortable in the throat but are more difficult in breath
energy required" (Christy 1967, p. 63). "The realization
that the lift exists helps the singer to know that tones that
are mistakenly called high tones are more easily produced
than the so-called low tones. The study of acoustics proves
to us that fast vibrations are created with less effort than
slow vibrations" (Williamson 1950, p. 23).

The Technical Approach

Sectional Treatment

     Empiricists, the voice scientists and professional
singers generally agree that the middle range of the voice
must be understood and developed first. Deliberate emphasis
on increasing the vocal range is often condemned.

> The very worst thing a singer can do is to try to ex-
> tend range by working at the reaches that need exten-
> sion. If you lack high tones, don't sing high or vice
> versa. Range is extended by not trying to extend.
> Work in the middle range and perfect that as to ease,
> freedom and control [Hatfield 1946, p. 286].

> It is the proper training of the middle voice that
> brings the beautiful head voice [W. Brown 1957, p.137].

> I had the privilege of knowing most of the great
> artists of my time, and their advice to me always
> was: the middle voice--always practice the middle
> voice, it will safeguard against undue forcing and
> preserve it for long usefulness [Gardini 1947, p. 4].

> The young teacher's general rule should be to com-
> mence training within the easy range of the voice,
> working at the extremes cautiously, and noting the
> kind of development which takes place [Field-Hyde
> 1950, p. 69].

The teacher must maintain exercises only on that
volume of tone in which the singer can sing with
facility [Vrbanich 1960, p. 8].

Restrict all pitch patterns to lower and medium range
of voice until responsive action is secure [Sister Mary
Rosemarie 1956, p. 15].

Training usually begins on the middle part of a vocal
compass [Freer 1959b, p. 19].

During the first practice period, it is better to concentrate the work in the well known 'middle voice'
[Treash 1948, p. 4].

Working from the middle of the voice we find we can
build a reliable 'song-range' long before the highest
and lowest tones could possibly be ready for use
[Mallett 1948, p. 291].

Directional Treatment

Downward practice is advised. --The use of more than
one pitch implies a directional movement.   Concerning extensive practice of descending or ascending scales or arpeg-
gios, most authors agreed that there was more value to be
gained in the regular use of descending vocalises.

The value of downward progressing scale passages
was well recognized.   This exercise is of especial
value as it tends to prevent overloading of the lower
scale and the consequent register difficulties [Lukken
1946, p. 295].

I got a great personal thrill out of coloratura singing,
but I have found that one must remember never to
force the voice!   Working downward is a great principle for equalizing the voice [Roberta Peters 1959,
p. 9].

The qualities of the upper voice can be coaxed down
and throughout the entire singing range.   The lower
voice, on the other hand, is incapable of expansion
[Rosewall 1961, p. 37].

At first, exercises descending in pitch are used rather

than ascending sustained exercises. In descending
exercises, there is less tendency for the larynx to
become tense [Bachner 1947, p. 81].

To articulare a student's voice in the beginning from
'high to low' is a golden rule already established and
fought for [Franca 1959, p. 16].

The tone acquired should be practised by proceeding
through a series of semitones, first and for a time
exclusively downwards, then upwards throughout the
easy compass of the voice [Field-Hyde 1950, p. 38].

        Approaching high tones. --In the literature concerned
with vocal pedagogy, there is a prevalence of statements
offering suggestions, devices, and approaches to the high
voice.   These suggest quite strongly that particular attention
should be afforded this portion of the vocal range.   The
following are representative of 34 statements gathered which
dealt with this subject:

    A singer should not sing a high note in public unless
    he has sung a whole tone higher in exercises.   In
    other words he should have a reserve [Fuchs 1964,
    p. 85].

    If you cannot sing a high note softly, you ought not to
    sing it at all--or at the most only two or three such
    notes a week [Punt 1967, p. 57].

    If, somehow, the voice box can be encouraged to re-
    main fairly well in place or even drop a bit as the
    singer approaches his high tones all sensation of
    squeezing will disappear, and the high tones will float
    out freely [W. Rice 1961, p. 38].

    Failure to drop the soft palate results in the blockage
    of the resonator with the result that high notes will
    be weak or strained [Klein and Schjeide 1967, p. 44].

    Be mentally and physically poised--develop the quali-
    ties of throat roominess and throat elasticity--add a
    comfortable abdominal lift--and ease into the upper
    range with a uniform flow of pure vowel sounds [P.
    Peterson 1966, p. 73].

Never sing your top notes needlessly while practicing, for when you do you are wasting your voice, using something which cannot be replaced [Roma 1956, p. 102].

The thought in singing the high tones should be to lift the tone or vibrating breath up and behind the soft palate and out through the nose. When this method is used, with an open relaxed throat, a ringing, vibrant tone will be felt in the bones of the head and face and little or no vibration noticed in the throat [F. Lawson 1944, p. 53].

Notes that can only be reached in staccato cannot help general vocal development. High notes should first be sung in legato, so that the right way to sing them can be embodied in the voice. Legato notes can be developed: staccato notes cannot [Fuchs 1964, p. 122].

After many years of study in the matter of high tones and their development, the author has found that the best progress is made by going slowly and carefully about it. Then, the progress is permanent [Freemantel 1946, p. 64].

For singers who have been discouraged by vain efforts to sing certain vowels at high pitches, it may be a comfort to learn that it is theoretically impossible. This should also be a warning to the music teacher who literally expects 'the impossible' from a student! Of course, this problem affects male voices much less than female voices [Howie and Delattre 1962, p. 8].

Robert Merrill has to think 'oo' for his top tones in order to make them come out right. However, this does not work at all for Jerome Hines. He has to think 'uh' for his top [Margolis, as quoted by Collins 1969b, p. 13].

Various Technical Devices

Importance of scale work. --The Harvard Dictionary (Apel 1969, p. 753) defines the scale as "the tonal material of music arranged in an order of rising pitches. " Scale practice as an aid in developing an extended vocal range, is mentioned by several writers, who frequently add limiting or qualifying factors:

> The slow ascending scale is the finest medium for
> building up the voice [Herbert-Caesari 1951a, p. 215].

> The first approach to a high note should be made
> through an arpeggio, not by means of an upward scale.
> In a scale each note is as near to, and so much like
> its predecessor that it tempts the singer to keep the
> vocal instrument in one position [Bairstow and Greene
> 1945, p. 49].

> There must be a note-by-note adjustment in singing
> up the scale, or there is no turning into the upper
> register [Whitlock 1968b, p. 10].

> The practice of scales and exercises over a suffici-
> ently long period of time makes the muscles so flex-
> ible that the ability of the pupil to adjust his reso-
> nators unconsciously is greatly increased [Rose 1962,
> p. 31].

> Until the student has quite a high degree of control
> of his voice, the use of scales and other singing
> exercises can be extremely dangerous [Rose 1962,
> p. 240].

> Fast scales do much for the voice. In time you can
> sing slowly with the same ease. Never sing fast
> scales legato [W. Brown 1957, p. 133].

> We cannot sing slow ones and gradually increase them.
> In this the voice differs from all instruments. We
> must sing the scales at a quick tempo and correct
> them with practise [Lamson 1963, p. 14].

> Daily warming up drills include much scale work. I
> vocalise the straight scale, up and down; first in the
> major and then in the minor [Steber 1946, p. 365].

Blending the registers. --The Singer's Glossary defines
"blending" as the "joining together the different segments of
the vocal gamut so as to avoid noticeable gaps or changes in
quality during the progression of the voice from one end of
its range to another" (Fields 1952, p. 9). Attainment of an
unbroken line throughout the compass of the voice is considered a desirable goal.

There are several important characteristics in a
change of register, or the passage over a break,
which vary in different individuals. In some the
change can be made at any point within a range of a
third or fourth or more, that is, there are several
optional tones, which can be sung in either the upper
or lower register. In others, the optional tones will
be fewer, while some show practically no such tones
at all [Field Hyde 1950, p. 77].

As in all correct singing, but especially in the bridg-
ing of the passaggio, DROP THE JAW BEFORE re-
leasing the tone. More than anything else, this will
nullify TENSION [Whitlock 1968b, p. 10].

Vowel modification is helpful or necessary in making
a smooth transition into the upper register of the
male singing voice [Taff 1965, p. 11].

To secure this continuity, one must forget about
range, or registers of voice; instead, think of the
voice as a single, unbroken tissue--a wonderful natural fabric, like many yards of shimmering silk,
without any break or change [Pescia 1948, p. 737].

It is well to follow this rule: When one feels a pull,
give way to that pull and take the higher resonance
[Levinson 1962, p. 29].

The method for uniting the vocal registers is to
bring the falsetto downward below the register break,
at E above middle C as far as possible. The falsetto
must overlap all tones of the lower register [Frisell
1964, p. 35].

In making the transition from middle register to chest
register descending, a female singer usually 'feels' a
change in mechanism, she decreases vocal force by
using less energy and by slightly lowering the jaw.
She attempts to 'ease' her voice into the lower registration mechanism. The basic vowel is always main-
tained through this pitch change--ascending or descending without modification [Appelman 1967, p. 93].

The teacher must not worry about co-ordinating the
registers. His problem is one of purifying, developing, balancing and resonating them properly, and

engendering the proper concepts.   When this has been
done co-ordination is automatic [Stanley 1950, p. 87].

In some cases, the attempt is made to isolate groups
of muscles and create a low and high register, while
in so doing the muscles are supposed to be purified
and then again be co-ordinated.   Without question,
this is the most vicious form of training the voice
[B. Taylor 1951b, p. 19].

The upper four tones of any register must partake of
the quality of the next four tones above without abandoning their own resonance.   This is 'equalizing the
registers' [W. E. Jones 1947, p. 3].

Covered tone. --Sometimes called a "closed tone, "
"covered tone" refers to a matter of tonal quality.   "In its
favorable aspect, it is acquired through the modification of
vowels to prevent blatancy.   In its unfavorable aspect the
term means one that is constricted in production" (AATS
1969, p. 11).   The controversial and confusing terms,
"covering" or "covered tone, " seem to evoke some of the
most dogmatic and unequivocal statements found in the literature on vocal instruction.   "Covering, " in its several meanings, has implications for blending the registers, the
approach to high tones, and vowel modification.

The covering mechanism used in the transition from
the chest voice to the head voice is used primarily in
male voices.   The contralto and dramatic soprano
may sometimes use it but the soprano and coloratura
soprano not at all, since the point of transition occurs
on the low pitches of the voice [Appelman 1953, p.34].

A man ... should gradually cover and close the upper
region of his voice; for his resonance should remain
forward to the top [Bairstow and Greene 1945, p. 50].

It is my opinion that the expression 'covering' is born
of an old-fashioned conception, and its use is more
likely to confuse beginners than to aid them [Vennard
1967, p. 155].

Assuming that covering is an aid to the emission of
high notes, it is a help at the expense of good diction
and the risk of 'voice disturbances. '   Any method injurious to the voice, that gives it unmusical qualities

and destroys good diction, cannot be acceptable and
should be discarded [Bollew 1956, p. 14].

By 'covering the voice' is meant a slight darkening of
the vowels on higher pitch levels to avoid excessively
bright timbre in singing. It serves to facilitate register transitions and is accomplished through lowering
of the larynx with simultaneous widening of the resonance tube [Luchsingor and Arnold 1965, p. 103]

Covering has to be used with great care because, in
its extreme form it is hard on voices [Brodnitz 1953,
p. 83].

In the first place, without abandoning the support of
his chest without which the voice loses its carrying
power, he must invoke all the head resonance he can
command ... and secondly he must begin to cover his
open vowel sounds [Graves 1954, p. 55].

The word cover is the most insidious, misleading and
harmful word in all vocal parlance [Whitlock 1967,
p. 30].

Covering originates in the coordination of different
muscle groups in the vocal apparatus [Fuchs 1951b,
p. 19].

SUMMARY, ANALYSIS AND INTERPRETATION

      In the literature used in this study, 257 concepts re-
lating to range were found. The writers were found to reflect a general interest in the compass of the voice; discussions of the complicated and controversial subject of vocal
registers are frequent.

      The concept of vocal registers was borrowed from the
terminology of the pipe organ. From the eighteenth century
and earlier, singing teachers have been interested in the
problem of registers of the human voice. Some teachers
and professional singers of this century are of the opinion
that the "natural" voice has only one register. According
to the views held by these adherents of the one-register
theory, the transitional notes between the registers, which
are apparent in most voices, result, more or less, from
faulty singing technique. On the other hand, the majority of

vocal physiologists subscribe to the idea that register differences in the human voice represent a physiological fact.
Accomplishing the equalization of the different registers, as
well as the perfection of smooth transitions from one register
to the next, is interpreted as an accomplishment of good
singing technique and a goal of singing instruction.

According to Luchsinger and Arnold (1965, p. 94), the
low chest register is especially well developed in low-voice
classifications, whereas the high head register is more extensive in the high vocal types.   Extending between these two
principal registers, is the middle register or mid-voice, also
spoken of as "voix mixte. "   At the borders of the principal
registers, transitional tones may be produced by the mechanism of either register.   This passage, or bridge is more
noticeable in the male voice, between the lower and upper
registers.   In the untrained, natural voice, an unpleasant
"break" separates, to varying degrees, these two registers.
The vocal technique of "covering" is used for the equalization
of these register passages.

The various theories concerned with registers can be
summarized around the framework of the two-register theory
and the three-register theory.   To a considerable extent, the
conflict in these two theories is more apparent than real.
In the hypothesis of some authors, the middle register functions as a separate register; to others, the middle register
is an extension of either the upper or lower register, de-
pending upon the directional approach to the note in question.
In this latter group, Vennard (1967, p. 76) offers for consideration the concepts of dynamic and static register adjustment.   "A dynamic emphasis allows for an extension of
either register into the appropriate middle range; a static
adjustment would, on the other hand, limit the agileness and
evenness of the vocal line. "

Scientific research studies after 1942, which contribute to the literature on vocal registers, are extensive.
Appelman (1953), by means of planigraph, radiograph and
spectrograph, studied the transition from the middle to the
upper register in vocal tones.   Hollien (1960) added to the
general knowledge of laryngeal correlates in regard to pitch
and voice classification.   Sonninen (1954, 1956) contributed
to the literature concerned with laryngeal action as it relates
to pitch and registers.   Husson (1956), among other findings,
disproved the theory of the "whistle" register.   Van den Berg
(1963) reported on a new concept of the origin of the main

registers.   Taff's study (1965) gave further information on
formant frequencies near the point of register transition, and
Large (1968) studied acoustic differences between the registers.

Comparative analyses of the statistical data of Fields'
research and that of this investigator (Table 6) reveals the
following observations:

1. There is less emphasis and concentration on the one
    register concept.   Fields listed 11 statements pro-
    posing one register; this study found five.
2. On the basis of 18 statements, the theory that three
    registers occur in the vocal range seems to be
    dominant.   Adherents to the two-registers theory
    were represented in 15 statements.   Fields found
    a slight preference to the theory of two registers.
3. Fourteen statements were found which accepted the
    legitimacy of the falsetto tone as a normal, useful,
    part of the vocal mechanism, while not entirely en-
    dorsing its use.   Fields found two statements on this
    subject.   This distinct increase may be due to the
    fact that the multi-register concept also asserts the
    usefulness of the falsetto in the methodology of most
    teachers.

It is interesting to note (Table 6) that the "high and
low fallacy" seems to be receiving less attention from
writers now and that more suggestions for approaching high
tones are available in the literature.   This researcher found
34 concepts on this subject, compared to 16 in the earlier
study.

In a general discussion of range and the related vocal
processes essential to an adequate vocal compass, it is necessary to remember the axiom that facts in themselves are
never dangerous, but interpretation and application often are.
According to Christy (1961, p. 79), the mistake appears to be
that teachers fail to understand that vocal production inherently remains an indirect empirical process controlled by
psychology and not by physiology.

Chapter VII

CONCEPTS OF VOCAL DYNAMICS

"Dynamics" is defined as: "A term of mechanics comprehending the laws of action and energy affecting the attack, sustaining and release of a tone. Volume, virility and intensity are a part of dynamics. Refers also to the loudness or softness of a tone" (AATS 1969, p. 12). Fields, in Training the Singing Voice (1947, p. 166), stresses the latter portion of the definition when he says: "Like most vocal and acoustical terms, dynamics has both subjective and objective connotations. Hence it is broken down into loudness and intensity. According to recent recommendations of the Acoustical Society of America, the term loudness should be used to designate the strength of the tone as heard, the mental or subjective impression, while intensity denotes the physical strength of the tone as measured objectively. Since both subjective and objective meanings of these terms are employed in training the singing voice, dynamics is also used to denote that department of vocal science that relates to the variation and control of either loudness or intensity factors in voice production. "

The American Academy of Teachers of Singing (1969, p. 23) has defined volume as: "The quantity, strength or loudness of sound; in music, fullness of tone. In gaining loudness, the quality must not be impaired, destroyed or interfered with. " Vennard (1967, p. 3) has said that "intensity refers to the extent to which equilibrium is disturbed by the sound.... Increase the intensity and you will increase the loudness, but the ear adjusts itself so that doubling intensity will not double loudness. "

THEORIES

The theories for attaining a wide range of dynamics are discussed to a lesser degree than other phases of singing. The reason for this may be that intensity, softness, and loudness are so closely allied to the breath, to phona-

120

Table 9. SUMMARY OF CONCEPTS OF VOCAL DYNAMICS

	Number of Statements in "Teaching Singing"	Number of Statements in "Training the Singing Voice"
I. Theories of vocal dynamics	8	9
II. Methods of controlling vocal dynamics		
A. A psychological approach to vocal dynamics		6
1. a mental conception of dynamic change	4	
2. an indirect approach to dynamic change	4	
B. The technical approach to vocal dynamics		
1. physical action in dynamic change	4	
2. resonance and vocal dynamics	13	9
3. breathing and vocal dynamics	28	18
4. loud versus soft singing as a practice technique		
a) loud tones should be used in practicing	27	18
b) loud tones should not be used in practicing	29	38
5. the _messa di voce_ as a device	17	10
Factors not covered in this research		2
TOTALS	134	110

tion, and to resonance.   In defining volume, the American Academy of Teachers of Singing (1969, p. 23) reaffirms a widely accepted theory: "Control of the breath is an integral part of the act requiring volume, because greater pressure of air must be exerted against the resisting vocal bands. " Reid (1950, p. 120) interjects the thought: "A properly pro-

duced soft tone is one of the major difficulties of vocal technique and can only be executed correctly after the registers
are developed, balanced, and perfectly united in their action."

> Experimental studies have recently demonstrated that
> if air flow is held constant, sound volume can be
> augmented by contraction of the glottal muscles alone.
> Applying this observation to the vocalist, if a tone is
> not properly supported and a subject vocalizes on a
> less than optimal flow of air, desired levels of loud-
> ness may be attained by greater muscular effort at
> the glottal level. Such a disturbance in balanced air
> flow-glottal resistance relationships will eventually
> manifest itself in some form of vocal strain. Exhala-
> tion must be ample and smooth, and no air should
> escape without giving up its mechanical equivalent in
> sound [Rubin 1966, p. 22].

METHODS OF CONTROLLING VOCAL DYNAMICS

A Psychological Approach

A Mental Conception

"All singers and voice teachers know that the quality
and volume of vocal tone may be regulated or controlled to
a considerable extent by mental concepts" (Wilcox 1944c,
p. 327). "The thought of speaking loudly or softly will bring
the desired result" (MacDonald 1960, p. 21). "All that he
needs to do is to conceive a pianissimo sound and the folds
will adjust themselves" (Appelman 1967, p. 14). "The demand for tone in all its aspects--pitch, intensity, volume,
concentration, etc. --comes from the auditory centres in the
brain" (Bachner 1947, p. 88).

An Indirect Approach

Sidney Dietch is quoted by John C. Collins (1969b,
p. 17): "The trouble with most singers is that they try to
make things happen and they can't. They've got to let it
happen. " "Always work for quality, and volume will gradually and naturally develop" (F. Lawson 1944, p. 44). "The
vowel that is free from consonant interference and throat
tensions and is allowed to 'swirl' in the resonators has a
feeling of power and projection" (P. Peterson 1966, p. 44).

"We do not consciously make tones soft or loud" (Montell 1950, p. 111).

The Technical Approach to Vocal Dynamics

Physical Action

Physical action, according to some authors, plays a distinctive role in dynamic change. "A forte tone depends largely on the proper use of the back muscles" (Tkach 1948, p. 4). "The greater the tension directed to the abdominal muscles, the greater the amplitude of the vibrations and thus the greater the power of the tone. Also the greater the closure of the glottis, which tends to increase the pressure" (Rose 1962, p. 91). "The only way to beautify the voice is to use a deeper and deeper activity of the coordinated torso and legs. Power can manifest itself only in proportion to our relaxation" (Beckman 1955, p. 121). "Volume or loudness ... is determined by the amplitude of vocal cord vibration" (Brodnitz 1961, p. 21).

Resonance and Vocal Dynamics

Vocal dynamics and resonance are closely allied; many pedagogues develop the two as one. "Correct piano singing is always based on sufficient head resonance and not pressure on throat and neck muscles" (Fuchs 1964, p. 107). "High forte notes should be ample, but they should consist mainly of resonance" (Herbert-Caesari 1965, p. 101). "A singer can be trained to express all the conflicting emotions of life, ranging from very soft and low to very high and loud tones by using the resonating sinus cavities which enable him to sing fortissimo with the greatest ease" (Lamberti 1954, p. 75). "A voice is the sound that is created by exhaling a column of breath which is set in vibration by its impact with the vocal cords and afterwards increased in volume by the various resonators through which it passes" (Baker 1963, p. 4).

Breathing and Vocal Dynamics

Breathing and its related processes (rate of emission, amount of pressure) are a factor in achieving an artistic change of dynamics. "When one is singing fortissimo, more

breath is used than when singing pianissimo" (Appelman
1967, p. 16). "Send the breath out as fast as possible at all
times whether ascending or descending a scale. These conditions must be invariable whether the tone is forte, pianis-
simo--high or low" (Alberti 1947, p. 6). "The less air used
for a certain sound--whether piano or forte--the better the
result will be" (Brodnitz 1953, p. 79). "The causal relationships without which intensity cannot exist are numerous.
Above all, a rise of intensity demands an increase of breath
pressure which in turn causes a muscular involvement en-
gaging the entire respiratory tract" (Reid 1965, p. 212).

Loud vs. Soft as Practice Technique

The use of soft singing as a practice technique and
in caring for the voice has had encouragement:

> The effect of excessive volume superimposed on
> basically good technique can be just as devastating
> to the larynx as poor technique alone [Rubin 1966,
> p. 22].

> Good singing is seldom loud singing [Freemantel
> 1946, p. 34].

> It is always risky to sing high notes as big notes
> straight away [Fuchs 1964, p. 84].

Loud singing practice is favored by almost half of
those writers and professional singers commenting on this
subject.

> I believe in practicing finished roles and songs in full
> voice ... quite as I would on the stage [Jeritza 1947,
> p. 185].

> No pupil should sing softly until pharyngeal resonance
> adjustment is completely established [Stanley 1950,
> p. 179].

> The pupil is well advised to master singing on the
> loud before he attempts singing on the soft. This
> does not mean overly loud practice. Remember that
> beautiful soft tones are not small tones, they are not
> devitalized tones, but are the most intense of all
> tones in respect to well-controlled pronouncing in-

tensity [S. Brown 1967, p. 79].

Both loud and soft practice are of value for good
vocal development, in the opinion of some authors:

> Soft singing helps to develop quality.   You hear ee
> and oo sounds better--thus helping the closed vowels.
> And you are also aware of the easy vibrato pulsations.
> Singing mezzo-forte, helps to produce a more natural,
> uninhibited, full tone.   It assists open vowel develop-
> ment.   Both soft and full singing are necessary for
> good vocal development [Angell 1952, p. 10].

> Another precept which has been of great value was
> the statement to sing ppp seldom and be equally
> frugal with ff.   One should use the singing voice as
> a well modulated speaking voice and surprise the
> listener with extreme dynamics [Rosalie Miller 1957,
> p. 18].

The Messa di Voce

The messa di voce is desirable, both as a vocalise
and as an example of a refined technique.   Schiøtz (1970,
p. 4) has defined it as "an Italian expression literally meaning the 'sending out of the voice.'   It consists of producing
a tone on a certain comfortable pitch with rising and falling
dynamics; make a long and even crescendo followed by a
long and even diminuendo ... [and] it will help you attain a
fine living tone."

> The number of notes on which the exercise can be
> performed, from top to bottom; the length of time to
> which it can be spun, divided equally between the two
> phases; the dynamic spread between pp and ff; the
> smoothness of laryngeal function in going from quasi-
> falsetto at the start to full voice and back again; and
> the purity with which any and all vowel sounds can be
> maintained--these are the considerations that make
> the exercise a thorough inventory of the vocal 'treas-
> ury' [Vennard 1967, p. 213].

Fuchs (1964, p. 114) suggests that "at first, exercises
for messa di voce should only be sung within a very small
compass, and never too high."   Reid (1950, p. 99) feels that
the messa di voce is suitable "for only two or three semitones comprising the immediate area of the break" and that

"F above middle C, therefore, is the highest note permitted for this exercise. "

The decrescendo within the _messa di voce_ presents one of the more difficult vocal feats.   Westerman (1955, p. 95) approaches the problem this way: "The decrescendo takes care of itself if the student merely stops increasing the support which he has at the height of the fortissimo, and holding that support, lets the tone diminish of its own volition by merely thinking the continued tone more nasalized as it decrescendos. "

> It is important for young singers to practice this skill faithfully, especially if they possess dramatic voices, because if they neglect it until after they have built a technic of power production for several years, it is much harder to learn this kind of _mezza voce_.   The trick is to shift into light production without a break, and without losing the 'edge' which characterizes the heavy mechanism [Vennard 1955, p. 5].

SUMMARY, ANALYSIS AND INTERPRETATION

Since the artistic demands of intensity, of loudness and softness are so interwoven into the total fabric of singing, the larger percentage of teaching helps are expressed in other areas of vocal pedagogy.   A portion of the literature gives only the principles involved and is vague concerning methodology.   In this study, 134 statements relating to the various aspects of dynamics were found (Table 9).   This number is similar to that tallied by Fields (1947, p. 174) in this area; he found 110 statements, of which 18 were from professional singers, 6 were from objective studies, and 2 gave authentic historical references.

Fields (1947, p. 174) found little information regarding the physiological controls of dynamics in singing.   Within the span of the present study, important contributions have been made in the experimental studies of Ekstrom, Husson, Isshiki, Ross, Rubin and others.   Rubin (1963, p. 412) found that "air flow is not the major factor in supporting a tone of increasing loudness"; his research revealed that "glottal resistance is far more important. "   Husson (1957b) detailed specific physiological explanations of the singer's effort to sing with power.   Ekstrom (1960, p. 11) found significant differences in levels of vocal intensity between the beginning singer and the experienced singer. The implication here is, of course, that control of intensity comes with practice and experience:

> The singers generally were more accurate in their abilities to control loud singing intensities than in their abilities to control soft singing intensities. The experienced singers claimed to rely heavily upon physical sensations for the control of singing intensity, whereas the inexperienced singers seemed to rely more heavily upon auditory sensations.

Isshiki (1964, p. 17) found that pitch level is significant in intensity control. "It was concluded that at very low pitches, the glottal resistance is dominant in controlling intensity (laryngeal control), becoming less so as the pitch is raised, until at extremely high pitch the intensity is controlled almost entirely by the flow rate (expiratory muscle control). "

Fields (1947, p. 175) ventured the idea that the control of loudness is an inherent rather than an acquired characteristic. If this theory could be substantiated by conclusive, objective evidence, the pedagogy of dynamics would be superfluous and the responsibility would resolve itself into a refinement of technical abilities which the singer already possesses, rather than a cultivation of new skills where none exist. There is no known evidence at the present to support this theory. Questions concerning the methodology of dynamic control continue to be asked. In this study, 28 statements were gathered which indicated that vocal volume is controlled by means of breath pressure. This is the most common opinion and it is supported by pronouncements from the American Academy of Teachers of Singing (1969, p. 23) and by experimental research.

The question of loud versus soft practice has supporters evenly divided. Writers often express caution concerning habitual practice at either end of the dynamic scale. Christy (1967, p. 13) adds another viewpoint:

> It is desirable that both loud and soft singing be practiced but always within the limits of safe technic. Exclusive use of either loud or soft singing will lead to one-sided development. The pupil is advised to find the dynamics and range at which he sings with the best quality and emphasize that at the beginning

of each practice period.... It is how we sing, not
how loud or soft, that is important.... Both extremely soft and very loud singing are good for the
growth and quality of the vocal instrument, providing
the production is free.

Within the general area of intensity and vocal dynamics, there seems to be no other technique so generally accepted as that of the messa di voce. Discussions concerning
this favorite device of the early Italian singing masters indicate that complete ease and command of the swell and
diminish effect generally demonstrates the singer's control
of his instrument.

Chapter VIII

CONCEPTS OF EAR TRAINING

"Ear training" in singing is "the process of becoming proficient and skillful in recognizing, receiving and retaining mental impressions of vocal tones and tonal relations through the medium of the sense of hearing. Ear training has as its primary purpose the building up of the power to feel, think and express in tone" (Fields 1952, p. 20). Appelman (1967, p. 141) gives further definition and comment on hearing when he suggests: "To hear is to interpret sound. To the physicist, sound is a form of energy.... The physicist's sound can be measured and controlled.... To the psychologist, sound is a sensation, something that exists only within ourselves. Such sensations create emotions and change our conduct. Sound is real but intangible. One cannot weigh it or see it; one can only feel the effects of it. "

THEORIES

General Considerations

The ear is the organ of hearing and is capable of discriminating a number of pitch tones and discerning an infinite variety of sounds. The sensitivity of the ear to pitch differences is significant as a measure of musical aptitude. "It is this sensitivity to minute pitch differences that contributes to the ear's perception of overtones and vocal quality. On the other hand, a poor ear can be insensitive to pitch differences as large as a semitone" (Fields 1952, p. 19). The ear monitors the entire process of singing. Francis Rogers (1943, p. 338) goes so far as to say "the training of the voice should be fundamentally the tireless training of the auditive imagination. "

Importance of Ear Training

Sergius Kagen (1950, p. 13) wrote that he would advocate the study of ear training as the very first step in the

Table 10. SUMMARY OF CONCEPTS OF EAR TRAINING

	Number of Statements in "Teaching Singing"	Number of Statements in "Training the Singing Voice"
I. Theories of ear training		
General considerations	12	16
1. the importance of ear training	32	23
II. Methods of ear training		
A. A psychological approach to ear training		
1. tonal imagery a factor	23	16
2. self-listening as a vocal aid		
a) self-listening is recommended	3	17
b) self-listening is not recommended	7	4
3. sound and sensation as guide to vocal action		
a) sensation is a reliable guide	17	15
b) sensation is not a reliable guide	4	20
B. The technical approach to ear training		
1. critical listening to vocal models	32	20
2. imitation as a factor		
a) imitation is recommended	3	12
b) imitation is not recommended	22	8
Factors not covered in this research		6
TOTALS	155	157

study of singing and he would "advisedly put the possession
of a good musical ear, or the ability to imagine and repro-

duce pitches, as the very first prerequisite necessary for a
professional singer, even above the possession of a pleasant voice. " The importance of training the ear for artistic
singing is frequently mentioned by authors; 32 statements
were found in its support. These opinions are summarized
in the following statements:

> The first need of the pupil ... is to learn to recog-
> nize what the quality of his voice is really like, and
> the first duty of the teacher is not to tell the pupil
> what his voice is like, but to teach him to realize
> this for himself. The training of the ear is the
> most important work in the early stages of study,
> because real success depends absolutely upon the ear,
> both in teacher and pupil [Field-Hyde 1950, p. 20].

> Students should be made to understand the necessity
> for aural concentration and to realize that without it
> they are wasting their time and risking failure [Judd
> 1951, p. 31].

> It is necessary to establish in the mind of the pupil
> the right concept of a beautiful tone [Winsel 1966,
> p. 25].

> One may observe a good singer, and one may build
> technique, but the end result is dependent upon one's
> ability to hear what beautiful tone and expression are
> [Trusler and Ehret 1960, p. 32].

> No student can sing well unless he can rise above the
> teacher's mechanical method, and anyone can sing
> who has a well-trained ear and a love of singing
> [Lester 1951, p. 4].

> Though breath pressure is under one's conscious con-
> trol, cord action is only very slightly so and reso-
> nator 'tuning' is largely automatic, the whole being
> guided by the ear [Punt 1967, p. 28].

> A singer may know all about the throat, nose and ear
> from the physiological point of view--but the knowledge
> will be entirely useless unless he can train his ear to
> appreciate the difference between right and wrong
> [Baker 1963, p. 10].

The best hints on how to keep tone pure, though, are

of small value unless the young singer has an idea of
tonal beauty in her ears [H. Shaw 1948, p. 15].

It is the ear that guides and directs; vocal tones come
only as the result of its dictates. This cannot be too
strongly emphasized [Tagliavini 1948, p. 581].

The teaching of singing is to a great extent the teaching of ear training [W. Rice 1961, p. 10].

METHODS OF EAR TRAINING

A Psychological Approach to Ear Training

Tonal Imagery

     "Tonal imagery" is defined as: "The reproduction in
memory or imagination of the likeness of an actual auditory
sensory experience, together with accompanying feelings. It
is the preconception or mental expectation of sound not
actually present to the outer sense of hearing" (Fields 1947,
p. 180). It is generally taught that the more nearly a student can conceive a perfect tone, the more nearly he can
arrive at the perfect muscular coordination which produces
this tone. First, the mind is to experience these desired
mental pictures.

You sing with your mind, not your throat [Rosewall
1961, p. 91].

It is the mind that leads the voice [Waters 1954, p.17].

The human mind is the singer's source of creative
power, therefore the act of singing is primarily a
mental process [Ewing 1950, p. 46].

The training of the mind is the most important because first there must be a mental picture of what
we want to express before we can execute it [Samuel
1948, p. 294].

Singing is more mental than physical [Ririe 1960,
p. 35].

If, in your mind, you can hear a pleasing tone, there
is a reasonable chance that your body will reproduce

a pleasant tone [T. Williams 1953, p. 17].

Beautiful vocal tone starts with the loftiest conceivable idealistic aesthetic values in the singer's brain. One cannot think with the throat [Cooke 1952, p. 15].

One statement was found which is contrary to the above expressed opinions.   Elster Kay (1963, p. 80) firmly states: "The true artist neither imagines his tone in advance nor consciously listens to it when it comes. "

Self-Listening as a Vocal Aid

Can the student hear himself as others do?   Can the pupil learn to hear himself as others hear him?   The opinions are varied:

> The ideal teacher is one who, in addition to [having] an ear that will never accept as beautiful a tone that is not beautiful, is able by one means or another to train the pupil to hear his own voice much as the teacher hears it, and to enhance to a high degree of discrimination the pupil's power of self-criticism [Rogers 1944c, p. 267].

> It is the great paradox of singing that a singer does not and cannot hear his own voice as others hear it [Rosewall 1961, p. 49].

> I cannot recommend too highly this practice of listening to oneself and judging critically of strong points and weak points alike [della Chiesa 1948, p. 531].

> The singer cannot hear himself as others hear him [McLean 1951b, p. 8; and Behnke 1945, p. 18].

> The student ... must realize that he cannot accurately hear his own voice [B. Taylor 1950, p. 33].

The popular use of tape recorders has vastly expanded the opportunities to hear one's own voice; the value of electronic recording equipment as an aid in the studio has not been fully explored; however, a few opinions were expressed regarding its use:

> The use of a good tape recorder in vocal training can

aid the student in the auditory evaluation of his own
vocal progress [Simmons 1969, p. 16].

Historically, the singer has heard himself only
through bone conduction and his inner resonances.
Today there is no excuse.   The tape recorder provides an excellent opportunity to listen, to detect,
and to correct [Varkonyi 1960, p. 415].

There are several reasons why the recorded voice,
regardless of how accurate the machine may be, will
never sound 'normal' to the singer.   In the first
place, the individual hears himself in two different
ways: As he sings, the sound is carried through the
air by reflection and refraction to the external
ear....   Another consideration in this reference is
the fact that the singer is always 'behind his voice'
whereas the microphone is usually directly in front
[R. Taylor 1958, p. 22].

As an aid to the singer ... it is suggested that the
tape recorder be used frequently in order for the
student to clarify in his own mind those faults which
are described by the teacher and to determine the
success of his own efforts to correct them [Belisle
1967, p. 8].

Sound and Sensation as Guides

"Sensation" is a change in awareness or a "feeling"
which is the result of a stimulus.   Vennard (1967, p. 261)
defines it as "the process of receiving stimuli which under-
lies perception. "   Sensation and sound, as reliable guides to
vocal action, are firmly defended and equally opposed:

It is a great mistake to base one's teaching primarily
or mainly upon such sensations [Field-Hyde 1950,
p. 88].

Seek to guide your own voice merely by sensation,
not by listening to it [Levinson 1962, p. 86].

The student of singing is liable to be seriously misled by the sensations of tone production; therefore
practical work should always be preceded by careful
explanation, and by a sorting out of cause and effect
[Behnke 1945, p. 17].

Singing is not a reasoned philosophy, but a sensory experience; and it is largely in terms of that experience that he has to be taught [Kelsey 1952, p. 448].

Any teaching theory that picks out a single sensation or movement as a guide to perfection leaves the firm basis of scientific fact [Brodnitz 1953, p. 37].

I strongly advocate that to develop the balanced musical tone, it is necessary to create 'sensation' in the various brain centers wherever a sensation can be located [Banks 1948, p. 23].

The method is based on ... establishing as habitual the thought and feeling sensations associated with the best musical results [Christy 1961, p. 137].

A positive self-control for the singer lies in the sensation of tonal vibrations and the inner-ear sound of his tone [Bachner 1947, p. 62].

When the tone is correctly produced through the use of a free automatic action of the vocal cords, you will hear good tones and you will also be conscious of a lack of feeling, or sensation, in the larynx [Bowen and Mook 1952, p. 7].

Students learn best in the actual doing. More often than not they are hazy about even clear explanations until they have actually experienced the proper sensations personally [Litante 1959, p. 11].

The fine teacher ... is aware of the individual differences of students and avoids a methodology built around a vocal sensation which may be uniquely his own [Rosewall 1961, p. 64].

The Technical Approach to Ear Training

Listening to Vocal Models

"The teacher must present the student with many good models of singing in different context. These models may range from teacher demonstrations to concert performances by artists in 'live' performances and on recordings" (Simmons 1965, p. 22). Opportunities to hear the finest singers

in excellent aural reproduction have improved with the availability of high-fidelity stereophonic recordings.

>It is so very important that you should listen, and
>listen, and listen again, to the recordings of the
>great singers [Winsel 1966, p. 78].

>A vocal method utilizing recordings can be a real
>help to the very serious student of voice [Hoffelt 1952,
>p. 11].

>The great development of the radio and phonograph
>makes it possible for the student to hear the inter-
>pretations of great artists of whom there are many
>[Granville 1950, p. 69].

>The more the student hears live performance by the
>best singers of his time, the clearer the picture gets
>of the standard expected [Frisell 1964, p. 11].

Imitation as a Factor

Imitation as an approach to improved singing is defined in Training the Singing Voice (Fields 1947, p. 185):

>The conscious or unconscious patterning of acts,
>feelings, attitudes or achievements after some model.
>In vocal training, the teacher often serves as an ex-
>emplar of vocal technique, illustrating with his own
>performance the archetypes of singing artistry that
>he wishes the student to follow or imitate.

In this study, the use of imitation as a teaching aid
has had an interesting reversal of Fields' findings. Twenty-
two statements were found in the present study (Table 10)
which rejected imitation as a method of learning; three
statements were found which endorsed the employment of
the device.   Ross (1959, p. 134) looks at both sides of the
question.   "A good singing environment will be reflected
through imitation in good singing; a poor singing environment, in poor singing.   The error in imitation is in imitating results instead of causes; that is, a singer should imitate not the tone but how the tone is produced. "

The following statements reflect opinions on the use
of imitation in training the ear:

With most pupils expression must, in the first
instance, be imitative, and no teacher will make
expressive singers unless he can himself pattern the
rendering he desires; in fact, most pupils will depend much on the teacher's patterns for a considerable time and up to a fairly advanced stage [Field-
Hyde 1950, p. 207].

Control of the voice in the early stages of training
may be a matter of listening and of imitation. As
training proceeds, the onus should be shifted to
physical sensation which is more accurate and renders
the singer independent of the acoustics of the various
rooms and halls in which he may be called upon to
sing [Kay 1963, p. 80].

The worst mistake we can make as beginners is to
try consciously to manipulate our sound-making apparatus to imitate vocal qualities and characteristics
we admire in others [McClosky 1959, p. 29].

I do not believe in teaching a pupil by imitation
[Golde, quoted by M. Craig 1952, p. 20].

Students often choose great singers as their models
and hope that by imitating them they also will become
great artists.   They do not realize that they are trying to incorporate incorrect patterns into their singing
which do not fit their own physical and psychological
make-up [Metzger 1966, p. 19].

Although it is possible to be a good teacher without
being one's self a singer, it goes without saying that
self-demonstration is the most effective way of showing a pupil exactly what one has in mind and what he
ought to do [E. Lehman 1945, p. 226].

Most knowledge of singing can be learned only
through imitation [Kipnis 1951, p. 21].

To the individual who seriously accepts the responsibility of talent must be added a note of caution: be
wary of imitation.   Do not lose your individuality.
That too is your responsibility [Whitlock 1967, p. 3].

Every voice is individual.   It is not like any other.
Nor do we want to make any imitations or replicas
[Duval 1958, p. 180].

Build your own tonal conceptions, imitating no one,
but taking a little from here, a little from there, and
adapting the best to your own needs [Tagliavini 1948,
p. 581].

Since problems can grow out of method, the vocal
student should never imitate the sounds produced by
other singers; the most easily imitated sounds are
most likely the outstanding flaws in a voice [Hines
1951, p. 16].

SUMMARY, ANALYSIS AND INTERPRETATION

The subject of ear training can be divided into separate, though quite related disciplines. The musical theorist
strives to train the ear in pitch perception, key relationships, harmonic structure and the ability to transcribe aural
pitch into musical notation. Sufficient knowledge and a practical command of these skills are vital to the singer. The
voice trainer, on the other hand, strives to train the ear
for quality of sound, for subtle changes in intensities and
dynamics, for purity in vowel production and for accuracy
in articulation and enunciation. This results in a dichoto-
mous relationship, which may be best described in terms of
aesthetics, as Christy (1967, p. 61) has expressed:

Aesthetic concepts of tonal beauty are not fixed but
subject to never-ending change and improvement.
There is no such thing as standing still in this re-
spect--we either go forward or fall back.... We
may be sure that progress in singing ability is in
direct proportion to growth in aesthetic discrimination.

Cornelius Reid (1950, p. 25) gives further support: "When
the aesthetic judgment is correct the voice will immediately,
if gradually, respond by a steady increase in power, resonance, range and flexibility."

The act of hearing is securely and inseparably linked
to other working phases of voice production. The ear is the
receptacle for sound waves. The ear is the interpreter of
what it hears. It then is not difficult to understand the common importance placed on this aspect of singing by the voice
scientist, the empiricist and the professional singer. There
were 155 statements directly related to ear training found in
the literature surveyed (Table 10).

In Training the Singing Voice, Fields (1947, p. 187)
found "little objective evidence concerning the relation of the
hearing function to the vocal act and most author opinions
grow out of empirical observations or guesswork." This
situation continues to exist. "With incredible versatility and
selectivity, hearing apparently plays an important role in the
vocal act, and it is doubtful whether any performance of the
singing voice can be entirely independent of the hearing function" (Fields 1947, p. 187).

Tonal imagery is considered to be a prime factor in
ear training by 23 writers. This concept continues to be
important, as it was in Fields' analysis. Statements by 17
writers consider sensation as a reliable guide in training of
the ear; this figure, compared to 15 statements found by
Fields (Table 10) indicates an acceptance of this concept.
"A singer cannot possibly sing a pitch knowingly without first
conceiving it as sensation" (Appelman 1967, p. 9).

A striking contrast in preferability for the use of
imitation as a technique bears comment. Fields reported
an acceptance of imitation as a desirable technique by 12
writers; eight statements were negative. This writer found
only three statements advocating the use of imitation as a
mode of learning and 22 statements rejecting its use. The
wide-spread availability of fine recordings, so true to the
original sound, has created an opportunity for students of
singing to hear professional singers in a variety of ways.
It is felt that repeated listening to selected recordings will
increase the probability of a parrot-like performance. This
element may be the source of increased caution expressed
in those statements objecting to imitation. "The practice of
listening to the recorded voices of great artists can be enjoyable and inspiring, but any temptation to imitate the
voices should be firmly resisted" (T. Williams 1953, p. 17).
The use of imitation as a learning aid is not unrelated to the
learning device of listening to vocal models, which is recommended by 32 writers. The differences in acceptance between the two techniques may be found in the phrase critical
listening to vocal models as opposed to imitation of vocal
models.

Chapter IX

CONCEPTS OF DICTION

"Diction," as defined in Training the Singing Voice, is:
"The clear and accurate formation, production, and projection of the elementary sounds of language and the combining
of these sounds into fluent, sequential patterns that are
suited to the tonal expression of the words and music of a
song" (Fields 1947, p. 190). The same writer defines articulation, enunciation, and pronunciation:

> Articulation--A method of producing vowels and con-
> sonants in intelligible syllabic and verbal patterns.
> Articulation is a formative or moulding process, in-
> volving organic mechanisms of the vocal tract that
> shape the phonetic patterns of the language (1952, p. 5).

> Enunciation--A projective, dynamic, or energizing
> process whereby vocal sonancy, audibility and dis-
> tinctness are applied to the vowels and consonants,
> for purpose of communication to a listener (1952,
> p. 20).

> Pronunciation--An integrative or combining process
> whereby vowels and consonants are united into large
> rhythmic groupings called syllables, words, and
> phrases (1947, p. 190).

"Diction, in its complete sense, means not only the
clear, beautiful, sensitive and intelligible communication of
language, but the whole technique and art of song-text de-
livery" (NATS, 1957). Others have added:

> The projection of the word idea by means of vowels
> and consonants is what we mean by enunciation
> [Schmidt 1950, p. 11].

> In general, it may be said that we pronounce words,
> enunciate vowels and syllables, and articulate con-

140

Table 11. SUMMARY OF CONCEPTS OF DICTION

	Number of Statements in "Teaching Singing"	Number of Statements in "Training the Singing Voice"
I. Theories of diction		
A. General considerations	28	23
B. Vocal factors in the singer's diction		
1. vowel as a vocal vehicle	30	25
2. vowel characteristics	40	16
3. importance of consonants	33	13
II. Methods of cultivating diction		
A. A psychological approach		
1. importance of mental imagery	11	7
2. speaking as a device	34	28
3. whispering as a device	1	2
4. chanting as a device	5	4
B. The technical approach		
1. value of sol-fa training	0	9
2. vowel techniques		
a) importance of ah vowel	11	26
b) lingual controls	24	17
c) other physical controls	14	7
d) various hints	14	13
3. vowel alteration		
a) high pitch vowels are altered	16	15
b) high pitch vowels are not altered	3	7
4. consonant techniques		
a) physical controls	14	9
b) consonants as tone-interrupters	22	23
c) interrupters of rhythm	4	5
d) exaggeration as a device	14	5
5. phonetic knowledge advisable	13	
TOTALS	331	254

sonants [Christy 1967, p. 75].

We may take diction to mean one word, and that
word is 'words' [Marshall 1953, p. 1].

A word consists of sounds. The science of producing
and pronouncing sounds is called phonetics; the enunciation of words and sentences synthesized from
sounds is called diction [Adler 1967, p. 3].

The textual element separates singing from the instrumental idiom. Because of this distinction, authors of
singing texts continually stress the importance of good diction
in singing.

The first requisite in singing a song is that its
words should be clearly understood [C. Scott 1954,
p. 424].

Perfect tone placement cannot be achieved in singing
without perfect diction [Wyckoff 1955, p. 30].

The secret of the whole thing lies first in the perfect
purity of the vowel sounds and second in a free and
untrammelled articulation [Eberhart 1962, p. 32].

I believe that most fundamental vocal ideas can be
sifted down to three fundamental principles--the
handling of the breath, the freedom of emission, and
the proper articulation of the vowels and consonants
[Treash 1947, p. 4].

Diction is inseparable from tone production, for singing requires the communication of ideas and moods,
verbally expressed, as well as the rendition of beautiful vocal tones [Fields 1957, p. 6].

Most of us believe that the most effective approach to
tone is the manner in which we pronounce the word
[DeYoung 1946, p. 304].

THEORIES

General Considerations

Vowels Are the Vehicle

Thirty statements (Table 11) refer to the vowel as the chief carrier of singing tone. McLellan, as quoted by John Collins (1969a, p. 33), states that "tone is nothing in the world but vowelized breath." Margolis adds emphasis to the vowel idea, according to Collins, with this comment: "Important as it is, the singer can have the most wonderfully developed breathing in the world and still not be able to sing, if the vowel mould is not right." The following statements are also relevant:

> The beauty of the voice and the expression of emotion is heard in the vowel sounds, the intensity and colour of which can be varied to a very great extent [Rose 1962, p. 225].

> The emphasis should be placed on the vowels, with comparatively little emphasis on the consonants [Ross 1959, p. 10].

> The procedure for obtaining good diction can be easily stated: produce a pure vowel without distortion or 'chewing,' attach the proper consonants quickly and clearly, and move instantly into the next pure vowel sound [W. Rice 1961, p. 46].

> Voice is beautiful only when there is a beautifully effective word. Beauty of voice and beauty of word are synonymous terms [DeYoung 1958, p. 67].

> I am convinced that beauty of tone is due to the color that we give to the vowels [Fonticoli 1951, p. 17].

> After all is said, when the pupil has learned to sing five vowels, absolutely pure, he has learned to sing. The early bel canto teachers held the premise that an absolutely pure vowel can have no fault in singing and time has, in no way, disproved this [Whitlock 1969, p. 13].

Vowel Characteristics

The function of the vowel is expressed briefly by Ririe (1960, p. 45): "Vowels are carriers of tone." Concerning the individuality of vowels, Young (1956, p. 25) says: "Different vowels result from different combinations of the resonances of the two cavities. Every vowel has its own

upper and lower ranges of pitch, or 'formants' as they are
called, and will be heard whenever the resonances of the
throat and mouth correspond respectively to these two
formants. " Trusler and Ehret (1960, p. 16) add: "One of
the most important things for the student to know is that each
vowel sound has its own individual quality.   Nothing is so
dull as a voice which has neutralized all vowels into one
consistently bright or dark color. "

The scope of this study does not permit an examination of all the details of each vowel used in singing.   The
following statements concerning the qualities of vocalized
sounds illustrate representative approaches:

> All six vowel sounds should be felt resonating high up
> and forward, just behind the upper front teeth. . . .
> The more brilliant ee, aye, ah, should pass out
> under the edge of the upper teeth, and the more
> somber awe, oh, oo under the upper lip.   The mouth
> should be kept symmetrical at all times [F. Lawson
> 1944, p. 23].

> The general principle which can be supplied to vowel
> positions ... that all the positions must be definite
> and capable of being held stationary, that is, they
> must not be positions to which the organs spring and
> immediately retire from; for instance, the oo position
> requires that the lips shall be held still, no matter
> what the breath may be doing, for any length of time
> [Aikin 1951, p. 81].

> The vowels ay, ah, and ee should be sung in the
> smiling position.   But oh and oo (ü) need the more
> mellow tone given by a rounded position, when the
> mouth is shaped into an exaggerated kiss [Fuchs
> 1964, p. 45].

> The selection of vowel sounds, then, indicates a de-
> parture from the neutral sound of uh.   It is from the
> position of uh that the various sounds of the voice
> begin to take shape.   This shaping of the vowels
> arises from two principal actions: (1) the raising
> and advancing of the tongue; (2) the closing of the
> lips [C. Scott 1954, p. 112].

> I have little patience with phonetics and the various
> ramifications of the vowel-school.   I want just FIVE

PURE VOWELS, seven for Italian.   All other off-
shoots can come later.   Just the AH, AYE, EE, OH
and OO.   When the young singer can sing these five
vowels pure, then the surest possible foundation for a
singing career has been laid [Whitlock 1968a, p. 20].

Concepts of physiological functioning pertinent to the
vowel process are often developed.   Adler (1965, p. 45) says
"a vowel is a voiced speech sound which originates in the
larynx and passes unhindered through the channel formed by
throat and mouth. " Other observations also are of interest:

> We are told that vowels are formed by the leaning
> over, backwards, of the epiglottis over the larynx.
> The changing of this 'leaning' of the epiglottis forms
> different shaped cavities, thus giving a combination of
> resonances at different pitches.   This is further in-
> fluenced by the change in shape of the throat and
> tongue.   It is the unconscious adjustment of these
> cavities that forms the different vowels [Whitlock
> 1968a, p. 20].

> The front wall of the laryngeal pharynx is the root of
> the tongue, and its primary function is to help form
> vowels; the primary function of the rest of the tongue
> is to produce consonants with the aid of the lips and
> teeth [MacCollin 1948, p. 3].

> The inter-play of volume and the conductivity factor
> of the connecting apertures determine, by appropriate
> resonance, the prominence given to certain overtones
> of the voice and these overtones determine the vowel
> [R. Taylor 1958, p. 29].

> When the laws of acoustics concerned with the com-
> position of a complex tone are satisfied, purity of in-
> tonation follows and a pure tone is produced.   There-
> fore, what is called a 'pure vowel quality' represents
> a condition of agreement between our mental concepts
> of quality and the laws of physics [Reid 1950, p. 38].

Importance of Consonants

Charles Kennedy Scott (1954, p. 157) defines "consonants" as "the distinguishing feature[s] of words, as
vowels are of music; the symbolic character of a word arises

from their use. " The Singer's Manual of English Diction
(Marshall 1953, p. 5) gives prominence to consonants: "You
may not have heard so much about consonants and their importance. They project the voice. They focus it. They
enhance its volume. They supply carrying power. They are
as vital to singing an effective pianissimo as in creating a
stirring fortissimo. " Kelsey, in Grove's Dictionary (p. 59),
calls consonants the identification marks of the word. Sarle
Brown (1967, p. 29) holds that a satisfactory vowel formation
is impossible apart from a skillful articulation of consonants
in respect to their neatness and rapidity. He adapts an old
cliché: "In a very real sense, as goes the consonant so
goes the vowel. " Other statements, giving importance to the
function of consonants, are:

> Weak consonants are by far the greatest enemies of
> good diction [Camburn 1962, p. 24].

> Consonants are starters, spacers and stoppers, but
> since there are twenty of them (four times as many
> as vowels) they need more than passing attention
> [Strickling 1951, p. 50].

> Spare no effort to achieve consonant clarity. It is
> essential to good diction and good diction is essential
> to intelligibility of speech in song [J. Lawson 1955,
> p. 58].

> All consonants must be produced with the right mus-
> cles. They should never interrupt the 'floating' of
> the notes. The more dramatic the way of singing,
> the more important the consonants [Fuchs 1964, p.56].

METHODS OF CULTIVATING DICTION

A Psychological Approach

Importance of Mental Imagery

In the opinion of 11 authors, the singer's diction may
be influenced by a mental prevision of the desired expression
before its actual production. This concept of mental imagery
finds support in statements by Cranmer (1957, p. 33), Bellows (1963, p. 97), and Baker (1963, p. 9). Kagen (1950,
p. 63) says, "Practically every aspect of singing and speaking is affected to a greater or lesser degree by the clarity

of the mental image of the sound the singer or speaker wishes to produce. The coordination of muscular activities, for instance, necessary for the production of an accurate vowel sound depends to a very considerable degree upon the formation of a precise image of the vowel. " "The vowel exists first in the singer's ear; if it does not, nothing in the world will enable him to produce it; all the shaping of resonators and learned talk about frequencies are helpless to achieve what the human ear can do, if left alone" (Judd 1051, p. 51).

Speaking as a Device

The relationship between spoken diction and diction for singing is discussed extensively in the material on voice pedagogy.   Helen Traubel (1943, p. 6) says, "Practice in elocution is helpful.   I did my own work in elocution with my singing teacher. " Vennard (1967, p. 185) suggests it is excellent discipline to "speak a line of a song two or three times as if you were on a stage, and then sing it. " As a help to pronunciation, Crystal Waters (1953, p. 61) suggests reading aloud for half an hour a day.   Authors frequently point out the influence of speaking on singing.   These are represented in the following statements:

Good diction is dependent upon beautiful speech [Sunderman 1958, p. 37].

What is singing?   First it is extended speaking in both range and power [Slater 1950, p. 6].

Those principles which apply to good speech are also applicable to good singing [Beckett 1958, p. 30].

Singing is merely a conscious refining of instinctive shouting.   It may be said that singing is finding the best mouth position for any vowel sound on any pitch [Beckman 1955, p. 76].

The slogan, 'sing as you speak' or at least, 'sing as you should speak' holds good in most vowels and almost all consonants [Vennard and Irwin 1966, p. 18].

'Study the mechanism' of the production of the sounds of speech [Judd 1951, p. 106].

The teacher should help the student to understand
that singing is basically the same as speaking [W.
Rice 1961, p. 11].

Do not feel any change take place when you pass from
speech to song.   Music is not put on to words; it
pervades them [Bairstow and Greene 1945, p. 34].

Stanley insists that his students speak pharyngeally,
that they speak almost in the same manner as they
sing, which means that the speakers breathe and establish tension during phonation.   This procedure
works wonderfully in preparing the student for his
singing [Stanley, Chadbourne and Chadbourne 1950,
p. 37].

Whispering as a Device

Whispering, as a technique to improve diction in
singing, is mentioned only occasionally by authors.

Audible whispering should be done frequently, especially with phrases that are difficult for the pupil,
as that provides the most helpful means of analyzing
the correct point of formation of words, the sensation
of breath constantly flowing across the teeth, and
freedom from voluntary physical effort to form or
speak words [MacDonald 1960, p. 29].

Concerning the practice of whispering, Fields (1947, p. 199)
says, "Since the vocal cords do not vibrate, whispering is
considered restful to the voice and conducive to relaxation
and freedom of the vocal organs. "   Caution is expressed in
a comment by Friedrich Brodnitz (1953, p. 156):   "If we
advise you to keep complete voice rest during laryngitis we
mean just that.   Whispering does not rest the voice.   Persistent whispering of the 'stage whisper' type may even
strain the vocal cords more than conversational voice. "
Luchsinger and Arnold (1965, p. 120) add: "Since the vocal
cords are closed to various degrees during whispering, un-
voiced speaking does not constitute voice rest....   Patients
should not be advised to whisper during attacks of acute
hoarseness.   Voice rest means silence. "

Chanting as a Device

Some writers consider practice in chanting to be
pedagogically helpful.   In Training the Singing Voice, Fields
(1947, p. 199) says that chanting is "the recitation of the
words of a song in a musical monotone.   The chanter under-
goes all the correct actions necessary for singing except that
he does not have to concern himself with variations in pitch,
intensity, and interpretation.   Thus ... he can give more
attention to problems of intonation and diction. "   Christy
(1961, p. 53) finds "practice in chanting or 'intoning' is a
natural transition to close the gap between speaking and
singing, and to enlarge the area of speech resonance as an
intermediary step to singing of songs. "   Ringel (1948, p. 8)
says to "chant a portion of a sentence or a line of poetry on
a comfortable pitch, and then ... speak the balance with
dramatic inflection. "   He comments that this device helps
stimulate greater responsiveness in an individual's speech
and singing, and creates an awareness of the phonetic pattern
of the words.   Freer (1961, p. 547) and Cates (1959, p. 7)
are other writers who add supportive comments on the use
of chanting as a device for acquiring better diction.

The Technical Approach

Vowel Techniques

The importance of the "ah" vowel. --The ah vowel is
similar to that spontaneous vowel sound uh, which is uttered
without any deliberate vowel mold.   The following are representative statements, which advocate the employment of the
ah vowel as an approach to singing diction:

> It has been acknowledged by all physiologists that the
> position of the resonator in the pronunciation of the
> vowel-sound ah should be regarded as the starting
> point whence all the positions of other vowels may be
> said to be differentiated [Aikin 1951, p. 44].

> It is the most natural vowel, and no school of sing-
> ing has any relationship with the old Italian school if
> it teaches anything else [Lamson 1963, p. 7].

> The phonetic symbol [ɑ] represents the vowel sound
> in the word father, and in such words as star, heart,
> calm.   This sound is basic to singing; it is the theme

of which other vowels are variations [Marshall 1953, p. 125].

The vowel ah is most frequently employed as a medium for voice discipline in the beginning stage of study [Wilcox 1945, p. 18].

Since the ah vowel is produced with the least tension, it follows that it should logically be the key sound in more natural voice production and it can be the approach to articulating all other phonation [Beckett 1958, p. 30].

Infrequently a statement rejects the value of the ah vowel.   "My personal experience has taught me that ... young voices should not be built on the vowels ah and oh. These are bad for practice, and especially bad for training. They tend to take the voice out of the mask and bring it down into the throat" (Welitsch 1950, p. 18).   "In the old days ... teachers began to work with all of their voice pupils on the vowel ah, asserting that this was the easiest one.   I claim that this is not true" (Margolis, as quoted by Sabin 1953, p. 19).

Lingual controls. --It is generally agreed that the tongue is the busiest organ in the process of good singing diction.   Beyond this point, writers are not agreed about the function of the tongue in vowel formation.

The vocal instrument is shaped by the positioning of certain mobile parts of the vocal mechanism, namely the pharynx, tongue and soft palate, the various adjustments of which mean simply one thing: vowels. Correct shaping of the vowels is correct shaping of the vocal instrument [Wragg 1956, p. 529].

The tongue should never feel limp; it is not something to be kept flat at all times, as is too often supposed, but something which makes very decided vowel gestures [Kelsey, Grove's, p. 52].

The general principles which can be applied to vowel positions are that the jaw should remain open for all vowel-sounds, thus relying upon the lips and the tongue for the various modifications of their shape [Aikin 1951, p. 81].

Vennard (1967, p. 130) is convinced that, directly or indirectly, the control of the tongue is the most important factor in good vowel formation. Marshall (1953, p. 122) apparently takes a different point of view and gives no stress to the tongue action in the study of English vowels. In The Singer's Manual of English Diction, she discusses the function of the tongue in the study of consonants, but indicates that, in her experience, most English-speaking vocalists make the tongue adjustments for vowels automatically.

Other physical controls. --Robert M. Taylor (1958, p. 29) says that one of the most misleading and prevalent of all fallacies in the world of singing is "the concept that the vowel is 'formed' by a certain shape of the mouth and the striving to attain a certain excellence in diction by using certain preconceived 'molds' has caused untold frustration. " This strong position is of interest in the light of the following statements:

> It is not always realized that the 'vowel-moulding machine' of the singer consists of the soft palate and the centre of the tongue [Kelsey, Grove's, p. 52].

> I personally feel that the resonance of the mouth is far more important than that of the neck in determining vowels; as well, it is far more constant [C. Scott 1954, p. 151].

> Pronunciation should be effected in the front half of the mouth, leaving the throat free [McLaughlin 1959, p. 11].

> The lips pronouncing the various vowels and their myriad composites do not change the form of the tone, and alter the sensations of resonance [R. Brown 1946, p. 90].

> The pharyngeal cavities assume shape and sizes highly characteristic and predictable for given sounds --especially vowel sounds [Truby 1962, p. 1978].

> The student must be firmly convinced that all vowels ... are formed ENTIRELY in the pharynx, that is the back part of the mouth with its soft palate rising and descending as required.... The front part of the mouth ... has no part in the actual vowel-shaping since this absolutely demands maneuverable adjustable

parts [Herbert-Caesari 1965, p. 128].

Various helps for improving vowel attack. --Margolis
(1951, p. 34) says that he chooses the most natural vowel
for each singer and later blends it into the other vowels. As
another device for improving vowel attacks, George Newton
(1954, p. 8) says that the object is to find the most beautiful
sound used in speech, which will still leave the vowel with a
distinctive quality; he adds that it is often necessary to
change one's speech habits to find a better way of making
some sounds.   Vennard (1967, p. 44) believes in deliberately
using an exaggerated [h] in many cases; this then is followed
by a sudden, firm loud vowel.   In staccato work, the valve
is then immediately loosened again before the tenseness has
time to develop.   Vennard goes on to say that an audible
[h] is only a crutch for learning the correct attack.   When
a clear, crisp initiation of the vowel is achieved, the amount
of time and breath that is wasted in the [h] should be reduced until there is only an "imaginary [h]. "   Consonants
are suggested by Dengler (1944, p. 22) as a means of improving vowel beginnings.   He says consonants are "positions
from which vowels spring.   They act as catapults for vowels.
You can sing bah, bah, bah ... much faster than ah, ah, ah...."

Vowel Alteration

Above the normal compass of the speaking voice, the
singing voice, particularly that of a beginning student, passes
from a stronger to a weaker portion of his range.   It is
generally accepted, both from an empirical viewpoint and
from experimental research that a degree of vowel modification is necessary in the top range.   "It is important that the
singer should understand that a certain modification of the
vowel is indispensable to the perfect production of sound in
certain parts of the voice" (Eberhart 1962, p. 9).   There is
indecision as to the manner of singing vowels in this part of
the voice:

When the singer has learned to shape the pure vowels
correctly, he will find that each is capable of being
modified in shape and color; this modification is necessary on all vowels when sung on the higher pitches
[Wragg 1956, p. 530].

Vowels modify to their shorter form with ascending
pitch [Bachner 1947, p. 70].

In climbing the scale, drop out some of the basic tone to gain altitude, but always retain enough to keep control at the top.   We do this, mainly, by modifying the vowel slightly as we go upward [Angell 1957, p.6].

Jean de Reszke advised tenors to use the vowel ü on high notes, but for some singers this would be fatal as the throat has to be free and relaxed [Fuchs 1964, p. 83].

Research has suggested that at points of transition to the upper mechanism, there is a tendency toward alteration of the vowel.   Taff (1965) points this out in a spectrographic analysis of selected male singers.   Within the framework of the study, it was revealed that the subjects made significant changes in the formant frequencies of all vowels at or near the transitional notes.   Bellows (1963, p. 97), however, believes "it is quite possible to sing all the pure vowels without modification throughout the range of the voice. "

The clarity of words at high pitch levels has been the subject of research, in which it is generally conceded that intelligibility of words is more difficult to achieve in the higher range of the voice.   Howie and Delattre (1962, p. 6) report that vowels generally lose intelligibility as the pitch rises.   Triplett (1967, p. 50) confirms this observation: "If a singer could learn to relegate voice quality to second place, and allow vowel color to predominate just for the split second it takes, at the beginning of a tone, to establish the vowel, more intelligible sound could be sung on high pitches. "

Consonant Techniques

Physical controls. --Consonant sounds are produced by the action of obstacles in the path of the tonal stream.   These obstacles, or controls, as they might be called, are the result of articulatory action of the tongue, lips and the jaw. "Consonants are responsible for word intelligibility.   The lips must be active" (Sunderman 1958, p. 37).   "Good, clean, crisp consonants demand an agile tongue and a jaw completely free of tension" (W. Rice 1961, p. 49).   "Consonants [are produced] by more or less complete interruptions of the stream by interposition in various ways of tongue, teeth, lips, etc. " (Punt 1967, p. 16).   "There can hardly be disagreement on the fundamental truth that the most beautiful

consonants and vowels are those that are pronounced with
complete relaxation of the lips and the throat muscles"
(Marshall 1953, p. 2).

Consonants as tone interrupters. --"Consonants are
produced in a general way by interference with the sounding
function of the resonator, that is, they are for the most part
constrictions and stoppages of the orifices of the resonator"
(Aikin 1951, p. 70). "Singing is at its best when the singer
conceives of the vowel sound in flowing speech as a series
of rectangular sections linked together by consonantal break
points" (Appelman 1967, p. 244). Ross (1959, p. 44), Eberhart (1962, p. 32), Paul Peterson (1966, p. 69), and George
Newton (1954, p. 8) are among those who add statements to
support this concept.

Exaggeration of consonants as a device. --Intelligible
consonants are often sought through exaggeration. Comments
on this concept vary:

> The amount of articulatory force necessary in some
> instances is almost impossible for the student to be-
> lieve [Christy 1967, p. 92].

> A teacher or coach does more harm than good by
> telling a student to articulate more distinctly [Fuchs
> 1964, p. 56].

> In order for consonants to be recognized as such the
> noise must be exaggerated [Vennard 1967, p. 182].

> Exaggeration is not the best means for clarity and
> tonal beauty. The best principle is relaxation
> [Marshall 1956, p. 18].

> Here I recommend the exaggeration of words as a
> help and not a hindrance on the road to good diction
> [Melton 1953, p. 15].

> A singer must exaggerate beyond the needs of normal
> speech but must do so without distortion [Cashmore
> 1961, p. 514].

> By teaching exaggeration of pronunciation of conso-
> nants ... one achieves what has been called the 'lum-
> inosity back of the word' [Sharnova 1947, p. 4].

Where phonetics are understood, the sentiment of the
text considered and the words articulated with feeling,
the consonants, which appear in song exactly as they
do in speech, take care of themselves surprisingly
well [R. Brown 1946, p. 96].

Phonetic Knowledge Advisable

The International Phonetic Alphabet was devised by
the International Phonetic Association in 1886 to provide a
phonetic symbol of every speech sound. This alphabet has
gained acceptance as a consistent and serviceable analysis
and classification of speech sounds of all standard languages.
Singers have been encouraged to learn the International
Phonetic Alphabet for the study of foreign languages and for
a precise knowledge of the proper sound and accent of syllables or words in their native tongue. During the period of
this study, the publication of The Singer's Manual of English
Diction has had influence in acquainting the student of singing with the International Phonetic Alphabet; Marshall (1953,
p. 123) comments that any singers who have been aided by
this alphabet in their study of French or German, for example, will find it a valuable basis for comparison with
English. Appelman's The Science of Vocal Pedagogy (1967,
p. 171) has also focused attention on phonetic science:

Careful study of the International Phonetic Alphabet
brings to the singer a discipline of the word. It
teaches the singer to become aware of the great variation of mechanical adjustments of the articulators,
for within this alphabet each symbol demands a particular articulatory position for most of the speech
sounds he will sing.

DeYoung (1958, p. 77) strongly urges teachers and singers to
study and learn the International Phonetic Alphabet to the
degree that they can not only recognize and pronounce the
symbols, but also so that they can transcribe any passage
or word into phonetic script. Walsh (1947, p. 555) says that
a study of phonetics will give exact direction for clean-cut
and distinct consonants.

Schiøtz (1970, p. 167), Ross (1959, p. 164), and
Govich (1967, p. 214) are among others who add comments
encouraging the use of the International Phonetic Alphabet.

SUMMARY, ANALYSIS AND INTERPRETATION

An examination of the theories of singer's diction reveals an interdependence of the sung word and a number of related fields. A study of speech-singing characteristics draws upon a sound knowledge and understanding of vocal anatomy and physiology; acoustical physics and psychology contribute to an understanding of the nature of uttered sounds. In singing diction, a study of speech sounds is vital to the best execution of pronouncing needs. In one sense, a study of diction is a study of symbols, on the written page or mentally conceived.

In a more direct manner, an important interrelation exists between tone production and enunciation; one fosters the other. "The singer who speaks freely and naturally in song produces better tones, and the singer who has mastered correct tonal emission, reveals no distortions in diction" (Thibault 1946, p. 669). Freedom of tonal emission and of enunciation results when constriction is absent.

A consensus is easily derived from statements relating the vowel as the vehicle of the voice. This may be stated in this manner: The beauty and purity of the vowel is the foundation of a singing tone. On this subject, there is found little disagreement among the writers. There is, however, considerable disagreement concerning the essential methodological approach to achieve the desired purity of vowels. Again, there exists a conflict between the physical action control theory and the "mind-mold" vowel approach of the empirical school.

Comparative figures in this study and in Training the Singing Voice are reflected in Table 11. The following inferences are drawn:

1. Consonants are receiving increased attention in an effort to achieve clarity of diction.
2. Vowels sung in the upper range of the voice often are, and should be, altered.
3. A degree of exaggeration in articulation is acceptable.
4. There is increased endorsement of the International Phonetic Alphabet throughout the span of this research.
5. The value of speaking as a device to aid diction is widely accepted.

6. The ah vowel, as an important basic technique, is
    not practiced as extensively as before.

On the basis of his research, Belisle (1967) derived
important factors that influence diction in singing. He found
that singers who have superior diction (1) use good vowel
contrast, (2) have very little vibrato distortion in the voice,
(3) use a type of voice production which could be described
as "forward and bright, " (4) have strong voices (5) form all
sounds--particularly single and multiple vowels--carefully and
deliberately, (6) sing correct vowels with a minimum of
modification, and (7) generally are advanced in vocal skill.

In conclusion, the singer sings to express an idea, a
narrative, a mood or a philosophy; this can only be accomplished through the words. It is fact that singing does not
exist without a voice, but the voice does not suffice without
lyric or dramatic diction; the voice can often be a hindrance
or a handicap in lucid understanding of verbal expression.
Magnificent vocal quality cannot compensate for smothered
consonants and ill-conceived vowels. With perfected diction
however, there is a tendency to overlook weakness of the
voice and the lesser endowed singer is able to make himself
both heard and understood.

Chapter X

CONCEPTS OF INTERPRETATION

"Interpretation" has been explained as: "The communication of mood and thought values: The final rendering
of a piece of vocal music so that its fullest meaning is intelligible to a listener" (Fields 1952, p. 29). The Harvard
Dictionary (Apel 1969, p. 418) defines interpretation in this
manner: "The personal and creative element in the performance of music, which ... depends upon a middleman forming
a link between the composer and the audience. " "Expression"
is closely allied to interpretation. This is described as:
"The quality that accounts for the peculiar emotional effect
of music. Expression is usually regarded as a basic and
universal attribute of music" (Apel 1969, p. 301). Aksel
Schiøtz (1970, p. 20) has said: "To interpret actually means
to explain ... true interpretation comes from within. "

Interpretation is that part of musical expression that
the singer shares equally with other performing musicians.
There are many areas of interpretation which are important
to singing, but, because of their general nature, are beyond
the scope of this study. Technical terms which are significant to all areas of music, such as grace notes, syncopa-
tion, rubato, phrasing, crescendo, for example, and which
are not applied exclusively to voice science, are not considered within the compass of this chapter.

THEORIES

General Considerations

Nature and Importance of Interpretation

"A singer's personal style of interpretation involves
many intangibles, but there are a few obvious characteristics
that every singer must have. He must have definite talent
not only for singing but also for making the audience listen
.... He should arouse the listener's mental activity and

158

Table 12. SUMMARY OF CONCEPTS OF INTERPRETATION

	Number of Statements in "Teaching Singing"	Number of Statements in "Training the Singing Voice"
I. Theories of interpretation		
General considerations		20
1. the nature and importance of interpretation	44	
2. individuality in interpretation	14	17
II. Methods of developing interpretational skill		
A. A psychological approach to interpretation		
1. emotional emphasis	42	25
2. personality emphasis	26	14
3. interpretational emphasis	26	22
B. The technical approach to interpretation		
1. mastery of the text		
a) text comes before tone	28	18
b) speaking the song	32	74
2. criteria of song selection	26	20
3. foreign language study		
a) foreign language study is essential	36	21
b) foreign language study is not essential	6	7
4. techniques used in interpretation		
a) memorization	8	5
b) note connection: legato and staccato	26	29
c) tone color	8	12
d) various factors in song analysis	8	7
5. performance aspects		
a) visible factors in performance	26	8
b) criteria of artistic performance	28	34
Factors not covered in this research		21
TOTALS	384	354

emotions by the music that he tries to re-create" (Schiøtz
1970, p. 19). Cranmer (1957, p. 37) feels that it is impossible to teach interpretation. He goes on to say that anyone
who professes to do so is "deluding himself and his pupil.
It is possible to guide a pupil by suggestions and constructive
criticism but it is of no use forcing your view on others."
Litante (1959, p. 89) agrees: "You are either born with it or
not. Nevertheless, it lies dormant or inhibited in many
singers and often needs only the right kind of stimulus to
bring it to life."

        The "re-creative" part of music is stressed by Kagen
(1950, p. 110): "The function of a musical performer is to
allow the music to sound. ... He re-creates music--music
which already exists in a very definite form but which, in
that form, is beyond the reach of most people." The nature
of interpretation is sometimes expressed in terms of the
physical being. "The more we know about the human voice
and how it functions, the better we shall be able to use it to
its fullest as a means of expression" (McClosky 1959, p.
xiii).

        Interpretation is a manner of communication. "The
principal requirement for efficient operation of the singing
voice is the same stimulus which operates the speaking
voice: the desire to communicate thought" (Widoe 1952, p.
31). "The art of singing, like every other art, is not a
series of techniques, but a unified human expression" (Novotna 1945, p. 406). "Singing instinct is really the important thing. You see it in life, you interpret it in song"
(Eddy 1943, p. 77). Commenting further on the nature of
interpretation, various writers stress certain elements of
music as a necessity in interpretation. This is best represented in the statement by LaForge (1950, p. 33): "Rhythm,
as the basis of all interpretation, is as important to singers
as it is to pianists. The constant striving for volume or
for isolated vocal effects, at the expense of rhythmic pulse,
beauty of phrase, and clarity of diction, leads only to
musical defeat." "In the last analysis, the object of both
singing and acting is to create illusion" (Middleton 1951,
p. 50).

Individuality in Interpretation

        Vocal authorities are solidly in favor of some artis-
tic deviation from the standardized interpretation of a song

in performance. "There is no such thing as only one way to interpret a composition beautifully" (Christy 1963, p. 6). "For better or worse, you must rely on your own interpretation of the songs you sing" (Sayão 1953, p. 59).

> Seek your own way! Do not become paralyzed and enchained by the set patterns which have been woven of old. No, build from your own youthful feeling, your own groping thought and your own flowering perception--and help to further that beauty which has grown from the roots of tradition.... Consider tradition not as an end but as a beginning [Lotte Lehmann 1946a, p. 11].

Duschak (1969, p. 30) interjects the thought that individual vocal taste, vocal style and tonal imagination are decisive for the complexity of vocal beauty. Cranmer (1957, p. 63) points out that if a student shows signs of individuality in interpretation, do not stop him even if it disagrees with your picture. Question him and find if it is a real picture or a stunt or perhaps a copy of someone else.

METHODS OF DEVELOPING INTERPRETATION

A Psychological Approach

Emotional Emphasis

A number of writers emphasize thoughts and emotions as a source of inspiration for effective interpretation of a song. Fields (1947, p. 221) clarifies the use of emotion in song: "To emphasize the emotional content of a song is to give force, prominence or vividness of expression to the more or less variable complex of feelings that accompanies its interpretation." Lester (1950, p. 178) says that there is no other human activity so keenly attuned to emotion as the vocal mechanism. "All will agree that vocal technique is merely a tool by which the emotional qualities of music are brought out" (Beckett 1958, p. 30).

Collins (1969b, p. 32) quotes Paul Althouse as saying: "The singer must have no inhibitions. He must study the song; double the emotions of the song, and finally become the living character in the song." "Unless we forget ourselves in our enthusiasm for the song and its emotion, we are not truly artistic" (Westerman 1955, p. 137). "Musicians

are of the emotional type.   Their job is to play upon feelings" (Nikolaidi 1962, p. 130).   "A person of emotional
sensitivity will project not only tone in an accurate manner,
but he will infuse it with the emotional quality that will
render it meaningful" (Leonard 1968, p. 41).   "Man can use
his voice to express a great variety of emotions without even
knowing how he does it.   Love and hate, anger and satisfaction, hope and despair, joy and sorrow, wooing and re-
jection, all can be expressed by a lilt of the human voice"
(Freud 1955, p. 50).   Ross (1959, p. 135) questions whether
a singer should actually feel the emotion he is trying to
portray, or should he simulate the emotion rather than give
way to it completely.   He suggests the singer must keep his
emotions from running away with his voice.

Personality Emphasis

        "Personality" is "the outward manifestation of indi-
viduality, or the sum of characteristic traits and patterns
of behaviour that outwardly distinguish one person from
another" (Fields 1947, p. 222).   "There is only one thing in
all the study of singing that can not be either taught or
learned and that is personality.   It must be developed, for
it is the crystallization of the soul of the singer.   It grows
as he grows and develops.   All else can be learned, or acquired" (Whitlock 1969, p. 11).   "The teacher should concentrate his efforts on developing the musical personality of
his student from the very beginning of his technical work
with the voice" (Schiøtz 1970, p. 6).   "Of course, the more
temperament and imagination the singer has, the more he
will be able to find the right accentuation for these different
emotions" (Duval 1958, p. 111).   "I feel that female artists
especially must study to develop a personality and that once
having become assured they understand the full potentials in
themselves the personality must never change.   Matters of
style are not important compared with matters of personality" (Thebom 1953, p. 50).

Interpretational Emphasis

        In order to develop excellence in interpretation, the
technical factors of voice production must be mastered.
"Freedom in interpretation comes only when the musical
values of a song or part are so completely mastered that
one can sing that song or part with perfect accuracy even

while thinking of something else" (Djanel 1943, p. 312). "To
my mind, good interpretation can begin only when voice
mechanics have been so thoroughly mastered that they become second nature and need not be thought of consciously"
(McClosky 1959, p. 106). "Learning the notes of a composition and performing them correctly mark only the initial
stage in the study of a musical work" (Schnelker 1956, p.
14). "Concentration is on the meaning of what is said and
not on how the voice sounds" (Manning 1940, p. 105).

The Technical Approach to Interpretation

Mastery of the Text

Text comes before tone. --As an avenue to effective
interpretation, 28 authors suggest learning the text first.
The following are representative statements reflecting this
concept:

> Study the text, memorize it, declaim it aloud, under-
> stand its every shade of meaning, before you even
> approach the music [Traubel, as quoted by Withers
> 1945, p. 463].

> One should remember that the poem generally pre-
> ceded the music and that it was conceived by its
> author as a unique and personal literary creation
> [Cates 1959, p. 16].

> I believe with all my conviction that the poem is al-
> ways the core of the song. If the poem of a song
> moves me, I will sing that song even if the music
> is only passable [Frijsh 1945, p. 135].

> The first step to be taken in studying a song is to
> learn the words [Stanley 1950, p. 242].

Others have taken a different point of view and stress
learning the musical elements before the text. On this subject, Maggie Teyte (1946, p. 16) says: "It is the greatest
possible mistake to begin a new song by learning the poem
first. No, the music comes first. " Stignani (1949, p. 382)
seems to agree: "Only when the musical study is done, do
I begin work on the words and the delineation of the character. "

Speaking the song. --Reading aloud the text of a song
or the general oral expression of fine prose and poetry, is
recommended by 32 authors.

> To read the text of a song out loud dramatically with
> full attention to its meaning and mood is the surest
> way to gain a proper concept of eloquent expression
> in song [Christy 1965, p. 58].

> I ask the pupil to read the words as a poem [L.
> Martin 1967, p. 29].

> It is impossible to be a good lieder singer if one
> cannot recite the poem as an actor would recite it
> [Lotte Lehmann 1946b, p. 74].

> First of all, I would suggest that he read the poem
> aloud before he looks at the music [Crammer 1957,
> p. 38].

> Every future singer or public speaker should be
> trained in the reading and reciting of poetry with an
> open and free throat [Franca 1959, p. 22].

> I find it a good practice to recite the poem of a song
> as a declamation [G. London 1953, p. 61].

> I often used to wonder why teachers did not instruct
> their pupils to read aloud sonorous sonnets and prose
> which gives to the vowels a very beautiful quality
> [Galli-Curci, as quoted by Seward 1964, p. 52].

Criteria of Song Selection

There are many opinions on the selection of songs
and arias. The following are representative statements:
"Avoid any material that is beyond you interpretatively, as
well as vocally" (G. London 1953, p. 19). "I recommend
assigning of character songs as soon as a pupil has a usable
range of an octave plus two or three other notes. A song
about a specific person is inherently more interesting and
stimulating than an obtuse love song or a mood song"
(Stocker 1964, p. 13). "At whatever cost a teacher must
not allow a pupil to sing works for which he is not fitted
vocally" (Cranmer 1957, p. 64). Klein and Schjeide (1967,
p. 106) seem to take an individual view of this when they say:

"The ability to sing one song correctly is very much like learning to ride a bicycle. If a student can ride one, she can ride them all. " Other opinions on the subject of song selection are summarized in the following, more comprehensive statements:

> Learning to strain through songs and arias beyond one's immediate physical capacity accomplishes only the following. (1) It makes the student feel the immediate inadequacy of his voice very acutely. This feeling of inadequacy increases the tension with which he sings. The increase of tension affects adversely his entire singing. (2) It also creates within the student a number of unpleasant, deeply ingrained associations, almost phobias, which this piece of music evokes automatically every time he is confronted with it [Kagen 1950, p. 73].

> For the first two or three years of the student's training exclusive attention should be paid to the development of vocal coordinations. His repertoire is only a by-product, and the selections of it should be based upon its application to his problems [Schmidt 1954, p. 13].

Foreign Language Study

Singing in a language that is not native to the singer's background presents opportunities and problems in interpretation. The statements listed here represent the variety of opinions found on this subject:

> The singer should perform only in languages he fully understands--to the point of being able to converse in them [Pinza 1953, p. 62].

> It is not necessary to speak the language fluently to be able to sing it well [Melchior 1949, p. 51].

> Learn foreign languages! Before I sing in a foreign tongue, I speak the words, many times, in recitation. This helps one to become fluent; it also helps to control the foreign speech-patterns which must sit normally upon the voice [Farrell 1952, p. 56].

> It is impossible to produce valid emotional impact in

a language one does not understand.   Hence, not only
pronunciation but languages must be learned [Niko-
laidi 1952, p. 13].

A parrot-wise study of song texts is worse than use-
less for an intelligent and moving interpretation
[Sabin 1952, p. 21].

I encourage and stress a solid foundation in the old
Italian repertoire [Harrell 1949, p. 479].

I encourage the study of languages if only to improve
English diction.   They make football players play
hand-ball and tennis to develop agility, speed and
timing [Protheroe 1950, p. 14].

Cannot a song in the English language serve just as
well to teach a youngster how to sing, how to understand and maintain a legato?   Without disparaging the
old Italian classics, why cannot any song in English
be just as good vocal medicine?   [Akmajian 1969,
p. 21].

It is better to begin by singing songs in Italian, and
to postpone battling with English vowels until real
mastery has been achieved [Fuchs 1964, p. 58].

Techniques Used in Interpretation

Memorization. --"The first step in interpretation, in
vocal music, is the thorough study and memorization of the
words.   This should always be done with special emphasis
on the meaning, the natural phrasing, the normal accent and
rhythm, and the location of energy surges in their relationship to the overlapping and blending of the consonants between words" (Westerman 1955, p. 135).   "Everything must
be memorized.   If one does not definitely know the message
he is to tell his audience, he can never present the thought
spontaneously and convincingly" (MacDonald 1960, p. 53).   "I
strongly recommend to my students that they write the words
of each song, over and over in preparation.   This usually
prevents forgetting, for then the words are implanted in the
subconscious mind" (Whitlock 1964, p. 31).

Note connection: legato and staccato. --"Legato, " defined in the Harvard Dictionary (Apel 1969, p. 465), is: "To

be played without any perceptible interruption. " From the
same source (p. 806), "staccato" is defined as "a manner
of performance ... calling for a reduction of its written
duration with a rest substituted for half or more of its
value. " "Technically speaking, legato is going from the
heart of one vowel directly to the heart of the next vowel,
in spite of the interruption of the consonants. ... We must
remember in singing that legato is the 'staple fare, ' staccato
the 'seasoning' " (Whitlock 1900a, p. 31). "The spark of
imagination must be the prime mover of the legato line"
(Richard Miller 1966, p. 16). "The first step towards establishing a firm legato is the realization that vocal tone
must always have a quality which, for want of another word,
we must call intensity" (Judd 1951, p. 75). "Correctly
used in good taste, the true portamento is the basis for fine
legato in Bel Canto style" (Christy 1961, p. 67).

Paul Peterson (1966, p. 70) gives three aids which
he considers useful in acquiring a true legato:

> (1) Allow the pure vowel to flow unhindered through
> the large open channel throat into the resonating
> cavities of the head. (2) Control the emission of
> breath with coordinated physical and mental activity.
> (3) Enrich the resonant qualities of sustained beauti-
> ful speech sounds as though you were singing directly
> from one pure vowel to the next without consonant
> interference.

"The long unbroken phrase is not taught today; teachers make it too easy on their students by breaking their
phrases up with breath marks. I am shocked by the frequency of the breath marks in modern editions of Concone.
Stop making the technique easy and instead, make the technique adequate" (Whitlock 1968a, p. 30). "It is better to
sing shorter phrases, making them somewhat marcato if
necessary, than to sing such a perfect 'line' that the words
are lost" (Vennard 1967, p. 184).

Tone color. --"Tone coloring is a mental process,
even as singing itself is. All tone has some sort of color."
(Gould 1958, p. 70). "There are two kinds of beauty in the
human voice. One is purely physical and depends partly on
a naturally fine organ, and partly upon the absence of any
strain employed in using it. The aesthetic beauty of a voice
springs from emotional tone colour" (Freer 1959b, p. 19).
"The emotional quality is accomplished more by tone color

variations than by any other factor or combination of factors" (Christy 1967, p. 66).

According to the Harvard Dictionary (Apel 1969, p.
857), each vowel in singing represents a different "instrument." This is in line with the formant theory, which plays
an important part in explaining the different timbre of the
vowels in singing. "No vowel sound can be correctly produced unless it carries the color of the mood that the composer felt when he created the music" (Williamson 1951d,
p. 59).

Various factors in song analysis. --"The singer should
be beyond merely a literal reading of the printed measures
and should try to absorb and convey the rhythmic impulse of
the composer's musical thought. The music and text each
have their own rhythmic impulse" (Bachner 1947, p. 108).
"Stress is the only semantic element which connects the
singer's psycho-physical sensation with the aesthetic meaning of the words he sings; through the use of stress, the
singer transforms his concept of the meaning of a word to
an audible declaration of its meaning" (Appelman 1967, p.
191). "Interpretative ability is retarded or destroyed unless
a correct impression of mood, style, melody, rhythm and
phrasing is gained at an early stage in the study of a song"
(Christy 1963, p. 6).

Performance Aspects

Visible factors in performance. --Singing is an aural
expression, but the related visual aspect is also a part of
the end product. Facial expression and body movement are
important to the total performance. Included here are representative statements reflecting a variety of views:

What does one do with the hands? Just what one
would do with them in polite conversation. Be spar-
ing of gesture, but do not be rigid like a cigar store
Indian. Let your eyes and facial expression carry
the mood along [Whitlock 1964, p. 31].

It is illogical for singers to distort features to produce sound since the facial muscles have nothing
whatsoever to do with the activation of tone and
grimaces will only interfere with the correct reso-
nancing of the voice [Stout 1955a, p. 10].

In singing, it is only of secondary importance that a
face should look 'nice.' Doubtless it is a happy co-
incidence when both ear and eye are pleased, but it
will seldom happen that the use of the voice leaves
the face in quite a natural, easy position. Tensions
are involved which prevent this, and it is just as well
to accept it straightaway [C. Scott 1954, p. 116].

I hate gestures in the concert hall, but I hate almost
more, an inanimate body, lifeless eyes, and expres-
sionless hands [Lotte Lehmann 1946b, p. 74].

No gestures are permitted to the concert singer and
any infraction of this rule is a serious offense against
platform manners. It is often tempting to lean
against the piano or to lay your hand on it, but the
temptation should be resisted [Graves 1954, p. 43].

All exaggeration should be carefully avoided. A
singer who constantly smiles is as bad as the singer
who always shapes his mouth like a fish [Fuchs 1964,
p. 46].

A smiling mouth without the inner smile of the eyes
is a fake, one smiles from within and then exter-
nalizes it [Lewis 1962, p. 59].

Criteria of artistic performance. --Writers have vari-
ously evaluated an artistic performance. "Artistic singing
is a product of the mind and the emotions" (Christy 1961,
p. 93). "Personality ... is the prime requisite of a great
artist, with second and third places going to intelligence and
hard work" (Whitlock 1960, p. 32).

It is usually said that one must have lived, to be a good
interpreter. Experience no doubt seasons the powers
of the interpreter, but a vivid imagination, one of the
attributes of a dramatic talent, can make up in part
for lack of experience [Ross 1959, p. 125].

In the bustle of our way with music we may forget
that repetition and more repetition finally make for
intuitive performance, neutralizing the ravages of
nervousness and of rhythmic insecurities [Van Grove
1969, p. 12].

All artful singing is conceptual [Appelman 1967, p. 9].

Singing and performing is a psychological feat if a
singer is to succeed in projecting words, drama and
meaning [Jacobson 1963, p. 32].

While a mind remains blocked and inhibited, the voice
will remain blocked and held back.   The singer must
be able to unbend and surrender himself to the sound
which will please his audience [Rose 1955, p. 637].

By continually striving to make ideal tones which
thereafter can be released when the vocal organs are
properly conditioned, is the best way to secure the
highest voice results.   That is, every tone must be
filled with the loftiest concept of musical beauty,
appropriate to the meaning of the text [Cooke 1952,
p. 63].

It is no use anyone thinking he will be an artist if
his technique is not as near perfect as he can make
it [Cranmer 1957, p. 21].

The good singer must be generosity itself--and give
his voice away [Hartley 1946, p. 88].

SUMMARY, ANALYSIS AND INTERPRETATION

The faculty of interpretation is the singer's way of
expressing his thoughts or embodying his conception of a
song.   The interpretative element permits the personality
of the singer to be the creative component in the musical
performance.   There is considerable latitude in transforming
the composer's work from the printed page into a vital performance.   This arbitrariness of artistic expression often
leads some performers deliberately or ignorantly to seek an
unusual or extreme interpretation of a composition.   This
results, not infrequently, in a warped, inappropriate, distortion of the composer's intentions.

There are no precise instructions by which a play-
wright can dictate to an actor the exact way his lines are
to be spoken; in like manner, there are few means whereby
a composer can notate his compositions and dictate to the
singer the precise way songs are to be sung.   Certainly
time values and pitch determining notation add more strin-
gencies than the descriptive instructions of the dramatist.
The ideal singer is one who can place upon the composer's

composition an expression in conformity with the conventional style and within the composer's intent.   However, complete control over a singer's interpretation of a composition is not possible and not to be desired.   There must be adequate leeway for the individual performer to adapt tempo, intensity and color to his liking.   The solution appears to be found in the education of the singer in matters of musicianship, musical style and good taste.

There were 384 interpretative concepts gathered in this study.   The numerical tabulation is reflected in Table 12.   With the exception of five categories, a proportionate increase was found between the tabulation of the earlier study and that of this investigator.   Categories which reflected a marked increase in emphasis between the two studies are emotional emphasis, text comes before the tone and visible factors of performance.   Some decrease in emphasis is seen in the categories of legato and staccato and criteria of artistic performance.   The consensus is that ability to interpret is innate and that it can be stimulated and awakened.   Music is a communicative art and meaning is conveyed from the artist to the listener through interpretation.

The degree of maturity of the interpreter is significant; dependent on this, an interpretation may be genuine or it may be superficial.   The writers generally agree that the interpreter must discover his own inner-developing approach to interpretation.   Forty-two writers indicate that emotion is an important factor in interpretation; some writers go on to say, as does Frank LaForge (1950, p. 33), that there is a paradox in using emotion in interpretation:

> He must not make the mistake of falling victim to his objective emotional reaction to the music; this is the most frequent error of inexperienced singers. If uncontrolled feeling is allowed to show itself in the voice, and to be-cloud the singer's conception and projection of the song, the audience will only resent or pity the singer, and will not be gripped by the poet's and composer's meaning.

A rather dominant thought, as mentioned earlier, is that the ability to interpret effectively is inherent; if this is so, then the influence of personality on interpretation is closely allied. The writers are in agreement that personality is a factor in interpretation.   It is not always clear, however, if reference

is made to personality traits in general or to the element
of interpretative expression through empathy.

The presence of the textual element separates the
song from other musical experiences. This fact is manifest in the prevalence of statements by authors urging full
consideration of the word content. A generally accepted
dictum is to memorize or to learn the text before the tonal
portion. This idea is given additional support from the
widespread acceptance of the category speaking the song. A
general concern is voiced by several writers that assigned
repertoire not be too difficult technically for the student.
Other factors mentioned in song selection were range and
tessitura, suitability of style and the appropriateness of the
text for the student.

There is a prevalent opinion that foreign language
study is important to the complete training of the student.
There appears a common opinion among those professional
singers whose native tongue is not English, that one cannot
sing effectively in a foreign language without being able to
converse in that language. American born teachers and
singers generally agree that foreign language study is important, yet they are not so insistent on a comprehensive
mastery of a language before its use in song.

Eight statements were gathered by Fields concerning
visible factors in performance. In the present study, 26
statements were found in the literature. A wide range of
opinions is expressed here. The majority seem to share
the thought that gestures are not inappropriate in concert
but discretion and good taste are advisable. The English
writers, more frequently than others, have a distinct disdain
for hand movements in recital. Experience, intuition, personality, mental concept, an open mind, a striving for ideal
tones, lifting of aesthetic tonal concepts, and a perfected
technique are some factors which are considered vital to
sensitive, artistic performance.

Chapter XI

OUTCOMES OF THIS STUDY

Within the framework of nine major subject areas, this work has analyzed data concerning the fundamental concepts contained in recent contributions to the literature of vocal pedagogy. Specific results of the research were reflected within the appropriate chapters. Conceptual ideas were arranged in theoretical and methodological groupings within the nine chapter divisions; methodological techniques were further subdivided into psychological and technical teaching approaches. Table 13 is a final numerical summation of concepts tabulated throughout the text. In all, 3,230 concepts were gathered from the bibliographic sources; this abundance of concepts is evidence that the texts and articles on the singing voice contain a wealth of pedagogical resources.

The bibliography was compiled from the sources listed on pages 177-8. In synopsis, there are 803 items: 167 books (including 21 reprints and two reference volumes), 90 scientific papers and documented studies, and 546 articles which include 107 published interviews by professional singers. Ninety-three publishers, exclusive of privately printed volumes, and 47 magazines and professional journals are represented. The bibliography lists works of 524 authors, representative of many areas:

303 Singing teachers and coaches, music educators, choral conductors
 95 Professional singers
 44 Physicians and physiologists
 43 Phoneticists and speech therapists
 19 Critics and editors
 12 Physicists
  3 Organizations and Associations
  2 Psychologists
  2 Music therapists
  1 Drama coach

Table 13. FINAL COMPARATIVE SUMMARY OF CONCEPTS USED

["Training the Singing Voice" is Column I; "Teaching Singing" is Column II]

	No. of Statements		Theories		Methods (Total)		(Psychological Approach)		(Technical Approach)	
	I	II	I	II	I	II	I	II	I	II
Table 1: Vocal Pedagogy	690	640	145	156	545	484	374	244	171	240
Table 2: Breathing	428	497	58	92	370	405	95	78	275	327
Table 4: Phonation	463	558	188	171	275	387	85	92	190	295
Table 5: Resonance	262	274	137	169	125	105	19	30	106	75
Table 6: Range	228	257	99	132	129	125	33	19	96	106
Table 9: Vocal Dynamics	110	134	9	8	101	126	6	8	95	118
Table 10: Ear Training	157	155	39	44	118	111	78	54	40	57
Table 11: Diction	254	331	77	131	177	200	41	51	136	149
Table 12: Interpretation	354	384	37	58	317	326	174	94	143	232
TOTALS	2946	3230	789	961	2157	2269	905	670	1252	1599

The nature and scope of the research, and the breadth
of the potential bibliography necessitated exhaustive reviewing
of the works tentatively listed and many valuable items, not
relevant to the subject matter, had to be foregone in the
selection of material. Ninety-two books and 178 articles
were examined and deleted, not falling within the categorical
limitation of the research. Of the articles, 46 were noted
as being published in at least two sources; when possible,
the original article was used in the bibliography. Systematic
and comprehensive digest of such a scope of material serves
to point out that many articles are repeated at a later date
in the same journal or duplicated in others and often under
various titles. The worthwhile works of authorities are especially vulnerable to this.

There are occasional titles in the bibliography which
would appear to indicate the item is not within the scope of
this work. In all cases, the entires contain relevant material. Discrimination was on the basis of subject matter
and date of publication; works of questionable literary or
scholarly worth are included along with reliable contributions.
The bibliography lists the sources pertaining to singing instruction which have been copyrighted from 1943-1971. These
entries comprise:

1. First editions of books and pamphlets in English, or
    first English translations, including original paper-
    back editions.
2. Editions other than the first, when that edition was
    revised, enlarged, or supplemented (in which case
    only material from the supplement was used).
3. Reprint editions of books long out of print and books
    and pamphlets which have new copyrights but contain
    no alterations of the original editions. No state-
    ments from these were used, nor are they reflected
    in the statistical data. They are listed for the sake
    of completeness, and are indicated in the bibliog-
    raphy with an asterisk.
4. Bulletins, proceedings, yearbooks, pronouncements
    of associations.
5. Encyclopedias and dictionaries of music, selected.
6. Articles in journals and magazines.
7. Newspaper articles.
8. Monographs
9. Doctoral theses and dissertations. Those subse-
    quently published are listed in their printed form.

The list of references is arranged alphabetically by surname of authors. When there are two or more works by the same author, they are listed chronologically. Two or more works by an author, published in the same year, are identified, for example, as 1964a, 1964b.

SOURCES OF BIBLIOGRAPHIC INFORMATION

American Doctoral Dissertations. Ann Arbor, Mich.: University Microfilms, Inc., 1056 1068.

Books in Print: An Index to the Publishers' Trade List Annual. New York: R. R. Bowker Co., 1952-1956; Subject Guide to Books in Print, 1957-1968.

British Books in Print. London: J. Whitaker and Sons, 1965-1968.

Cumulative Book Index: World List of Books in the English Language. New York: H. W. Wilson Co., 1943-1969.

Datrix Reference Listing. Ann Arbor, Mich.: University Microfilms, Inc., 1970.

Dissertation Abstracts. Ann Arbor, Mich.: University Microfilms, Inc., 1943-1968.

Doctoral Dissertations Accepted by American Universities. Vols. X-XXII. New York: H. W. Wilson Co., 1943-1955.

Education Index. New York: H. W. Wilson Co., 1943-1949.

Gordon, Roderick D. "Doctoral Dissertations in Music and Music Education, 1957-1963." Journal of Research in Music Education, 12 (Spring, 1964), 4-112. "Supplement, 1963-1964," 13 (Spring, 1965), 45-55. "Supplement, 1964-1965," 14 (Spring, 1966), 45-57. "Supplement, 1965-1966," 15 (Spring, 1967), 41-59.

Larson, William S. Bibliography of Research Studies in Music Education, 1932-1948. Chicago: Music Educators' National Conference, 1949.

_____. "Bibliography of Research Studies in Music Education, 1949-1956." Journal of Research in Music Education, 5 (Fall, 1957), 64-225.

Music Index: The Key to Current Music Periodical Litera-
    ture. Detroit: Information Service, Inc., 1949-1968.

National Association of Schools of Music. List of Books on
    Music. Ann Arbor, Mich.: Edwards Brothers, 1943-
    1957.

"Peabody Bi-Monthly Booknotes" and "Book Reviews." Pea-
    body Journal of Education. Vols. XXI-XLVI. Nashville,
    Tenn.: George Peabody College for Teachers, 1943-
    1969.

"Quarterly Book-List." Musical Quarterly. Vols. XXIX-
    LIII. New York: G. Schirmer, 1943-1967.

Southern Regional Education Board. College Teachers and
    College Teaching: An Annotated Bibliography on College
    and University Faculty Members and Instructional
    Methods. Atlanta: Southern Regional Education Board,
    1957-1967.

The Library of Congress. The Library of Congress Catalog:
    Music and Phonorecords, Subject Index. Washington:
    The Library of Congress, 1958-1969.

ANNOTATED BIBLIOGRAPHY*

Adler, Kurt. The Art of Accompanying and Coaching. Minneapolis, Minn.: University of Minnesota Press, 1965.
       In addition to the titled area, an historical back-
ground is given and the mechanics of the principal instruments used for accompanying are explained. Extended pronouncing helps for singing in the Romance
languages will be useful to those who have some fam-
iliarity with languages. This is a distinctive contribution to the art of coaching and accompanying.
_____. Phonetics and Diction in Singing. Minneapolis,
Minn.: University of Minnesota Press, 1967.
       This book is based on chapters four through eight
of Adler's larger volume, The Art of Accompanying
and Coaching. Following an introductory section about
the general aspects of singing diction, the larger portion of the book gives pronouncing guides for Italian,
Latin, French, Spanish and German.
Aikin, W. A. The Voice: An Introduction to Practical
Phonology. Revised by H. St. John Rumsey. London:
Longmans Green and Co., 1951.
       A standard reference book first published in 1910.
It contains a precise analysis of the organs of speech
and breathing, as well as the phonetics of the English
language.
Akmajian, Diran. "Foreigners in Their Own Land." The
NATS Bulletin, 26 (December, 1969), 21.
       The author encourages singing in English by Eng-
lish speaking people.
Albanese, Licia. "How Much of Singing Can Be Taught."
An interview by Myles Fellowes. Etude, July, 1944,
p. 387.
       Miss Albanese expresses the belief that unless
one has an exceptional natural voice, there is little
justification for attempting a career in singing.
Alberti, Helen. "Facts Concerning the Art of Bel Canto or
the Basis of Bel Canto." The NATS Bulletin, 4 (November-December, 1947), 4.

_____
*Entries with asterisks, see p. 175, item 3.

Good breathing is stressed as the basis of <u>bel</u>
<u>canto.</u>

American Academy of Teachers of Singing. <u>Classification of</u>
<u>the Singing Voice.</u> Forest Hills, N. Y. : American As-
sociation of Teachers of Singing, 1956.

_____. <u>Terminology in the Field of Singing.</u> New York:
G. Schirmer, 1969.

By this means, the respected American Academy
of Teachers of Singing recommends a uniform but
simple guide to terminology in terms defined with
clarity and exactness.

"Anatomy of Voice. " <u>Choral and Organ Guide</u>, 21 (October,
1968), 4-30.

The issue is devoted to a reproduction of selected
material on voice from the 1888 edition of <u>Grove's Dic-</u>
<u>tionary of Music and Musicians</u> and an informative
selection from <u>Garcia, the Centenarian.</u>

Angell, Warren M. <u>Vocal Approach.</u> Nashville, Tenn. :
Broadman Press, 1950.

A small volume briefly touching several areas of
vocal instruction. It is designed for class instruction
of church choir members.

_____. "Sing Fully--Sing Softly. " <u>The Southwestern</u>
<u>Musician,</u> 18 (July, 1952), 10.

Values of loud and soft practice are given.

_____. <u>The Beginning Vocalist.</u> Nashville, Tenn. : Con-
vention Press, 1956.

_____. <u>The Progressing Vocalist.</u> Nashville, Tenn. :
Convention Press, 1957.

_____. <u>The Advanced Vocalist.</u> Nashville, Tenn. : Con-
vention Press, 1959.

Three class study books designed for use by
church choir members.

Apel, Willi. <u>Harvard Dictionary of Music.</u> 2d ed. , rev.
Cambridge, Mass. : The Belknap Press of Harvard
University Press, 1969.

A standard book of music literature; the revised
second edition has been updated and substantially enlarged.

Appelman, D. Ralph. "A Study by Means of Planigraph,
Radiograph and Spectrograph of the Physical Changes
Which Occur During the Transition from the Middle to
the Upper Register in Vocal Tones. " Unpublished
Ph. D. dissertation, Indiana University, 1953.

The author observed a lowering of the larynx in
the transition to the upper register. This results in
the pharynx becoming the primary resonator.

_____. "Science of Resonance." Music Journal, 17 (March, 1959), 44.

Appelman's approach to resonance and phonetics is reflected in this article.

_____. The Science of Vocal Pedagogy. Bloomington, Ind.: Indiana University Press, 1967.

Designed as a comprehensive textbook for a two-semester study, this work describes the scientific theories of vocal pedagogy in detail. A phonetic system of teaching voice based upon the International Phonetic Alphabet is exhaustively formulated. Some aspects of voice pedagogy not available elsewhere are found in this significant book.

_____. "Whither Vocal Pedagogy." The NATS Bulletin, 24 (May, 1968), 17.

The author attempts to provide bridges of transition which can be used as an objective system for teaching or for singing. The discussion is complex and involved.

Arant, Everett P., Jr. "The Development and Evaluation of a Method of Voice Instruction Utilizing Tape-Recorded Lesson Material." Unpublished Ed. D. dissertation, University of Georgia, 1970.

Both experimental tape-recorded lessons and traditional methods of instruction have been effective in producing improvement in singing ability.

Arment, Hollace E. "A Study by Means of Spectrographic Analysis of the Brightness and Darkness of Vowel Tones in Women's Voices." Unpublished Ed. D. dissertation, Indiana University, 1960.

Spectrographic analysis reveals that, of 240 sung tones supplied by five soprano voices, the qualities of bright and dark may be partially influenced by such factors as the vowel, the pitch and the intensity; of these the vowel appears to be the most influential.

Armstrong, Wm. G. "The Art of Classifying Voices." Etude, February, 1944a, p. 87.

The author relies strongly on physical characteristics in determining voice classification. Vocalises are given to encourage the free emission of the voice in order to determine the classification.

_____. "Weak Low Tones." Etude, October, 1944b, p. 567.

Suggestions for improving weak low tones particularly in the soprano voice.

_____. "The Use of the Palato-Pharyngeal Muscles in Singing." Etude, February, 1945a, p. 75.

A convincing rationale for lifting the soft palate in singing.

_____. "Singing for Health." Etude, July, 1945b, p. 375.
A combination of clavicular, costal and diaphragmatic breathing is advocated.

_____. "The Soft Palate in Singing." Etude, December, 1945c, p. 679.
The author asserts actual nasal resonance is achieved with a high, arched palate. The theory is interesting, though controversial.

_____. "Chest Support in Singing." Etude, March, 1947, p. 135.
Armstrong puts extreme emphasis on chest resonance. Chest resonance is synonymous with chest register in this article.

Ashworth, A. H. "The Nude in Music." Musical Opinion, 79 (February, 1956), 275.
The nude in music is the human voice; the unaccompanied voice has a human intimacy no instrument can achieve.

Auerswald, Adrienne. "How Singers Think They Sing." Annals of the New York Academy of Sciences, 155 (November, 1968), 230.
A singer speaks to voice scientists gathered at the 1966 conference, "Sound Production in Man."

Austin, Herbert W. "Blending the Registers." Etude, November, 1943, p. 762.
A brief article with six exercises for blending the registers.

Bachner, Louis. Dynamic Singing. London: Dennis Dobson, 1947.
After an extended condemnation of faulty teaching methods, the author promises to give the fundamental laws of voice production. This is confined to one word --freedom. Overuse of this word and of all its derivatives encumbers the argument. Finally, he suggests the use of devices similar to those he earlier condemned.

*Bacilly, Bénigne de. A Commentary upon the Art of Proper Singing. Translated and edited by Austin B. Caswell. Brooklyn, N. Y.: The Institute of Medieval Music, 1968.
Insight into the singing style, vocal ornamentation and voice instruction of the seventeenth century is provided in this translation. It is humorous, historically quaint and often apropos to voice instruction in the

twentieth century.   Originally published in 1668.
*Bacon, Richard Mackenzie.   Elements of Vocal Science.
Edited by Edward Foreman.   Champaign, Ill. :   Pro
Musica Press, 1966.
   A new edition of the 1824 publication on the prin-
ciples of singing.   It is written in the stilted style of
the time.   The philosophical rationale of singing receives an erudite treatment, but the vocal helps are
often elementary.
Bagley, Silvia R.   "About Unclassifiable Voices. "   The NATS
Bulletin, 3 (June-July, 1947), 2.
   We would in many cases get better results with
voices if we did not insist that they go into one of the
recognized classifications.
_____.   "The Singer and Stage Fright. "   Etude, May,
1949, p. 291.
   Stage fright is a force which good performers
use instead of avoid.   With its help, they turn routine
preparation into inspired performance.
_____.   Viewpoint for Singers.   Denver: World Press,
1955.
   A useful book written for the student and the aspiring teacher as well.   The writer is well-acquainted
with the techniques and methods of the better teachers.
Personal experiences are included.
Bairstow, Edward C. , and Greene, Harry Plunket.   Singing
Learned from Speech.   London: Macmillan and Co. ,
1945.
   The authors suggest that it has been the custom
to teach singing from the wrong end--to begin with
notes and to finish with words.   A proper textual consideration will help to improve rhythm, diction and interpretation.
Baker, George.   This Singing Business.   London: Ascher-
berg, Hopwood and Crew, 1947.
   Some practical advice from 38 years as a professional singer.   The author addresses himself to
"ordinary people who like singing. "
_____.   The Common Sense of Singing. Oxford: Pergamon
Press, 1963.
   This book deals mainly with the activities of a
singer's life and is, as the author states, "the plain
man's guide to singing. "   His opinions on technique are
often dogmatic.   The book is interesting reading.
_____.   "Singers and Teachers. "   Opera, 16 (July, 1965),
473-478.
   An interesting attempt to trace the pedagogic

lineage from Garcia I to the contemporary scene.
Bakkegard, B. M. "Speech and Singing." Educational Music
    Magazine, 33 (November, 1953), 25.
        The author concludes that the study of singing
    does not have direct correlation to speech adequacy.
Bampton, Rose. "Sound Vocal Development." Etude, March,
    1947, p. 125.
        Vocal problems and how they were overcome com-
    prise the worthwhile aspects of this article.
    _____. "What is Your Vocal Problem?" Etude, Decem-
    ber, 1949, p. 23.
        Questions from readers are answered.
Banks, Louis. Voice Culture. Philadelphia, Pa.: Elkan-
    Vogel Co., 1948.
        The author asserts a new approach to voice cul-
    ture that is based upon utilizing neuro-muscular energy
    with the brain as the center of gravity for the voice.
    His ideas concerning resonance and voice classification
    are particularly extreme and unorthodox.
Barbareux-Parry, Mame. Education from Within. Boston:
    Christopher Publishing House, 1948.
        The second of two volumes on the "Barbareux
    System" presents the voice and its development as a
    stringed instrument. An understanding of this system
    purportedly liberates the production of the human voice
    entirely from all need and consciousness of breath,
    pitch, tone, syllables, and physical sensation.
Barrett, Clara. "Putting Over a Song." Etude, May, 1945,
    p. 255.
        Often-repeated suggestions concerning interpreta-
    tion and ease of performance.
Bassett, G. Willard. "Organization and Business: Aspects
    of the Voice Studio." The NATS Bulletin, 16 (May,
    1960), 14.
        Contains helpful information on business practices
    and studio policies.
Beachy, Morris J. "Are Choral and Vocal Studio Rehearsal
    Techniques Compatible?" Choral Journal, 10 (Septem-
    ber-October, 1969), 24-28.
        From a study which dealt specifically on the use
    of the voice in choral singing, the author found, to a
    surprising degree, a large majority of respondees did
    not feel that there was any basic difference in the
    pedagogical approaches of the vocal teacher and the
    choral director.
Beasley, B. "The Art of 'Hollywood' Singing." Music
    Journal, 21 (January, 1963), 46.

The serious singer must learn effective use of the microphone for recordings.

Beckett, Willis W. "Vocal Methods. " Music Journal, 16 (February, 1958), 30.
A short, well-written exposition of the author's basic tenets.

Beckman, Gertrude W. Tools for Speaking and Singing. New York: G. Schirmer, 1955.
Advocating a "chair lift" exercise purported to achieve remarkable results, the author presents her method of teaching singing. Many ideas are not well presented and are therefore of limited value; other ideas make the volume worth reading.

Behnke, Kate Emil. The Technique of Singing. London: Williams and Norgate, 1945.
Local effort procedures are most prominent in this book written by the daughter of an early voice scientist. Exercises are given for breathing, the soft palate, the tongue, and the lips.

Belisle, John M. "Some Factors Influencing Diction in Singing. " The NATS Bulletin, 24 (December, 1967), 4.
Findings of this research are summarized: "Singers who have superior diction (1) use good vowel contrast, (2) have very little vibrato distortion in the voice, (3) use a type of voice production which could be described as 'forward' and 'bright', (4) have strong voices, (5) form all sounds carefully and deliberately, (6) sing correct vowels with a minimum of modification, (7) generally are advanced in vocal skill. "

Bellows, E. LeRoy. "As to Vocal Standards. " Music Journal, 18 (November-December, 1960), 40.
The author writes a fervent plea for the elevation of vocal standards.

_____. "Voice; The War between the Methods. " Music Journal, 21 (January, 1963), 97.
This is one of several articles enumerating the extreme teaching methods used by some singing instructors.

*Bérard, Jean-Baptiste. L'Art du chant. Translated and edited by Sidney Murray. Milwaukee, Wis. : Pro Musica Press, 1968.
An important early treatise on the fundamentals of voice production; the art of ornamentation in the style of the day is included. First published in 1755.

Berglund, Joel. "Some Problems of the Deep Voice. " Etude, September, 1947, p. 495.
Useful suggestions for the bass-baritone are given,

including a discussion on blending the registers.
Bergman, Adolph. Creating and Developing a Singing Voice.
New York: By the Author, New York, 1950.
    The author makes strong claims but fails to relate
them to facts. "Far from having discovered a new
method, I have rediscovered a very old one. And to
bear me out in this, I call to witness none other than
Enrico Caruso, who, as far as can be established, was
the first and last to whom we can trace this method."
_____. "Problems of Voice Training in Connection with a
New Interpretation of Enrico Caruso's Vocal Method."
Voice, 7 (March-April, 1951), 10.
Berkman, Al. Singing Takes More than a Voice. Alhambra,
Calif.: Wilshire Book Co., 1961.
    A practical guide for the singer in radio, tele-
vision, films and musical comedy; it also has helpful
suggestions on interpretation for the serious student.
Best, Jack. "Do Singers Qualify as Musicians." Music
Journal, 15 (September, 1957), 24.
    The author implores the singing student to improve
his general musicianship.
Bjöerling, Jussi. "Your Vocal Problem." Etude, June,
1950, p. 21.
    Questions from readers on vocal problems are
answered.
Bjørklund, Adolph. "Analyses of Soprano Voices." Journal
of the Acoustical Society of America, 33 (May, 1961),
575-582.
    The study shows a distinct correlation between
levels of training and vibrato of the voice.
Bollew, Joseph A. "Sing as You Speak." Etude, August,
1951, p. 58.
    A strong defense of the approach expressed in the
title. This article was written in response to Franklyn
Kelsey's "What Is Singing" (Etude, June, 1950, p. 13).
_____. "Breathing and Breath Control in Singing." Etude,
February, 1952a, p. 22.
    A "full, rich, ringing tone--the hall-mark of all
well-produced voices," is the result of good breath
control.
_____. "A New Approach to Voice Teaching." Etude,
December, 1952b, p. 15.
    Bollew has outspoken personal opinions about
singers who become teachers of singing.
_____. "Attack and Emission in Singing." Etude, April,
1953, p. 14.
    Accepted ideas and some controversial precepts

are suggested in this article.

_____. "What Price Vocal Longevity?" <u>Etude</u>, April, 1954a, p. 17.

Correct vocal production, a good musical education and strict adherence to dietary, bodily and hygienic rules are essential factors in vocal longevity.

_____. "Is the Falsetto False?" <u>Etude</u>, July, 1954b, p. 14.

A defense of the falsetto is made by mentioning its use by a variety of great singers.

_____. "Diction in Singing." <u>Etude</u>, May-June, 1956, p. 14.

"Covering" is sharply condemned as the enemy of clear, understandable singing diction.

Bolstad, Donald S. "The Role of the Otolaryngologist in Relation to the Problem Voice." <u>Music Therapy.</u> Yearbook of the National Association for Music Therapy. Lawrence, Kansas: National Association for Music Therapy, 1955.

An examination of problems which affect voice production.

Borchers, Orville J. "Practical Implications of Scientific Research for the Teaching of Voice." Music Teachers National Association. <u>Volume of Proceedings for 1947.</u> Pittsburgh, Pa., 1947.

The writer believes that no voice teacher can trust his hearing unless he has a complete scientific as well as musical knowledge of singing.

_____. "What Is an Open Throat in Singing?" <u>The South-western Musician</u>, 16 (July, 1950a), 16.

An excellent brief treatment of the subject.

_____. "What Causes a Breathy Voice?" <u>The South-western Musician</u>, 17 (September, 1950b), 17-18.

Contains information on probable causes and corrections of breathy tones.

_____. "The Phenomenon of Vocal Tone Quality." <u>The NATS Bulletin</u>, 8 (November-December, 1951), 15.

The author provides an acoustical analysis of the voice.

Bori, Lucrezia. "Technical Proficiency in Singing." An interview by Annabel Comfort. <u>Etude</u>, June, 1947, p. 324.

A helpful routine of technical exercises.

Bouhuys, Arend; Proctor, Donald F.; and Mead, Jere. "Kinetic Aspects of Singing." <u>Journal of Applied Physiology</u>, 21 (March, 1966), 483-496.

A study of the mechanical behavior of the respiratory system during phonation by means of a volume-displacement body plethysmograph.

Bowen, George O., and Mook, Kenneth C. Song and Speech.
New York: Ginn and Co., 1952.
A textbook designed for classes in fundamentals
of tone production for singing and speaking.

Briggs, John. "Mystery of the Voice." The New York
Times, 104 (January 9, 1955), Section 2, 9.
The author reviews the problems of teachers and
singers "still striving to solve the secret of the proper
method." He observes that the more scientific the
method the worse the pupils sing.

Brodnitz, Friedrich S. Keep Your Voice Healthy. New
York: Harper and Brothers, 1953.
A popular book on a medical subject. Chapter
Six is extremely helpful to the singer.

_____. "Scientific Knowledge and Singing." The New
York Times, 103 (January 10, 1954), Section 2, 10.
Dr. Brodnitz encourages the singing teacher to
seek scientific knowledge of vocal production so that he
may avoid being trapped by extreme theories often propagated by uninformed persons. This was written in
reply to an earlier article by Fraser Gange, "Is the
Laryngoscope Necessary?" The New York Times, 103
(January 3, 1954), Section 2, 7.

_____. "The Singing Teacher and the Laryngologist."
The NATS Bulletin, 13 (February, 1957), 2-3.
Some tenets from the author's Keep Your Voice
Healthy are expressed.

_____. Vocal Rehabilitation. 2d ed. American Academy
of Ophthalmology and Otolaryngology. Rochester,
Minn. : Whiting Press, 1961.
Prepared for the use of graduates in medicine,
this book is most informative and valuable to the student of singing. Scientific facts and recent research
concerning the several aspects of breathing, phonation
and resonance are given.

_____. "The Holistic Study of Voice." Quarterly Journal
of Speech, 48 (October, 1962), 280-284.
The author provides a review of the prominent
literature related to voice research.

Brody, Viola A., and Westerman, Kenneth N. "An Emergent Concept of the Singing Act." The NATS Bulletin,
8 (November-December, 1951) 7.
Growth and development of the singing art is correlated to growth of the physical and mental being.

Brown, Oren Lathrop. "Principles of Voice Therapy as
Applied to Teaching." The NATS Bulletin, 9 (May-

June, 1953), 16.

Since the function of vocal therapy is that of re-
storing vocal health, it seems increasingly important
that nothing involved in this process should be over-
looked in the training of the singing voice.

_____. "Causes of Voice Strain in Singing." The NATS
Bulletin, 15 (December, 1958), 20.

Brown, Ralph Morse. The Singing Voice. New York: Macmillan Co., 1946.

Among the many areas discussed, resonance and
voice classification are two of the most thoroughly
covered. This authoritative book could be a particularly helpful ally of the inexperienced teacher.

Brown, Sarle. Super-Pronunciation in Singing. Fort Worth:
By the Author, 1315 Edgecliff Road, 1967.

Pronunciation is the foundation of a good vocal
production; therefore, great stress is placed upon a
comprehensive and workable knowledge of singing diction.

*Brown, William Earl. Vocal Wisdom--Maxims of Giovanni
Battista Lamperti. 6th ed. Supplement edited by
Lillian Strongin. Brooklyn, N. Y.: Lillian Strongin,
Publisher, 1957.

Vocal maxims of the famed Italian teacher which
were not included in the earlier (1931) edition are included in the supplement.

Bryant, Chauncey Earle. Scientific Singing versus Individualized Guessing. Chicago: F. R. Hunt, 1962.

To the author, perfect singing is scientific singing. His approach, however, is basically empirical.

Buchanan, W. "Expressive Singing." Music of the West, 4
(August, 1949), 13.

Buckingham, Raymond J. "Is a Voice Teacher Necessary."
Music Journal, 23 (December, 1965), 28.

The writer feels it is dangerous to study with 75
percent of the voice teachers today. After this condemnation, he offers sound criteria for choosing a good
teacher and he considers the problems of a singing
career.

Bull, Inez. "Vocalizing Is an Art." The Southwestern
Musician, 18 (October, 1951), 12.

The title is misleading; the author's personal
philosophy of singing is expressed.

Bullard, Edith. "Breathing in Relation to Vocal Expression."
Etude, February, 1947, p. 75.

Burroughs, J. J. "The Blueprint of Fulfillment." Voice,
6 (September-October, 1950), 13.

A perspective on the "how" and "why" of singing.
The joys of achievement are stressed.

Cady, H. L. "We Are Only Human. " The NATS Bulletin,
22 (October, 1965), 16.
Inter-personal relation of teacher to student is
discussed.
Camburn, John. "Voices in Class. " Music in Education,
26 (March, 1962), 24.
Weak consonants are the greatest enemies of
good diction.
Campbell, E. J. Moran. The Respiratory Muscles and the
Mechanics of Breathing. Chicago: The Year Book
Publishers, 1958.
Although the author makes no claim to deal spe-
cifically with speech and singing physiology, this
standard reference work for the medical profession is
also helpful to the voice pedagogue.
Carp, Louis. "The Physiology and Psychology of the Sing-
ing Voice. " Music Journal, 14 (October, 1956), 10.
A surgeon writes about the singing voice.
Carson, Leon. "Song ... Its Role in the Vocal Studio. "
Music Journal, 8 (March-April, 1950), 15.
Use of the song as a technical aid in vocal study
is firmly advocated.
Cashmore, Donald. "Some Practical Observations. " Musical
Times, 102 (August, 1961), 514-515.
Nontechnical explanations of singing diction.
Casselman, Eugene. "The Secret of Bel Canto. " Etude,
September, 1950, p. 20-22.
After a short history of singing, from Tosi to
Stanley, the author provides an excellent review of
basic teaching guides used by early Italian masters.
_____. "The Singer's Breath. " Etude, Part I, October,
1951a, p. 22 and Part II, November, 1951b, p. 20-21.
Teachers from the "Golden Age of Bel Canto"
throw light on the correct manner of breathing.
_____. "Choral Singing and the Solo Voice (Does Singing
in a Chorus Cause Injury to the Solo Voice?)" Etude,
October, 1952, p. 20.
Potential dangers of singing in a choir are enu-
merated. The author cites more dangers than ad-
vantages.
Cates, Millard. Guide for Young Singers. Ann Arbor,
Mich.: University Music Press, 1959.
This class approach is designed for college

students whose majors are other than voice. Basic
objectives of vocal training, vocalises, and lists of easy
repertoire add to the book's usefulness.
Cecil, Winifred. "The Joy in Singing. " Music Journal, 18
(November-December, 1960), 22.
The emphasis of the article is preparation for a
singing career; there are some brief thoughts on vocal
principles.
Charles, Henry   "The Effects of Wind Instrument Training
upon Vocal Production. "   The NATS Bulletin, 3 (Septem-
ber-October, 1946), 3.
Results of a survey among teachers of singing
reveal "expected correlation in breathing and conflict in
the playing of brass instruments. "
_____. "Singers and Musicians. " American Music
Teacher, 3 (September-October, 1953), 6.
The author forcefully suggests several ways the
singer can combat the adage "singers and musicians. "
Christiansen, O. C. "Solo and Ensemble Singing. " The
NATS Bulletin, 21 (February, 1965), 16.
Personal philosophy, reminiscences, methods and
devices to improve voice production are written by an
exponent of "straight-tone" singing.
Christy, Van A. Expressive Singing. Vol. II. Dubuque,
Iowa: Wm. C. Brown Co. , 1961.
This advanced, expanded companion to Expressive
Singing Vol. I is primarily for the teacher. Compre-
hensive song lists are included.
_____. "Learning and Teaching Interpretation. " American
Music Teacher, 13 (September-October, 1963), 6-7.
Principally excerpted from the author's Expressive
Singing.
_____. Foundations in Singing. Dubuque, Iowa: Wm. C.
Brown Co. , 1965.
A condensed version of the author's Expressive
Singing, this is designed for students who plan one or
two terms of vocal study. Thirty-six songs are in-
cluded.
_____. Expressive Singing. Rev. ed. Vol. I. Dubuque,
Iowa: Wm. C. Brown Co. , 1967.
This text provides a comprehensive course for
class voice that is equally adaptable to private teaching.
Correlated song anthologies are available.
Clark, Edgar R. "Pardon, Your Voice is Showing. " Music
Journal, 9 (January, 1951), 14.
The author laments confusion and unethical prac-
tices within the ranks of singing teachers.

Coffin, Berton. "The Singer's Diction. " The NATS Bulletin,
    20 (February, 1964), 10.
        One of the most persistent problems faced by the
    serious teacher of singing is examined with reference
    to the author's text Phonetic Readings of Songs and
    Arias.
Cohen, Morris. "Get Your Vowels Right. " Etude, Novem-
    ber, 1944, p. 627.
        The most basic aspects of vowel production are
    reviewed.
Coladarci, Arthur P.   "The Psychology of Personality and
    the Teacher of Voice. " The NATS Bulletin, 7 (Febru-
    ary-March, 1951), 8.
        Personality traits and psychological factors are
    considered; the significance of this knowledge to the
    voice teacher is stressed.
Coleman, Henry. "Tuning for Voices. " Music in Education,
    25 (January, 1962), 183.
        This article is highly recommended because of
    its practical helps for singing on pitch.
Collins, John C. "Singing: A Comparative Analysis. " The
    NATS Bulletin, Part I, 25 (February, 1969a), 32-34
    and Part II, 25 (May-June, 1969b), 12.
        A comparative analysis of the singing principles
    taught by five recognized voice teachers of nineteenth-
    century Europe and eight contemporary New York voice
    teachers.
Conley, Eugene. "How to Build a Voice. " An interview by
    Rose Heylbut. Etude, March, 1950, p. 14.
        One of the best and most useful articles which
    have resulted from interviews with noted singers.
_____. "The Value of Applied Phonetics in the Teaching
    of Singing. " American Music Teacher, 3 (May-June,
    1954), 11.
        A basic statement and rationale of phonetics in
    singing instruction.
Conner, Nadine. "Mental Projection in Singing. " An inter-
    view by Rose Heylbut. Etude, May, 1945, p. 249.
        Strong emphasis is given the mental projection
    necessary for the singer's communication with his
    listener.
Cooke, James F. "The Golden Chalices of Song. " Etude,
    September, 1952, p. 15.
        Reminiscences of the author's long association
    with great vocal artists reveal vitally important vocal
    precepts for the contemporary singer.

Cooper, Morton. "Vocal Suicide in Singers." The NATS
    Bulletin, 26 (February-March, 1970), 7.
        Singers do not transfer the concepts and elements
    of the singing voice into practice for the speaking voice.
    Correct speaking helps the singing voice and affords the
    possibility for carry-over of good vocal habits from
    speaking into singing.
Cor, August F. The Magic of Voice. Los Angeles: De-
    Vorss and Co., 1944.
        Emotion (the origin of vocal tone) and an ab-
    horence of "method" are the prevalent thoughts through-
    out this book. The author's suggestions for voice pro-
    duction are unorthodox and extreme.
Corelli, Franco. "Records Are My Teachers." Music
    Journal, 19 (October, 1961), 79.
        The author tells why and how he uses recordings
    as a form of instruction; he discourages imitation of
    the recorded artist, however.
Cornwall, Burton. "A Natural Approach to Voice." Music
    Journal, 29 (January, 1971), 28-29.
        Breathing and certain aspects of diction are the
    main points of this brief article.
Cox, Ernest L. "Visual Aids in the Teaching of Voice."
    The NATS Bulletin, 6 (September, 1949), 7.
        Explanation of a well-planned class session; the
    dancing teacher, golf coach and films are suggested to
    illustrate correct posture.
Cox, George. "A Matter of Semantics." The NATS Bulletin,
    17 (October, 1960), 16.
        Some useful terms are mentioned as replacement
    for the confusing professional jargon used by some
    singing teachers.
Craig, Don. "Say Something When You Sing." Music
    Journal, 12 (March, 1954), 31.
        Communication of words and ideas should be the
    uppermost goal of the singer.
Craig, Mary. "Vocal Methods of Past Offer Guide to Artis-
    try." Musical Courier, 142 (October, 1950), 16.
        An interview with Arthur Gerry. He deplores the
    tendency to hasten the young singer.
_____. "Outlining a Credo for Fine Vocal Production."
    Musical Courier, 143 (May, 1951a), 16.
        A vignette of the teaching methods of Bianca
    Saroya and her husband, Dimitri Onofrei.
_____. "Vital Importance of Correct Voice Appraisal."
    Musical Courier, 143 (June, 1951b), 20.
        An informal interview with Paul Althouse. The

importance of correct voice classification is discussed.

_____. "Walter Golde Tells His Teaching Credo. "
Musical Courier, 145 (April, 1952), 20.
        Only brief insight into Golde's teaching credo is
revealed; the article is primarily biographical.

_____. "Factors in Voice Training Told by Sperber,
Hopkins. " Musical Courier, 148 (November, 1953), 20.
        Succinct statements by Sperber and Hopkins give
insight into their teaching procedures.

_____. "A Tone Is a Tone Is a Tone. " Musical Courier,
149 (March, 1954), 7-8.
        An informative review of the purported conflict
between the empirical and the scientific approach to
singing.   There is some levity in enumerating the extremes of both positions.   The author concludes with a
defense of the empirical approach.

Cranmer, Arthur. The Art of Singing.   London: Dennis
Dobson, 1957.
        After reading many volumes on singing technique,
this annotator found this book a refreshing oasis, unique
and stimulating in content and style.

Crawford, Hadley R.   "Treatment of the Immature Voice. "
Music Teachers National Association.   Volume of Proceedings for 1948.   Pittsburgh, Pa. , 1948.
        The principles given are intended to take the
young voice through the formative period to a coordinated unity.

_____. "Thoughts on Muscular Coordination. " The NATS
Bulletin, 8 (September-October, 1951), 14.
        Good vocal coordination may be achieved through
ear training.

_____. "Choral Devices or Vocal Techniques. " American
Music Teacher, 16 (February-March, 1967), 17.
        The writer warns against certain choral methods
that are contrary to basic vocal techniques.

Culver, Charles.   Musical Acoustics.   New York: Blakiston
Co. , 1951.
        The substance of the scientific material is de-
signed as a text for students majoring in music.

Daghlian, G. K.   "Song and Its Acoustics. "   The NATS Bulletin, 8 (November-December, 1951), 6.
        A fundamental article about acoustical properties
of auditoriums.

*Davies, David Ffrangcon.   The Singing of the Future.   1905.
Reprint.   Champaign, Ill. :   Pro Musica Press, 1968.

A vocal commentary of the first decade of this
century. Ffrangcon-Davies's insistence on careful pronunciation is the principal theme of the book.

Davis, Kenneth, Jr. "The Function of the Primary Resonating Areas and Their Relation to the Third Formant in
the Singing Tone." Unpublished Mus. D. dissertation,
Indiana University, 1964.
The study, among other things, reveals that the
origin of the vowel formants is the coupled system as
a complex unit rather than a specific cavity. There
seem to be no points along the vocal tract at which
energy concentrations are found around certain partials.

De Bidoli, Emi. "Old Methods of Voice Teaching versus
New Ones." The NATS Bulletin, 3 (March-April, 1947),
3.
A brief survey of old and new methods, as understood by the author.

De Bruyn, John W. "The Voice Teacher and the Speaking
Voice." Etude, November, 1943, p. 713.
The voice teacher can add resonance and careful
enunciation to the speaking voice.

DeJonge, James. "Are You Guilty?" Educational Music
Magazine, 25 (March, 1946), 39.
"Let us have inspired singing," the author en-
courages.

Delattre, Pierre. "Vowel Color and Voice Quality." The
NATS Bulletin, 15 (October, 1958), 4-7.
An acoustic and articulatory comparison that shows
what compensations the shape of the vocal tract can
make in order to preserve vowel color while producing
voice quality.

della Chiesa, Vivian. "The Start of a Vocal Career." An
interview by Myles Fellowes. Etude, September, 1948,
p. 531.
A brief discussion of the principles of good voice
production that are requisite for a vocal career.

de los Angeles, Victoria. "Singing Must Be Natural." Etude,
March, 1957, p. 13.
Interesting biographical material forms the bulk
of this article. The order of practice is briefly discussed.

DeLuca, Giuseppe. "Singing at Sixty-Nine." An interview
by Stephen West. Etude, August, 1946, p. 435.
Many helpful reflections from the experience of a
great singer.

_____. "Good Singing Takes Time." Etude, November,
1950, p. 13.

This article, written two months before DeLuca's death, gives valuable insight into his method of vocal production.

Dengler, Clyde R. Read This and Sing! Philadelphia, Pa.: T. Presser Co., 1944.
A combination of fundamentals of music notation, elementary and advanced vocal methods and some unique procedures. The implication of self-instruction in the title is not actually intended.

Deutsch, J. A., and Clarkson, J. K. "Nature of the Vibrato and Control Loop in Singing." Nature, 183 (1959), 167-168.
This study indicates that the voice is largely controlled by the auditory message generated by the voice itself.

DeYoung, Richard. "Teaching Devices and Their Value." Music Teachers National Association. Volume of Proceedings for 1946. Pittsburgh, Pa., 1946.
A forthright plea for the sharing of teaching methods among the profession.

_____. "First the Word." Voice, 7 (January-February, 1951), 11.

_____. "Some Practical Aspects of Educational Psychology." The NATS Bulletin, 9 (January-February, 1953), 7.
An alert analysis of the various situations experienced by the teacher and pupil and some practical advice on improving the teacher-pupil relationship. This article should be read by aspiring but inexperienced teachers of singing.

_____. "Communication." The NATS Bulletin, 14 (December, 1957), 23.
A helpful article emphasizing mutual respect between the pupil and teacher--the bridge over which suggestion and inspiration pass.

_____. The Singer's Art. Chicago: DePaul University Press, 1958.
The writer provides an open-minded discussion of the techniques of singing. The text is well-written, nontechnical and interesting.

Dickenson, Jean. "Make Haste Slowly." An interview by Rose Heylbut. Etude, March, 1944, p. 136.
Sensible and often-repeated advice is given the young singer.

Dickson, David R. "An Acoustic and Radiographic Study of Nasality." Unpublished Ph. D. dissertation, Louisiana State University, 1961.

This speech research emphasizes the variableness
in the acoustic characteristics of nasality from person
to person.
Diercks, Louis H. "Critical versus Creative Listening."
The NATS Bulletin, 19 (May, 1963), 22-24.
Effective and accurate choral auditions provide
helpful information to the voice teacher in regard to
effective song learning.
Di Tullio, Eileen. "The Voice Is an Instrument." Music
Journal, 18 (October, 1960), 30.
The fashion of loudness and dramatics in singing
is condemned.
Djanel, Lily. "Freedom in Singing." An interview by
Stephen West. Etude, May, 1943, p. 298.
Interesting aspects of interpretation make this
article useful.
Donath, Ludwig. "Voices for Opera." Music Journal, 17
(September, 1959), 88-90.
Rambling thoughts on various aspects of vocal
development.
Douglass, Ruth. "Adaption of the Teaching of Singing to the
Liberal Arts Pattern." Music Teachers National Asso-
ciation. Volume of Proceedings for 1948. Pittsburgh,
Pa., 1948.
A rationale of the teaching of singing in the
liberal arts curriculum.
Douty, Nicholas. "Singing After the Removal of the Tonsils."
Etude, April, 1949, p. 257.
A brief comment from Dr. Douty's "Voice
Questions."
Downes, Olin. "Problems of Diction." The New York
Times, 103 (February 14, 1954), Section 2, 7.
The author laments that American singers often
model their diction after their European counterparts.
The problems of singing in English will disappear when
the genuinely American opera is written.
Drew, W. S. "How to Become an Artist in Song." Musical
Times, 91 (April, 1950), 156.
Interpretation, one aspect of artistic singing, is
helpfully discussed.
Duey, Philip A. Bel Canto in Its Golden Age. New York:
King's Crown Press, 1951.
This study catalogues some of the things that were
said and done about the art of singing during the period
of its greatest virtuosity. Here is a valuable com-
parative survey of the writings of the bel canto period.
_____. "Science and Voice." Music Journal, 16 (Feb-

ruary, 1958), 29-30.

    A worthwhile history of vocal instruction concludes with a defense of the empirical method.

————. "Teacher-Pupil Interaction in the Studio. " The NATS Bulletin, 16 (October, 1959), 16.

    A forceful plea for a personal, individual approach to each student.

Dunham, Rowland W. "Vocal Tone. " The American Organist, 36 (December, 1953), 411-412.

    Fundamental characteristics of vocal tone are outlined for the church organist.

Dunkley, Ferdinand L. "Pitch Controlled Voice. " Voice, 6 (September-October, 1950), 5.

    The concept of a specific sensation related to a specific pitch is discussed. The idea is not clearly presented.

Durgin, Cyrus. "Singing in Its Elementary and Other Aspects. " The NATS Bulletin, 9 (January-February, 1953), 19.

    A noted music critic provides an interesting discussion of some problems confronted by the vocal teacher, student and the artist-singer.

Duschak, Alice G. "New Aspects of Coordination and Correlation in Vocal Teaching. " The NATS Bulletin, 11 (February, 1955), 7.

    Concentration on the vocal act may be enhanced by the performance at the same time of some physical act. These coordinations are drawing, conducting, dancing, touching and deep breathing. These are encouraged to foster better vocal coordination.

————. "Reflections and Aphorisms on Singing Followed by Psychological and Physiological Explanations. " American Music Teacher, 10 (May-June, 1961), 10.

    The author examines some of the difficulties that confront an aspiring vocalist.

————. "Influence of Instrumental Playing on Singing and Vice Versa. " American Music Teacher, 11 (January-February, 1962), 16.

    An interesting enumeration of several problems inherent in dual performance.

————. "Musical Style as a Stimulant to Vocal Technique. " The NATS Bulletin, 26 (December, 1969), 30.

Duval, John H. Svengali's Secrets and Memoirs of the Golden Age. New York: Robert Speller and Sons, 1958.

    Duval's method of voice production is revealed in the role of the fictional Svengali. His approach to vocal problems is non-arbitrary and his solutions seem

too simple.   Reminiscences of famous singers provide
the bulk of the text.
Dwyer, Edward J.   "Concepts of Breathing for Singing. "
The NATS Bulletin, 24 (October, 1967), 40-43.
The author has compiled statements on breathing
which represent teaching concepts of the most knowl-
edgeable vocal authorities.   The material is striking
and impressive.

Eastman, J.   "The Physical Factors of Vocal Virtuosity. "
Music of the West, 13 (December, 1957), 5.
_____.   "Some Secrets of Singing. "   Music of the West,
14 (December, 1958), 6-7.
This brief article emphasizes that sound vocal
technique is essential to quality performance.
Easton, Florence.   "Let Us Sing in English!"   An interview
by Stephen West.   Etude, June, 1944, p. 326.
Persuasive argument is given to encourage sing-
ing in English and the use of adequate translations.
Eberhart, Constance.   "Diction. "   The NATS Bulletin, 18
(May, 1962), 8.
Sound fundamental concepts of good singing diction
are interspersed with the author's personal judgment
concerning books on singing diction.   Some artists are
mentioned who sing English admirably.
Ebersole, A. S.   "Your Voice and You. "   Educational Music
Magazine, 24 (March, 1945), 29.
Unless the teacher gives constant attention to
vocal personality and enhancement, he is failing his
pupils.
Eddy, Nelson.   "Who Should Have a Singing Career?"   An
interview by Doron K. Antrim.   Etude, February,
1943, p. 77.
Good singing is the result of "singing instinct"
and the desire to sing.
Ehret, Walter.   "Vocal Instruction through Recordings. "
Choral and Organ Guide, 12 (January, 1960), 12.
Ehrhart, Gertrude.   "Mumbo Jumbo in the Studio. "   The
NATS Bulletin, 16 (December, 1959), 22.
A satirical writing about the nebulous professional
jargon used by singing teachers.
Ekstrom, E. Ross.   "Control of Singing Intensity As Re-
lated to Singer Experience. "   The NATS Bulletin, 17
(December, 1960), 8.
Significant differences in levels of vocal intensity
and in reliance upon the acoustical environment for the

control of singing intensity were found to be related to
singer experience.

Elmo, Cloe. "Natural or Impossible." An interview by
Myles Fellowes. Etude, June, 1948, p. 347.
The gift of an adequate vocal instrument must be
present before the student of singing can prepare for a
professional career.

El Tour, Anna. "The Art of Singing." The Southwestern
Musician, Part I, 16 (April, 1950a), 7 and Part II, 16
(May, 1950b), 5.
These articles illustrate the extreme claims of
teachers who profess to teach "the Italian method" and
all teach different methods.

Ettinger, Leon. "Why Study Singing." Music of the West,
10 (September, 1954), 7.
A realistic essay which explores the emotional
and intellectual aspects of the singing art.

Ewing, J. Ralph. "The Sources of Power and Expression in
Singing." Music Journal, 8 (March-April, 1950), 46.
The author writes that desire to accomplish is
requisite for power and expression in singing.

Farley, Charles R. "Contrasts in Vocal Pedagogy: 1940 and
1970." Unpublished D. M. E. dissertation, University of
Oklahoma, 1971.
The author sought to identify contrasts and to indicate changes which have occurred in methods of
teaching singing since the 1940's.

Farrell, Eileen. "Keep It Natural." An interview by Bates
Rudwin. Etude, December, 1947, p. 670.
_____. "After the Studio." An interview by Gunnar Ask-
lund. Etude, July, 1952, p. 13.
Interviews with noted singers tend to be much the
same. Miss Farrell, however, has fresh and interesting advice.

Felderman, Leon. "Spare the Calories and Save the Voice."
Etude, March, 1943, p. 161.
Harmful effects of over-eating are explained by a
physician.

Fellowes, Myles. "Here is Mary Garden." Etude, April,
1952, p. 14.
Appealingly open advice and interesting vocal tips
are scattered throughout a biographical article.

Ferguson, George B. "Organic Lesions of the Larynx Produced by Mis-Use of the Voice." The Laryngoscope,
65 (May, 1955), 327-336.

Students of singing will find the initial pages of
this paper are helpful.

Field-Hyde, Frederick C. Vocal Vibrato, Tremolo and
Judder. London: Oxford University Press, 1946.
A slim pamphlet in which the author reviews
varied and contradictory opinions on vibrato problems.
He describes six kinds of unsteadiness of voice and
offers his own theory of the loss of control that leads
to excessive vibrato.
_____. The Art and Science of Voice Training. London:
Oxford University Press, 1950.
Obvious knowledge and experience are displayed
in this book. Valuable suggestions are made for correction of vocal faults and developments in voice
science are listed.

Fields, Victor A. Training the Singing Voice. New York:
King's Crown Press, 1947.
A pioneering attempt to correlate all the diversi-
fied theories, methodologies and procedures used in the
teaching of singing. Selections, chosen from the literature on singing methods published in English within the
period 1928-1942, are impartially presented in the form
of a vocal compendium.
_____. The Singer's Glossary. Boston: The Boston
Music Co., 1952.
Through this means, the author of Training the
Singing Voice seeks to encourage the adoption of a uni-
form terminology for singers. Terms frequently used
by singers are defined in deference to the most widely
recognized usage.
_____. "The Road Ahead for the Career-Minded Pupil."
The NATS Bulletin, 14 (December, 1957), 6-7.
The author reviews the requisites for a professional singing career.
_____. "Review of the Literature on Vocal Registers."
The NATS Bulletin, 26 (February-March, 1970), 37.
A digest of the ideas now in print that will point
up a possible cause of the register break, if and when
it occurs, and information that will suggest prevention
or cure. Both physiological and psychological aspects
are approached. Although pedagogical procedures are
not discussed, the information presented will be useful
in the training of the singing voice.
_____, and Bender, James F. Voice and Diction. New
York: Macmillan Co., 1949.
Exercises for overcoming speech difficulties will
be helpful to singers concerned with effective use of the

voice. This book is designed as a text and reference manual on principles of speech correction.

Fisher, Charles. "The Four Freedoms in Singing." Choral and Organ Guide, 18 (May, 1965), 13.

  Freedom from constriction, slump, technique and inhibition is suggested. The author adequately outlines the problems but not the solutions.

Flack, Nannette, and Sherman, Leila. Singing Can Be Ecstasy. New York: Exposition Press, 1965.

  In an informal manner, the authors combine an instruction digest for singers with recollections of days in the theatre. The material is sensible in its approach.

Flechtner, Adalene S. "Low Vowel Formant in Soprano Voices." The NATS Bulletin, 26 (December, 1969), 23-26.

  On the basis of the author's experiment with certain vowels, it was concluded that: (1) Two or three formant areas are present in sung vowels as in spoken vowels. (2) The first formant regions in the sung vowels agreed in a general way with the average first-formant values for spoken vowels. (3) Intelligibility of vowels is affected by other factors besides first formant.

Fonticoli, Michele. "Good Pronunciation Holds Key to Beautiful Singing Tone." Musical Courier, 144 (October, 1951), 17.

Foote, Bruce. "New Horizons in the Teaching of Voice Pedagogy." The NATS Bulletin, 19 (February, 1963), 22-23.

  A singular article that gives the author's ideas on teaching the private lesson. A procedural outline of a course in vocal pedagogy is included.

*Foreman, Edward, ed. The Porpora Tradition. Milwaukee, Wis.: Pro Musica Press, 1968.

  Facsimiles of Domenico Corri's The Singer's Preceptor and Isaac Nathan's Musurgia Vocalis give insight into the methods of Niccolò Porpora, celebrated 18th-century Italian teacher.

Fox, William H. "Some Psychological Principles Involved in the Teaching of Singing." The NATS Bulletin, 7 (September-October, 1950), 8-9.

  The principles suggested are succinct, practical and well worth deliberate study.

Fracht, J. Albert, and Robinson, Emmett. Sing Well, Speak Well. Brooklyn: Remsen Press of Chemical Publishing Co., 1948.

A very basic approach to vocal technique pre-
sented as a dialogue between teacher and pupil.
_____. You, Too, Can Sing. New York: Chemical Pub-
lishing Co., 1960.
An approach for the beginner in voice technique.
A large portion of the book deals with music funda-
mentals. Great stress is placed upon breathing and
relaxation.
Franca, Ida. "Is the Human Voice an Instrument." Choir
Guide, 2 (November-December, 1949), 24.
_____. "Adventures of the Trill." Etude, June, 1951a,
p. 22.
He who is complete master of his lower jaw,
which has to be very mobile in its sockets, can easily
possess a faultless trill.
_____. "The Vocalist's ABC's--Breathing, Sound Attack,
Sound Detachment." American Music Teacher, 1 (No-
vember-December, 1951b), 1.
A helpful breviary of the first steps in learning
to sing.
_____. Manual of Bel Canto. New York: Coward-Mc-
Cann, 1959.
Vocal technique, expressed in many nebulous
phrases, comprises the first part of the book. Part 2
is a study of technique and style of bel canto and Part
3 is biographical sketches of noted castrati.
Frankfurter-Karnieff, Maria. "Cardinal Rules for the Singer
Outlined." Musical Courier, 144 (November, 1951), 23.
Freeman, J. J. "Formulas for Fame." Opera News, 14
(October, 1949), 6-10.
In a panel discussion, six Metropolitan Opera
singers relate personal experiences and opinions.
Freemantel, Frederic. High Tones and How to Sing Them.
New York: Freemantel Voice Institute, 1946.
Helpful hints and exercises are given that are de-
signed to increase range and make high notes easier.
The approach is sound and conventional.
Freer, Dawson. "Singing in the Vernacular." Musical
Times, 97 (October, 1956), 538.
Strong encouragement is given to singing in the
vernacular and some objections to this are effectively
answered.
_____. "Phrasing and the Singer." Musical Opinion, 82
(May, 1959a), 521.
Dynamics and breathing are discussed as the prin-
cipal components of phrasing.
_____. "Emotion in Song." Musical Opinion, 83 (October,

1959b), 19-23.

    Following a brief history of language develop-
ment, the author urges sincerity of emotional expression.

_____. "Rhythm and the Singer. " Musical Opinion, 84
(June, 1961), 545-547.

    An excellent insight into the subtle aspects of
rhythm and words.

Freud, Esti D. "Voice Physiology and the Emergence of
New Vocal Styles. " Archives of Otolaryngology, 62
(July, 1955), 50-58.

    An interesting history of vocal styles. The prim-
itive, the castrato, the European classical, the blues
singer and the crooner are discussed in the light of
voice physiology.

Frijsh, Povla. "Why Do You Sing?" An interview by Myles
Fellowes. Etude, March, 1945, p. 135.

    A noted Danish soprano comments that a singer
is unwise to attempt any song in which he does not believe.

Frisell, Anthony. The Tenor Voice. Boston: Bruce Humphries, Publishers, 1964.

    The principal contribution of this publication is a
detailed discussion of the use of the falsetto in the development of the tenor voice.

_____. The Soprano Voice. Boston: Bruce Humphries,
Publishers, 1966.

    The author provides a second volume on a specific
voice classification. The structure and text are similar
to that of The Tenor Voice.

Fry, D. B., and Manén, Lucie. "Basis for the Acoustical
Study of Singing. " Journal of the Acoustical Society of
America, 29 (June, 1957), 690-692.

    As a basis for spectrographic and X-ray studies
of singing, tones which singers produced were classified according to the type of voice, the mood expressed
and the vowel sung.

Fuchs, Viktor. "The Musical Education of the Singer. "
Music of the West, 5 (January, 1950a), 3.

    General musicianship, conducting and keyboard
knowledge are discussed.

_____. "On a High Note. " Etude, February, 1950b, p.
13.

    A useful article stresses the dangers of increas-
ing the range by singing high tones that are uncomfortable for the voice.

_____. "Technique and Pseudo Technique of Singing. "

Music of the West, Part I, 5 (August, 1950c), 5 and Part II, 6 (September, 1950d), 7.
Vocal tricks are contrasted with the underlying principles of good vocal technique.

_____. "A Dialogue between a Conductor and a Voice Teacher." Music of the West, 6 (August, 1951a), 4.
Coaches and conductors need to have a clear idea of their responsibilities to the singer.

_____. "The 'Covered' Tone--What Is It?" Etude, December, 1951b, p. 19.
"To cover or not to cover, seems to be a question among many voice authorities." This concept is discussed later in his book The Art of Singing and Voice Technique.

_____. "First Steps in Studying Singing." Music of the West, Part I, 7 (May, 1952a), 5 and Part II, 7 (June, 1952b), 6.
The importance of a good beginning is stressed and sensible guidance about first lessons is given the teacher.

_____. "The Importance of Functional Hearing." The Southwestern Musician, 20 (November, 1953), 21.
The voice teacher must have a sensitive, analytical ear to discern in what way a tone is produced. This "functional hearing" is inborn.

_____. "Chest Tones in Women's Voices and Falsetto in Men's Voices." Music of the West, 9 (July, 1954), 6.
An excellent discussion and helpful clarification of two problem areas of voice production.

_____. "The Falsetto Tone." Music of the West, 12 (December, 1956), 5.

_____. "Make Music with Your Voice." Music of the West, 12 (June, 1957), 7.
The singer often forgets that his real task is to transform the notes he makes into music.

_____. The Art of Singing and Voice Technique. New York: London House and Maxwell, 1964.
Among the books on singing technique published during the span of this research, this is one of the most helpful. It is readable and explicit. Sensible advice on technique and on a singing career is in abundance. The author writes from a background of reading, performing, and teaching.

_____. "The Microphone and Head Resonance." The NATS Bulletin, 22 (December, 1965), 12.
The article is generally concerned with head resonance; head resonance is "the singer's microphone."

Gafni, Miklos. "Tenor Is a Disease." Music Journal, 19
(November, 1961), 50.
   A brief, interesting article about tenors and their
idiosyncrasies.
Gamber, Eugene. Your Guide to Successful Singing. Chicago:
Windsor Press, 1950.
   Since he believes that everyone should be en-
couraged to sing and should know about the voice
whether he sings or not, Gamber has made this a book
for everyone--from the disinterested bystander to the
professional vocalist.
Gange, Fraser. "Is the Laryngoscope Necessary?" The
New York Times, 103 (January 3, 1954), Section 2, 7.
   The author laments the use of the laryngoscope
as a teaching device. The historical references do not
bear the stamp of careful research.
*Garcia, Manuel. Hints on Singing. 1894. Reprint. Canoga
Park, Calif.: Summit, 1970.
Gardiner, Julian. A Guide to Good Singing and Speech.
London: Cassell, 1968.
   The fundamental principles of vocal production
taught in this volume were derived from the teachings
of Franklyn Kelsey. It is a thorough volume; the ma-
terial is logically presented in precise detail.
Gardini, Nelli. "Voice Foundation." The NATS Bulletin, 4
(September-October, 1947), 4.
   The most important foundation of any voice is development of the middle range.
_____. "Will Scientific Knowledge Make Us Better Teach-
ers of Singing." Music Journal, 8 (March-April, 1950),
32.
   Two favorite subjects of the author are simplicity
and naturalness.
Garlinghouse, Burton. "Rhythm and Relaxation in Breathing." The NATS Bulletin, 7 (February-March, 1951),
2.
   Four points suggested are: (1) the development of
automatic expansion instead of conscious inhalation, (2)
the relaxation of tensions above the chest during the inflow of breath, (3) timing the inflow of breath to avoid
holding, and (4) the element of relaxation in the breathing cycle.
_____. "The Musical Approach." The NATS Bulletin, 12
(September, 1955), 5-6.
   All technical efforts should be musically motivated.
Voice teachers should first of all be teachers of music.
_____. "Dialogue on Vocal Pedagogy." The NATS Bulle-

tin, 26 (February-March, 1970), 25.

 An impassioned plea for tolerance and for knowledge of the <u>bel</u> <u>canto</u> and scientific approaches to singing instruction.

Garns, John Seaman. "Voice Training through Emotions." An interview by Annie S. Greenwood. <u>Etude</u>, January, 1945, p. 23.

 Coordination in singing is enhanced by natural emotions such as sniffing a fragrant flower, chuckling and a few deeper emotions.

German, Francis. "What a Judge Has Learned at Contests." <u>Music Educators Journal</u>, 39 (September-October, 1952), 32.

Gerry, Arthur. "The Importance of Technique." <u>The NATS Bulletin</u>, 5 (September-October, 1948), 6.

 Observations from long experience emphasize the importance of a solid technical foundation before operatic repertoire is attempted.

_____. "Pathways to Vocal Pedagogy." <u>Music Journal</u>, 7 (March-April, 1949), 36.

 A plea for continued emphasis on building vocal technique before the serious study of repertoire. This important article appears in <u>The NATS Bulletin</u>, 6 (October-November, 1949), 2 and in slightly expanded form in a later issue of <u>The NATS Bulletin</u>, 11 (May, 1955), 7.

Gigli, Beniamino. "Breathing and Vowels: An Interview." <u>Choral and Organ Guide</u>, 18 (May, 1945), 13.

 A few informative and personal observations from the famed tenor.

Gilliland, Dale V. "Concomitant Learning in the Teaching of Singing." <u>The NATS Bulletin</u>, 11 (November, 1954), 5.

 The total training of the voice student should include emotional growth, moral training, the development of a sense of beauty, culture, and social opportunities.

_____. "Beliefs and Knowledge in the Teaching of Singing." <u>The NATS Bulletin</u>, 12 (September, 1955), 7-8.

 Stimulating examination of recent assumptions and practices pertaining to teaching of singing.

_____. "Fundamental Precepts for Voice Educators." <u>The NATS Bulletin</u>, 21 (February, 1965), 11.

 A concise restatement of salient goals of singing instruction.

_____. "Adding to the Meaning and Improving the Quality of Vocal and Musical Experience." <u>The NATS Bulletin</u>, 24 (October, 1967), 56-58.

 Preparation and inspiration must be a large part

of all instruction.   This can partially be gained from
observations of great teachers.

_____. Guidance in Voice Education.   Columbus, Ohio:
By the Author, Ohio State University, School of Music,
1899 N. College Road, 1971.

A treatise presenting and explaining the principles
of teaching solo singing, teaching the individual singer
in a choral situation, and the operation and techniques
of class voice.

Glaz, Hertha.   "Do It Yourself!"   An interview by Myles
Fellowes.   Etude, August, 1943, p. 503.

The aspirant to professional honors must be will-
ing to work and to devote homage to his art.

Golde, Walter.   "Cultivated Spontaneity."   The NATS Bulletin, 8 (March-April, 1952), 12.

In the beginning was spontaneity, so the singer
must return to "cultivated spontaneity"--a principle of
tone production in singing.

Gorin, Igor.   "Singing with Philosophy."   An interview by
Rose Heylbut.   Etude, December, 1943, p. 786.

A distinguished baritone gives words of encouragement to the young.   The mental approach is featured.

_____. "Use Those Precious Moments."   An interview by
Annabel Comfort.   Etude, January, 1949, p. 15.

Interesting and informative reminiscences.   Some
requirements of an operatic career are mentioned.

Gould, Herbert.   "Phonation."   The NATS Bulletin, 5 (May-
June, 1949), 6.

Some areas other than phonation are also discussed.   The ideas are sensible and prevalent.

_____. Handbook for Voice Students.   Columbia, Mo.:
Lucas Brothers Publishers, 1958.

The book takes a middle ground on the approach
to voice instruction.   The author's theory is that the
teaching of voice often requires trial and error in some
instances, even as it does the exaction of absolute
technical adherence in others.

Govich, Bruce M.   "Voice Science for Teachers of Singing."
Unpublished D. Mus. A. dissertation, University of Illi-
nois, 1967.

The purpose of the study was to synthesize the
basic subject matter on voice science.   An integrated
course of instruction was suggested in order to make
prospective voice teachers aware of the scientific rationale of singing.

Granville, Charles N.   The Granville Vocal Study Plan.
New York: Remick Music Corp., 1950.

A basic "home study" approach to singing that in-
cludes recorded aids. When the workbook is completed
the student is urged to seek further development under
the guidance of a competent teacher.
Graves, Richard M. Singing for Amateurs. London: Oxford
University Press, 1954.
The author's principal purpose is to warn ama-
teurs of the hardships and hazards of the singing pro-
fession. The book is interesting.
Graveure, Louis. "Vocal Beauty. " Music of the West, 4
(August, 1949), 13.
Green, Spencer. "Diction. " The NATS Bulletin, 4 (June-
July, 1948), 2.
A basic approach to good diction is suggested in
language and phrases which are often repeated though
appropriate.
*Greene, Harry Plunket. Interpretation in Song. 2d ed.
New York: St. Martin's Press, 1956.
Highly regarded and authoritative. Written in
1912, this unique volume on interpretation has con-
tinued to be current, despite the occasional dated ref-
erences. Few other books approach song interpretation
as well as this.
Greene, Margaret C. L. The Voice and Its Disorders. New
York: Macmillan Co. , 1959.
Though primarily concerned with speech and voice
disorders, the first chapters on normal voice are
helpful.
Griesman, B. L. "Mechanism of Phonation Demonstrated by
Planigraphy of the Larynx. " Archives of Otolaryngology, 38 (1943), 17-26.
Basic demonstrations of the use of X-ray to study
physiology of the larynx during phonation.
Griffith, James Francis. "Time an Important Consideration
in Vocal Training. " The NATS Bulletin, 8 (March-
April, 1952), 8.
Salient problems are discussed concerning the
ever-recurring question of enough time. Abbreviated
approaches to vocal study are deplored.
Guarrera, Frank. "Opera Singers Must Act. " Music Jour-
nal, 20 (January, 1962), 62.
The high demands of operatic interpretation are
stressed by a professional singer.
Gunn, George H. , Jr. "An Acoustical Analysis of Quality
Variations in Sung Vowels. " Unpublished Ph. D. dis-
sertation, University of Michigan, 1961.
The research is concerned with analysis of six

voice quality variations termed bright, dark, spread,
nasal, head and throaty.

Gunnison, Paul R.   "The Art of Singing." American Music
    Teacher, 3 (March-April, 1954), 5.
        Bold, controversial procedures of breathing and
    of vowel production are suggested; they are not con-
    vincingly substantiated.

Gurney, Henry B.   "Meeting Daily Vocal Problems." Etude,
    August, 1944, p. 447.
        "Free control" of the tongue, posture, and the
    head voice are mentioned.

Gutman, Julius.   "The Common Sense of Singing." Musical
    Courier, 159 (January, 1959), 17.
        Generally a philosophical treatment of the singing
    voice.   Hints and comments on building the voice are
    added by this noted singer and teacher.

Hardy, Lee.   "The Physiology of Breathing." The NATS
    Bulletin, 15 (December, 1958), 12.
        The physiological processes of breathing are ac-
    curately explained.

Harper, Andrew H., Jr.   "Spectrographic Comparisons of
    Certain Vowels to Ascertain Differences Between Solo
    and Choral Singing, Reinforced by Aural Comparison."
    Unpublished Ph.D. dissertation, Indiana University,
    1967.
        The study was made to determine harmful differ-
    ences, if any, of choral singing and the approach to the
    solo voice.

Harper, Ralph M.   G-Suiting the Body.   Boston: E. C.
    Schirmer Music Co., 1945.
        Harper's 1945 edition of The Voice Governor
    (1940) includes two additional chapters called "G-Suiting
    the Body"; these are published in this pamphlet.

Harrell, Mack.   "Strictly American Vocal Problems."   An
    interview by Allison Paget.   Etude, August, 1949,
    p. 479.
        Harrell attempts to explain why "our vocal ma-
    terial does not always reach the artistic heights to
    which it might reasonably aspire."   The steps are
    listed that must be taken to bridge the gap between
    having a voice and using it correctly.

Hartley, Maude H.   "Thoughts Culled from a Singer's Mem-
    oirs." Musician, 51 (June, 1946), 88.
        Interesting reflections are combined with useful
    hints regarding interpretation.

Harvey, Richard. "Beware of Voice Teachers." Educational
     Music Magazine, 34 (March-April, 1955), 29.
          Suggested are some conventional as well as ex-
     treme ideas about choosing a voice teacher.
Hatfield, Lansing. "The Control of the Voice." An inter-
     view by Gunnar Asklund. Etude, May, 1946, p. 254.
          Vocal talent must be artistically combined with
     intelligence.
Haugh, Harold. "Professional and/or Professor." The
     NATS Bulletin, 13 (October, 1956), 10-11.
          Convincing, argumentative points are used to
     justify lightening the teaching load of the college sing-
     ing teacher.
Haury, Elsa. "Producing the Beautiful Tone." The South-
     western Musician, 18 (March, 1951), 9.
          Various aspects of vocal production which con-
     tribute to beautiful tone are discussed. A middle-of-
     the-road position is urged in regard to diction.
*Haywood, F. H. Universal Song. 1933. Reprint. New
     York: G. Schirmer, 1957.
          Graded lesson plans about the fundamentals of
     singing that range in difficulty from elementary exer-
     cises to advanced studies.
Heaton, Wallace, and Hargens, C. W., eds. An Interdis-
     ciplinary Index of Studies in Physics, Medicine and
     Music Related to the Human Voice. Bryn Mawr, Pa.:
     Theodore Presser Co., 1968.
          This index is intended to refer the reader to the
     wealth of information in print about vocal research.
     Persons interested in the human voice will find refer-
     ences to a variety of investigations of the vocal tract.
Hempel, Frieda. "Preserving the Voice." An interview by
     Gunnar Asklund. Etude, November, 1947, p. 605.
          Regularity of practice is the most significant as-
     pect of preserving the voice.
Hemus, Gladys. "Drama in Song." Etude, April, 1957,
     p. 20.
          A discussion of the importance of clear enunciation
     on the part of singers.
*Henderson, William James. The Art of Singing. 1938.
     Reprint. Freeport, N. Y.: Books for Libraries Press,
     1968.
          First copyrighted in 1896 by the author. The
     1938 edition, compiled by Oscar Thompson and Irving
     Kolodin, contains Art of the Singer (1906) as Part I.
     Part II is a collection of articles principally from The
     New York Sun. This highly respected work continues

to have practical application to voice culture.
Hensellek, Gunter. "Dramatic Training for Opera Singers."
Music Journal, 18 (November-December, 1960), 20-21.
     The concepts of Biogymnastics and Theory of
Dramatic Performance have been developed by the
author.   These areas of study for singers are not altogether clearly explained.
Herbert-Caesari, Edgar F.   "The Pharyngeal Voice. " Etude,
November, 1950, p. 58.
     The pharyngeal voice is the author's terminology
denoting the head voice.
_____. The Voice of the Mind.   London: Robert Hale,
1951a.
     A wordy, detailed treatise to support the concept
of mental power over the voice.   Involved discussions
of the physiological-acoustical factors of tone production
weaken the author's own premise.
_____. "More About the Pharyngeal Voice. " Etude,
April, 1951b, p. 17.
_____. "The High Larynx--Hazard for Singers. " Etude,
July, 1951c, p. 64.
_____. The Alchemy of Voice.   London: Robert Hale,
1965.
     Essays on the state of singing in the mid-twentieth
century, a short history of opera, some philosophical
musings, a biography of Margaret Sheridan, and other
"relevancies" are inserted among various chapters on
vocal technique.
*_____. The Science and Sensations of Vocal Tone. 2d
ed. , rev. Boston: Crescendo Publishers, 1968.
     An attempt is made to form a theory on the use
of "sensations of vocal tone" as a reliable guide to
singing.   First published in 1936.
_____. Vocal Truth.   London: Robert Hale, 1969.
     With less verbosity than in former books, the
author writes "some of the things I teach. " Although
rambling and unorganized, the material is assimilable.
Hill, Robert P.   "Responsibilities of the Coach on Song Literature Toward Teacher and Singer. " The NATS Bulletin, 9 (May-June, 1953), 7.
     The author voices in a logical and a realistic
manner the position of the vocal coach in his professional relationship to the singing teacher and the singer.
Hines, Jerome.   "Don't Imitate Your Teacher. " Etude,
September, 1951, p. 16.
     Vocal students often copy the mannerisms, rather
than the virtues, of more experienced singers.

Hinman, Florence L. "The Use of Fundamental Tone and
Overtone for the Singer." Music Teachers National
Association. Volume of Proceedings for 1945. Pittsburgh, Pa., 1945.
In the vocal instrument the oral cavity or mouth is
the "home" of the fundamental or basic tone, while the
upper cavities provide the area for the overtone.
Hisey, Philip D. "Scientific versus Empirical Methods of
Teaching Voice." The NATS Bulletin, 27 (December,
1970), 14.
"Every teacher is compelled to speak with author-
ity and conviction. This can be done only through the
joint efforts of both the scientific approach and the empirical approach."
_____. "Head Quality versus Nasality: A Review of Some
Pertinent Literature." The NATS Bulletin, 28 (Decem-
ber, 1971), 4.
An evaluative review of a portion of the literature,
scientific and empirical, which deals with the correlation
or relationship between "head quality" and "nasality."
Hoffelt, Robert O. "Vocal Study through Recordings." Choral
and Organ Guide, 15 (March, 1962), 11-14.
A practical article on the use of recordings in
vocal study.
Hohn, Robert W. "A Study of the Relationship between Vowel
Modification and Changes in Pitch in the Male Singing
Voice." Unpublished Mus. Ed. D. dissertation, Indiana
University, 1960.
The researcher used certain vowels taken from
recordings of recognized singers at three different pitch
levels. After analysis, almost all singers showed significant changes in formant frequencies on all vowels at
three pitch levels. Each voice type has a pattern of
modification and the position of the pitch in the vocal
range is more significant than the specific pitch.
Holler, G. Frederick. "Using the Total Being in Singing and
Teaching." The NATS Bulletin, 20 (February, 1964),
4-8.
An element in singing higher than the mind or the
flesh is the spirit. This element, often ignored or for-
saken, is the topic of this discussion.
Hollien, Harry. "Some Laryngeal Correlates of Vocal Pitch."
Journal of Speech and Hearing Research, 3 (March,
1960), 52-58.
Results showed significant trends for laryngeal
size to be smaller as pitch level becomes higher.
_____, and Curtis, James F. "Elevation and Tilting of the

Vocal Folds as a Function of Vocal Pitch. " Folia
Phoniatrica, 14 (1962), 23-36.
    Laminagraphic studies of laryngeal function car-
ried out on 24 normal male and female subjects yielded
research data which showed that both the elevation and
the tilt of the vocal folds increase progressively with
increasing pitch.
Holst, Harald B.   "Interpretation in Singing. " American
    Music Teacher, 12 (September-October, 1962), 14.
    Using a quotation from Michelangelo, "The soul
longs to dwell with the body, " the author urges the
singer to develop a sincere, natural interpretation.
Hopkins, Edwin.   "Twenty Practical Exercises to Improve
    Your Voice. " Etude, April, 1943, p. 235.
    Some suggestions about how to produce far-carry-
ing tones in the most effective manner.
Horowitz, Michael S.   "Concerning Voice Physiology. " Music
    Journal, 15 (March, 1957), 40.
    Cooperation of the knowledgeable voice teacher
and the laryngologist is urged.
*Howe, Albert P.   Practical Principles of Voice Production.
    2d rev. ed.   London: W. Paxton and Co. , 1947.
    A slim book containing a brief guide to funda-
mentals of singing.   Some exercises are included.
First published in 1940.
Howie, John, and Delattre, Pierre.   "An Experimental Study
    of the Effect of Pitch on the Intelligibility of Vowels. "
    The NATS Bulletin, 18 (May, 1962), 6-9.
    This interesting study has direct practical impli-
cation for the voice pedagogue.   The research, among
other things, provides usable charts showing specific
vowels and pitch levels that will give difficulty in vowel
discernment.
Huls, Helen Steen.   "A Philosophy for the Teacher of Sing-
    ing. "   Music Teachers National Association.   Volume
    of Proceedings for 1947.   Pittsburgh, Pa. , 1947.
    A plea for the acceptance of new ideas and for
ethical conduct among teachers of singing.
Huntley, E. A.   "Class Singing--Assessing the Performance."
    Music Teacher, 43 (May, 1964), 221.
    An excellent listing of self-evaluation points.
Husler, Frederick, and Rodd-Marling, Yvonne.   Singing, the
    Physical Nature of the Vocal Organ.   New York:
    October House, 1965.
    Based on the works of Goerttler and Husson (the
vocal folds are capable of spontaneous vibration), the
authors deal almost entirely with the nature of the voice

and only incidentally with the art of singing.

Husson, Raoul. "A New Look at Phonation." The NATS
Bulletin, 13 (December, 1956), 12-13.
The human larynx is a neuro-muscular effector
constructed of vocal cords that manifest, in phonation,
a vibrating phase of opening at each action potential
reaching them from the recurrent nerve. A summary
of the author's theory.

_____. "The Classification of Human Voices." The NATS
Bulletin, 13 (May, 1957a), 6-11.
Experiments, compiled between 1953 and 1956,
establish that all the tonal characteristics of the human
voice are a function of a solid and unique physiological
factor--the excitability of the recurrent nerve.

_____. "Special Physiology in Singing with Power." The
NATS Bulletin, 14 (October, 1957b), 12-15.
Physiological conditioning for the singer who copes
with the demands of stage performance singing.

_____. "The Pharyngo-Buccal Cavity and Its Phonatory
Physiology." The NATS Bulletin, 16 (February, 1960),
4.
The phenomena analyzed show how much, in
phonation, pharyngo-buccal acoustic phenomena react
powerfully on the attack mechanism.

_____. "How the Acoustics of a Hall Affect the Singer
and the Speaker." The NATS Bulletin, 18 (February,
1962), 8-13.

Isshiki, Nobuhiko. "Regulatory Mechanism of Voice Intensity
Variation." Journal of Speech and Hearing Research,
7 (July, 1964), 17-29.
On the basis of the data, it was concluded that at
very low pitches, the glottal resistance is dominant in
controlling intensity (laryngeal control), becoming less
so as the pitch is raised, until at extremely high pitch
the intensity is controlled almost entirely by the flow
rate (expiratory muscle control).

Jacobi, Peter. "I Must Sing for Myself. An Interview with
Elizabeth Schwarzkopf." Musical Courier, 163 (May,
1961a), 10-22.
Schwarzkopf emphasizes her need to forget the
audience. Interesting aspects of her career are related.

_____. "A Lesson from Pierre Bernac." Musical

<u>Courier</u>, 163 (August, 1961b), 46-47.
Interesting biographical insights into the singing
career of Bernac and most useful comments on his
procedures and methods in the master class.
Jacobson, Robert. "The Gist of Jennie (Opinions of Jennie
Tourel). " <u>Musical America</u>, 83 (June, 1963), 32-33.
Some concepts which are based on Miss Tourel's
teaching experiences.
Jagel, Frederick. "Developing the Tenor Voice. " An in-
terview by Stephen West. <u>Etude</u>, August, 1947, p. 444.
Jeritza, Maria. "The Singer Faces the World!" An inter-
view by Rose Heylbut. <u>Etude</u>, April, 1947, p. 185.
Mme. Jeritza comments on the vocal and artistic
habits which make achievement possible.
Johnson, Donald E. "The Correlation between Certain
Physical Traits and the Singing Ranges of Selected Male
Students. " Unpublished Ph. D. dissertation, Teachers
College, Columbia University, 1950.
Physical traits measured were confined to those
involved in the vocal process. The findings indicate
that natural pitch extremes can be predicted from known
larynx length vocal cord rating and larynx prominence
with small standard error of estimate.
Johnson, Merion J. "An Investigation of the Effect of Training in the Articulation of Vowels by the Speaking Voice
upon the Articulation of Vowels by the Singing Voice. "
Unpublished Mus. Ed. D. dissertation, Indiana University,
1966.
Results of this experiment suggest that it is not
profitable to teach the production of a sung vowel by
using the spoken vowel as a model.
Jones, Arthur J. "A Study of the Breathing Processes as
They Relate to the Art of Singing. " Unpublished D. M.A.
dissertation, University of Missouri, 1970.
The author sought to isolate the anatomical and
physiological processes involved in the art of singing
and to define their functions through illustration and
verbal explanation.
Jones, William E. "Leaves from My Notebook. " <u>The NATS</u>
<u>Bulletin</u>, 3 (June-July, 1947), 3.
Contains comments on resonance and breathing.
Judd, Percy. <u>Vocal Technique</u>. London: Sylvan Press,
1951.
Although the author decries the use of "so-called
scientific facts, " his book frequently contains physiological diagrams and references to points of physiology.
Of particular interest is chapter 3, a consideration of

the importance of aural control.

_____. Musicianship for Singers. London: Novello, 1957.
The volume deals with basic musicianship as
needed by the singer.

Judson, Lyman, and Weaver, A. T. Voice Science. 2d ed.
New York: Appleton-Century-Crofts, 1965.
A study of how speech is normally produced, this
textbook is based upon known scientific fact and accepted experimentation. The exhaustive bibliography is
valuable to the serious researcher in singing as well
as in speech.

Kagen, Sergius. On Studying Singing. New York: Rinehart
and Co., 1950.
Not a book on how to sing; its main purpose is to
help the student find a way to study singing intelli-
gently. The writer discusses the minimal natural
equipment necessary for the serious study of singing
as well as goals, purposes and procedures of training.
Written from a long and distinguished career of guiding
young musicians.

Kantner, Claude E., and West, Robert. Phonetics. Rev. ed.
New York: Harper and Brothers, 1960.
An introduction to the principles of phonetic sci-
ence; authoritative and useful to the voice teacher.

Kay, Elster. Bel Canto and the Sixth Sense. London:
Dennis Dobson, 1963.
A technical essay on the "Italian Physical Style
of Singing" and a rambling glorification of the singers
of the twenties. The subject matter is disorganized,
self-contradictory and condemnatory. Exaggerated
claims are never explained for fear of revealing "a
trade secret."

Keep, C. H. "Understanding the Human Voice." Voice, 6
(September-October, 1950), 13.

Kelsey, Franklyn. "The Riddle of the Voice." Music and
Letters, 29 (July, 1948), 238.
Retrogression in vocal skill is caused by a fundamental error in the generally accepted view of the
human instrument. The author strives to point out this
error.

_____. "What Is Singing?" Music and Letters, 30 (July,
1949), 216-230.
The author decries the English "small voice" and
comprehensively writes how his countrymen may increase the fullness and quality of tone.

_____. The Foundations of Singing. London: Williams
and Norgate, 1950.
    Breath-pressure, the coup de glotte and articula-
tion in the throat are principal points on which the
author pins his faith.
_____. "The Nature of the Singing Voice." Music and
Letters, 32 (April, 1951a), 140-146.
    An article, which tells how not to breath for
singing, fails to make clear the correct style of
breathing.
_____. "The Tremolo." Music and Letters, 32 (April,
1951b), 203.
    The nature of breathing and tone production is
compactly presented.
_____. "The Singer and the Song." Musical Times, 92
(August, 1951c), 348-350.
    A number of worthwhile aspects of song interpre-
tation are covered in a scholarly manner.
_____. "Science and the Singing-Master." Musical
Times, 93 (October, 1952), 446-449.
    The author feels that the voice scientist is pri-
marily responsible for much of the confusion in voice
training. The article is excellently written.
_____. "Voice-Training." Grove's Dictionary of Music
and Musicians. 5th ed. Vol. IX.
    After an extended section on the technical aspects
of singing, an overview of voice training theories is
impressively given.
Kester, George. Your Singing Potential. New York: The
William-Frederick Press, 1953.
    The author-teacher speaks in dialogue with the
student. In 31 pages, he provides lessons for the beginner and progresses to professional activity. The
techniques suggested are conventional; the terminology
is unorthodox and confusing.
Kipnis, Alexander. "The Art of Mezza-Voce Singing."
Etude, January, 1951, p. 20.
    "Dependable breath control and endless practice
are the requisites for mastering this indispensable part
of singing," in the opinion of the famous bass.
Kirsten, Dorothy. "Be Your Own Guide!" An interview by
Myles Fellowes. Etude, June, 1945, p. 324.
    Sensations and the importance of vowels are
stressed.
Klein, Joseph J., and Schjeide, Ole A. Singing Technique:
How to Avoid Vocal Trouble. Princeton, N. J.: D. van
Nostrand Co., 1967.

The authors alternately address the teacher and
the student. Emphasis seems to dwell on correction of
ever-abounding vocal faults. External manipulation of
the larynx is advocated.

Klein, Max. "How Jean de Reszke Taught Singing. " Etude,
Part I, October, 1950a, p. 14 and Part II, November,
1950b, p. 21.
In a sequence of articles the author illustrates
the many diversities of de Reszke's teaching and his
individualized approach to each voice.

Kockritz, Hubert. "The Problem of Musicianship and the
Modern Singer. " Music Teachers National Association.
Volume of Proceedings for 1944. Pittsburgh, Pa. ,
1944.
An attempt is made to correlate the study of
singing and the growth of musicianship.

Koppel, Elsa. "Freedom of Voice Production. " The NATS
Bulletin, 12 (May, 1956), 15.
One can learn to use the vocal apparatus with
ease by essentially intuitive methods.

Korst, Robert. "Normal Breathing in Singing is Result of
Specific Training. " Musical Courier, 144 (October,
1951), 16.
Unaccentuated breathing is the background of good
singing.

Kwartin, Bernard. Vocal Pedagogy. New York: Omega
Music Co. , 1952.
A reprint of an address given before a conference
of singers and vocal teachers in New York. The author
seeks to make an inquiry into current methods and to
present new principles, but there is not space in the
brief pamphlet to clarify many points.

_____. New Frontiers in Vocal Art. New York: Carlton
Press, 1963.
The volume, which promises "an original theory
of tone production, " stresses focus, forward placement, and several points of local effort. Controversial
theories and devices are prevalent.

LaForge, Frank. "Interpretation and Emotional Control (As
Told to Robert Sabin). " Musical America, 70 (October,
1950), 33.
The singer must not fall victim to a subjective
emotional reaction--the most frequent error of inexperienced singers.

Lagourge, Charles. The Secret. 2d ed. Boston: Meador

Publishing Co., 1945.
"The tree of voice and its orderly growth." This
is a slightly enlarged edition of a 1924 publication.
Lamberti, Carlo. Improving Your Voice. New York:
Vantage Press, 1954.
A devoted advocate·of the theory of sinus tone
production, the author finds almost everyone and every-
thing to be wrong concerning orthodox vocal pedagogy.
He is also generally condemnatory of singers and sing-
ing.
Lampe, Sister Laura. "The Impact of Effective Singing."
Musart, 23 (September-October, 1970), 13.
The teacher of singing is urged to engage in fre-
quent study of his art in order to apply basic principles
and techniques that are fundamental to vocal instruction.
Lamson, Martha, ed. Duval's Svengali on Singing. New
York: Robert Speller and Sons, 1963.
This booklet contains excerpts from J. H. Duval's
first book The Secrets of Svengali on Singing, Singers,
Teachers and Critics (1922). Through the imaginative
use of DuMaurier's fictional character, Duval conveyed
his principles of teaching singing.
Landeau, Michel. "Voice Classification." The NATS Bulletin, 20 (October, 1963), 4.
Theories of voice classification are reviewed in
an historical survey of classifying researches. The
empirical and the scientific forms of procedure are discussed at length.
_____, and Zuili, H. "Vocal Emission and Tomograms
of the Larynx." The NATS Bulletin, 19 (February,
1963), 6-11.
A complex and technical study of limited value to
many voice instructors.
Large, John W. "An Acoustical Study of Isoparametric
Tones in the Female Chest and Middle Registers in
Singing." The NATS Bulletin, 25 (December, 1968),
12-15.
Acoustic differences in those areas of the singing
range where registers overlap are the subject of this
sonographic research. Within the same register,
marked similarities were found in the distribution of
energy among partials; conversely, marked differences
were found between registers.
_____. "Observations on the Vital Capacity of Singers."
The NATS Bulletin, 27 (February-March, 1971), 34.
The vital capacities of 20 male and 20 female

singers were measured by a Collins respirometer. A
wide range of results were obtained; on the average,
the singers showed roughly 16 percent greater measured vital capactiy than predicted for the corres-
ponding age and height.

_____; Iwata, S.; and von Leden, Hans. "The Primary
Female Register Transition in Singing: Aerodynamic
Study." Folia Phoniatrica, 22 (1970), 385-396.
  The results of this study support the theory that
the key to the register problem is primarily laryngeal,
not pharyngeal.

Lawson, Franklin D. The Human Voice. New York: Harper
and Brothers, 1944.
  A physician, formerly a professional singer,
writes about the proper use of the singing and speaking
voice.

Lawson, James Terry. Full-Throated Ease. Vancouver,
B. C. : Western Music Co. , 1955.
  A compact guide to the fundamentals of singing.
Written by a physician, the approach is primarily phys-
iological; the section on breathing is of instructional
value.

Lee, William J. "Hail, Demosthenes!" The NATS Bulletin,
17 (February, 1961), 6-7.
  A short article stressing the use of declamation
for the perfection of enunciation.

Lehman, Evangeline. "Reflections on the Art of Singing. "
Etude, April, 1945, p. 195.
  Sensible teaching methods are combined with per-
sonal reminiscences.

*Lehmann, Lilli. How to Sing. 7th ed. Translated by
Richard Aldrich. New York: Macmillan Co. , 1962.
  Controversial and difficult to read, this highly
personal account has enjoyed repeated editions.

Lehmann, Lotte. More Than Singing. London: Boosey and
Hawkes, 1946a.
  A foremost interpreter of German lieder puts into
words her ideas on the interpretation of songs: 140
lieder, as well as a few French, English, Italian and
Russian songs, are individually discussed. A thorough
study of the interpretative suggestions found in this book
will prove invaluable to all singers.

_____. "Teaching the Singer to Become an Interpretative
Artist. " An interview by Annabel Comfort. Etude,
February, 1946b, p. 74.
  Beyond technique and a fine instrument lies the
further goal of an interpretative artist.

Leonard, Ray. "The Trinity of Singing." American Music
    Teacher, 18 (September-October, 1968), 41.
            A well-written article. The goals of singing are
    compared with three aspects of the nature of man--
    physical, intellectual and emotional.
Lester, John L. "Hygienics of the Voice." Music Teachers
    National Association. Volume of Proceedings for 1950.
    Pittsburgh, Pa., 1950.
            For the student, this is a useful article on the
    best healthful care of the voice.
_____. "The Key to Coordination." The NATS Bulletin,
    8 (November-December, 1951), 4.
            The teacher is urged, despite the complexity of
    vocal training, to remember the spontaneous expression
    that is derived from good technique and coordination.
_____. "Getting Good Results from a Variety of Ap-
    proaches." The NATS Bulletin, 11 (November, 1954), 3.
            The author feels that any sense of imagery that
    helps get freedom of sound is good.
_____. "Breathing Related to Phonation." The NATS
    Bulletin, 14 (December, 1957), 26.
            Breathing should be very carefully studied. The
    beauty of singing will depend on how the forces of the
    breathing mechanism are coordinated with phonation.
Levinson, Grace. The Singing Artist. Greenville, S. C. : By
    the Author, Bob Jones University, 1962.
            The author's views on breathing, rhythm, tone,
    diction, interpretation and communications serve as
    principal chapter headings. Common vocal faults and
    practice aids are helpfully discussed.
Lewando, Olga Wolf. "Dramatizing Song Lyrics." Music
    Journal, 17 (September, 1959), 24.
            Practical ideas of visible interpretation are given.
Lewando, Ralph. "Vocal Technique for the Stage and Screen."
    Music Journal, 14 (April, 1956), 53.
            The author writes on some noted pupils and briefly
    on vocal technique.
Lewis, Robert M. "Voice Training through Singing." Edu-
    cational Theatre Journal, 14 (March, 1962), 59-63.
            A convincing rationale of the inclusion of singing
    in the experience of all serious students of the theater.
    A fascinating letter from Otis Skinner to his daughter
    on the value of singing is included.
Li, Chau-yuan M. "A Spirometric Mensuration of Forced In-
    halation Employed in Three Methods of Voice Instruc-
    tion." Unpublished Ph. D. dissertation, Southern Illinois
    University, 1970.

According to the author, the three most commonly practiced methods of breathing for singing are the costal, the diaphragmatic and the abdominal methods. The results showed that, on the average, the costal method gave a significantly greater lung capacity than did the other two methods, and the abdominal method provided the least lung capacity.

Liebling, Estelle. "So You Want to be a Singer." Music Clubs Magazine, 29 (April, 1950), 12.

The requisites for a successful singing career are given. These are followed by examples of famous singers who were exceptions to the rule.

_____. The Estelle Liebling Vocal Course. Edited by Bernard Whitefield. New York: Chappell and Co., 1956.

An elementary approach to vocal study. Four separate books for each major classification of voice were published.

Lindquest, Allan R. "Security in Singing." Music Journal, 7 (March-April, 1949), 36.

A brief biographical sketch of the noted Swedish voice teacher, Dr. Gillis Bratt. The theory of "total response" is discussed.

_____. "An Axiom for Vocal Pedagogy." The NATS Bulletin, 11 (May, 1955), 3.

Singers must train for and achieve "good form through the feel of it." His axiom is a complex statement of purpose.

Litante, Judith. A Natural Approach to Singing. Dubuque, Iowa: Wm. C. Brown Co., 1959.

The author's premise is that singing should be a natural, spontaneous act. The portions of the book pertaining to singing technique are direct and sensible.

London, George. "Don't Look for Short Cuts." An interview by Stephen West. Etude, May, 1953, p. 18.

Mr. London's attitudes toward improving vocal standards are clearly and forcefully expressed.

London, S. J. "Vox Humana: Theme and Variations." The NATS Bulletin, Part I, 21 (February, 1965a), 21; Part II, 21 (May, 1965b), 10; and, Part III, 21 (October, 1965c), 34.

A significant and unique treatise on the evolution of singing and historical style. Written originally for the readers of the medical profession, it will, however, be readable to the searching mind of an enlightened voice teacher.

Long, Newell H. "Some Things a Voice Teacher Should Know about Sound." The NATS Bulletin, 9 (March-

April, 1953), 6.
    Selected acoustical principles related to the prob-
lems of voice are discussed.
Longo, Teodosio.   Fundamentals of Singing and Speaking.
    New York: S. F. Vanni, 1945.
    The premise of this book is that singing and
speaking are based on the same fundamental principle.
The author states that his is the first book ever written
that explains the mechanics of the voice.   The concepts
are not always clearly defined.
Luchsinger, Richard, and Arnold, Godfrey.   Voice-Speech-
    Language.   Translated by Godfrey E. Arnold and Evelyn
    Robe Finkbeiner.   Belmont, Calif. : Wadsworth Publish-
    ing Co. , 1965.
    A comprehensive, encyclopedic volume based on the
broad aspects of human communication.   Here is an
amazing breadth of detail which should serve as a principal source of information for the voice pedagogue.
Lueders, Perry H.   "Toward Freedom and Discipline for
    Singers. "   Choral and Organ Guide, 21 (June-August,
    1968), 5-8.
    A convincing design for the use of improvisation;
"just fun" and "anything goes" is an approach for the
first lessons in singing.
Lukken, Albert.   "A Plea for Simplicity in Singing. "   The
    NATS Bulletin, 2 (December, 1945), 3.
    One of many articles urging the clearing away of
conflicting terms and nebulous concepts of singing instruction.
_____.   "Vocalization in Modern Teaching. "   Music Teach-
    ers National Association.   Volume of Proceedings for
    1946.   Pittsburgh, Pa. , 1946.
    In the light of recent statements implying that
there now exist new techniques and short cuts conceived
from research--which abrogate former methods of train-
ing--this article provides an affirmation of the value of
vocalization in modern teaching.
_____.   "The Vocal Vibrato: Its Use and Misuse. "   Music
    Journal, 14 (September, 1956), 54-57.
    Considered opinions of the cause of extreme vi-
brato are given; suggestions for the correction of the
problem are outlined.
Lynch, Christopher.   "The Secret of Singing. "   An interview
    by Myles Fellowes.   Etude, February, 1947, p. 69.
    An interesting, personal philosophy of singing.
Lyon, John Thomas, Jr.   "An Experimental Investigation of
    the Relation between Personality and Vocal Character-

istics of Selected Beginning Adult Singers. " Unpublished
Ph. D. dissertation, Indiana University, 1966.
    High college grades and college ability were found
to be significant factors of better voice. Better voice
accompanied high manifest needs of heterosexuality and
achievement, while poor voice paralleled the needs of
deference, order, intraception and nurturance.

McClosky, David Blair. Your Voice at Its Best.   Boston,
    Mass. : Little, Brown and Co. , 1959.
    The book provides a simple and clear explanation
of the processes involved in correct vocal-sound production.
MacCollin, Paul. "Tongue Action and Diction. " The NATS
    Bulletin, 4 (February-March, 1948), 3.
    The author suggests if vowels are formed in the
laryngeal pharynx, the consonants will take care of
themselves.
McCollum, John. "The Wonderful Rotary Singing Coach. "
    High Fidelity, 7 (March, 1957), 46.
    A useful article relates the value and danger of
using recordings in vocal study.
McCook, Lilian Gerow. "The Vocal Students Imagination,
    Its Development and Training. " Music Teachers Na-
    tional Association. Volume of Proceedings for 1947.
    Pittsburgh, Pa. , 1947.
    Vocal imagery and careful self-analysis of tonal
concepts help develop the imagination of the vocal
student.
MacDonald, Florence. Think Intelligently--Sing Convincingly.
    Rev. ed. New York: Vantage Press, 1960.
    The author especially emphasizes that the mind
controls almost every facet of singing. The book is
interesting and helpful.
McDonald, Katherine G. "Advice for the Beginning Student. "
    The NATS Bulletin, 17 (May, 1961), 32.
    A brief article containing a number of practical
helps.
McGinnis, C. S. ; Elnick, M. ; and Kraichman, M. "A Study
    of the Vowel Formants of Well-Known Male Operatic
    Singers. " Journal of the Acoustical Society of America,
    23 (July, 1951), 440-446.
    The formant regions of vowels sustained by well-
known male operatic singers were compared with each
other and with those of untrained voices. Three important formants were found in the male voices, although

the third of these was more prominent in trained voices.
Mackenzie, Mignon B.   "Challenge the Voice Student with
    Teaching. "   Music Journal, 8 (March-April, 1950), 33.
        The author urges the use of proper methods and
    materials and concludes with a plea for the inclusion of
    voice pedagogy classes for the senior voice student.
McLaughlin, D.   "Who Has Seen the Voice?"   The NATS
    Bulletin, 16 (October, 1959), 30.
        Physical features and their bearing on voice
    character and diction are discussed.
McLean, Cameron.   "Causes for Confusion in the Teaching
    of Singing. "   The NATS Bulletin, 7 (June-July, 1951a),
    15.
        Among the several "causes for confusion" are "the
    tone placers. "
_____.   "Starting Right in Vocal Study. "   The South-
    western Musician, 17 (July, 1951b), 8.
        Requisites for vocal study are well defined.
_____.   "What Have You to Declare?"   The NATS Bulle-
    tin, 20 (February, 1964), 2-4.
        Using the analogy of a customs declaration, the
    author issues a stimulating challenge to members of the
    National Association of Teachers of Singing.
MacNeil, C.   "Singing from a Suitcase. "   Music Journal, 20
    (May, 1962), 23-24.
        Though primarily biographical, there are a few
    concepts of training the singing voice.
MacRae, Tolbert.   "Breathing and Its Effect on Singing. "
    The NATS Bulletin, 4 (February-March, 1948), 2.
        A brief statement on how the "breath becomes
    voice. "
Madeira, Jean.   "The Trend is Up. "   Music Journal, 21
    (October, 1963), 22-23.
        The basic concepts of correct voice classification
    are found in this interesting article.   Disapproval of the
    fad of wishing to be a "high" singer is expressed.   The
    author mentions many operatic roles that are more
    satisfying than some of the roles for coloratura range.
Madsen, Clifford K.   "Toward a Scientific Approach. "   The
    NATS Bulletin, 22 (December, 1965), 22.
        The author urges the sharing and using of knowl-
    edge among teachers of singing in a similar attitude as
    among the physical scientists, who learn from each
    other's work.
_____.   "The Effect of Scale Direction on Pitch Acuity. "
    Journal of Research in Music Education, 14 (Winter,
    1966), 266-275.

On the basis of this study, the researcher found that vocal pitch acuity is highly superior in a descending direction, that subjects with greater formal training perform with greater pitch acuity than untrained subjects, and that practice sessions do not significantly improve intonation.

Mallett, Lloyd. "Encouraging Legato Singing." Etude, May, 1940, p. 291.
Principles of legato singing are reviewed and a variety of scale exercises are included.

_____. "In the Beginning." The NATS Bulletin, 18 (May, 1962), 30-31.
Practical helps for first lessons are given. Included is a long list of pertinent questions which should be asked the student. A very useful article.

_____. "Some Vocal Training Ideas Re-Explored." The NATS Bulletin, 20 (October, 1963), 8.
The teacher and singer, in search of new ideas or improved technique, will do well to study this relevant article.

*Mancini, Giambattista. Practical Reflections on Figured Singing. Translated and edited by Edward Foreman. Champaign, Ill.: Pro Musica Press, 1967.
The editions of 1774 and 1777 are compared, translated and edited by Foreman. Diverse topics about the singing art are discussed in a manner appropriate to our own use.

Manley, Ronald R. "A Comparative Analysis of the Vocal Intensity Developed Through Beginning Class and Individual Voice Instruction of University Students." Unpublished Ph. D. dissertation, Indiana University, 1967.
In this study no significant differences were found in the vocal intensity of the subjects who received individual voice instruction from those who received class instruction.

Manning, Irene. "Salesmanship in Singing." Etude, March, 1946, p. 135.
Concentrate on telling the story; this will enhance communication of the song.

Mansion, Madeleine. How to Sing. Translated by Frank Jackson. London, Falcon Press, 1952.
Conventional and often repeated platitudes on singing are prevalent. There seems to be little that is fresh and stimulating. The vocal ideas are generally sound.

*Marafioti, P. Mario. Caruso's Method of Voice Production. 1922. Reprint. Austin, Texas: Cadica Enterprises, 1958.
A somewhat extreme approach, allied to the track

228 Teaching Singing

of the speaking voice, was formulated by Caruso's per-
sonal physician.
Margolis, Samuel. "Exercises of Vowels May Yield Clue on
Voices." Musical Courier, 114 (November, 1951), 34.
   Some aspects of Samuel Margolis' teaching are
enumerated. He proudly speaks of his famed pupils.
Marshall, Madeleine. The Singer's Manual of English Diction.
New York: G. Schirmer, 1953.
   A recognized and highly respected treatise on the
sounds of the English language as they are used in singing.
_____. "Is Exaggeration Required for Good English Dic-
tion." Diapason, 47 (November, 1956), 18.
   Exaggeration is a matter of perspective. It is a de-
vice usable with knowledge and discretion. The author
provides a concise statement of the principal tenets
found in her book.
Martin, Anna Y. "The Physiological and Psychological Con-
comitants of State Fright." The NATS Bulletin, 17
(December, 1960), 18-23.
   A psychologist gives a comprehensive analysis of
stage fright. This is one of only a few articles on this
worthwhile subject.
Martin, Leonard B. "The Preparation of a Song." The NATS
Bulletin, 14 (December, 1967), 28.
   The author's individual approach to song analysis
is explained. A useful article full of good suggestions.
Martinelli, Giovanni. "Advice from the Golden Age." An in-
terview by Aida Favia-Artsay. Etude, January, 1954, p. 16.
   One of the greatest tenors of all time speaks
directly and simply of many subjects.
Martino, Alfredo. Today's Singing. Rev. ed. New York:
Executive Press, 1953.
   In an amplified edition of the 1938 publication, the
author continues his censorious attack upon the bad teachers of singing. As a contribution to vocal instruction, the
author presents some good, but poorly organized, principles.
M. Laudesia, Sister. "The Impact of Effective Singing."
The NATS Bulletin, 21 (February, 1965), 10.
   Brief comments on four areas a singing teacher must
discuss; these are breathing, resonance, phonation and
diction.
Mary Rosemarie, Sister. Vocal High Fidelity. Chicago: By
the Author, Mundelein College, 1956.
   An approach designed to help the student achieve
natural coordination by timing--a method calculated to
reduce or eliminate tension and timidity. Without first-
hand guidance by the author, the procedure would be

difficult to use effectively.

_____. See and Sing. Chicago: By the Author, Munde-
lein College, 1962.

A supplement to the author's Vocal High Fidelity.

Mason, R. M., and Zemlin, W. R. "The Phenomenon of
Vocal Vibrato." The NATS Bulletin, 22 (February,
1966), 12.

Although there is a large amount of literature
pertaining to vocal vibrato, there is little knowledge of
the physiology of the vibrato. This important research
contributes significantly toward providing that knowledge.

Matthen, Paul. "Scientific Method." Music Journal, 16
(February, 1958), 28-29.

The question at hand is the validity of the scientific method in the teaching of singing. An alert discussion of the subject.

Maurice-Jacquet, H. "Voice Classification and Some of Its
Freaks." Musician, 48 (November, 1943), 130.

The author lists the conventional classifications
and relates personal accounts of voices that are freak-
ish in range and defy normal classification.

_____. "Singer's Attitude Toward His Art." Musician,
49 (August, 1944), 141.

Various loosely-connected aphorisms on singing
and on a singing career are discussed.

_____. The Road to Successful Singing. Philadelphia:
Oliver Ditson, 1947.

From his experience as conductor-pianist-coach,
the writer hopes to inspire in the singer the highest
artistic expression. Spiritual aspects of singing are
coupled with a high emotional plane.

Meano, Carlo. The Human Voice in Speech and Song. Revised, edited and translated by Adele Khoury. Springfield, Ill.: Charles C Thomas, Publisher, 1967.

The writer, a physician, commands a unique
knowledge of singers' and actors' vocal problems. The
translator has provided a very lucid account from the
original Italian and the physiological illustrations are
exceptional. This volume should be among the first to
be studied concerning physiology of the vocal mechanism.

Melchior, Lauritz. "The Little Touch of God's Finger."
An interview by Gunnar Asklund. Etude, April, 1946,
p. 185.

The great need for the maintenance of artistic
expression--the little touch--is stressed.

_____. "What Is Your Vocal Problem?" Etude, Novem-
ber, 1949, p. 11.

Personal answers to some readers' questions on
vocal problems.
Melton, James. "Do You Put the Words Across?" An in-
terview by Annabel Comfort. Etude, June, 1953, p. 15.
Melton suggests that it is the words which carry
the tonal message to the audience.
Merrill, Robert. "Requisites for the Young Singer." An
interview by Burton Paige. Etude, June, 1947, p. 315.
Breathing concepts and the importance of experi-
ence are the principal discussions.
_____. "Your Vocal Problem." Etude, April, 1950,
p. 19.
Questions on vocal problems are answered.
_____. "The Singer's Development." An interview by
Rose Heylbut. Etude, January, 1955, p. 13.
Sensible advice, step-by-step with the singer's
development.
Metzger, Zerline Muhlman. Individual Voice Patterns. New
York: Carlton Press, 1966.
The author suggests that "every singer has a po-
tential ideal sound wave pattern for every pitch, vowel
and consonant, and also for every vowel-consonant
combination on each pitch. The best tones in an in-
dividual's voice are those whose 'pitch extent waves'
follow an inborn pattern that suits him best. This is
his 'Individual Voice Pattern'." Detailed procedure is
given in order to discover these voice patterns.
Middleton, Ray. "Singing Voice--Speaking Voice." Etude,
November, 1951, p. 13.
Middleton says that the singing voice is produced
"in exactly the same way as the speaking voice, only
more so; and that 'more so' makes a great difference."
Miller, H. Thomas. "Relationship of Singing to Speech."
Choral and Organ Guide, 13 (June-August, 1960), 11.
The author contends that if one desires to speak
well, one can, but one must think and listen. He
applies the same principle to singing.
Miller, J. Oscar. "English Language in Singing." Music
Teachers National Association. Volume of Proceedings
for 1946. Pittsburgh, Pa., 1946.
A brief but convincing argument for the singing
of English language songs. "More and more I have
come to realize that good singing and good diction are
synonymous, that the student whose diction is good will
have correct tone placement and a pleasing line of tone."
Miller, Mildred. "It Isn't Luck Alone." An interview by
Gunnar Asklund. Etude, January, 1953, p. 6.

The real luck in a vocal career lies in finding at
the start of study the correct teaching and the general
formative influences which will enable you to go forward.

Miller, Richard. "Legato in Singing." American Music
Teacher, 15 (February-March, 1966), 16.
The spark of imagination must be the prime mover
of the legato line. Fundamental principles of diction
are reviewed as an aid to legato singing.

Miller, Rosalie "Listen to Yourself." Music Journal, 8
(October, 1950), 15.

_____. "Every Voice Is a Problem." Etude, March,
1951, p. 15.
The goal today, as in the past, is to be reached
only through painstaking and persistent effort continued
through years of study.

_____. "The Violin Helps the Voice." Music Journal, 15
(March, 1957), 18.
A correlation of good practice precepts for the
violin and the voice.

Mills, Tom. "Singing from Memory." American Music
Teacher, 19 (February-March, 1970), 27.
If we teach or sing from a memory, which might
synonymously be termed an influence, we find that all
things are characterized by technical excellence and a
goodly portion of self-confidence.

Moe, Kate E. "What Makes a Good Singer?" Music Journal,
8 (November, 1950), 11.
An intelligent, but brief, discussion of the requisites for becoming a good singer.

Montell, Marjorie. Montell Vocal Technique. Miami, Fla.:
Montell Foundation, 1950.
The book stresses that the vocal channel must be
completely passive. The breath, throat, lips, tongue,
face and diaphragm are reflexes. A "magic spot" is
emphasized. The author claims a new and unique
technique. She is generally condemnatory of most
singers and singing teachers and advances the Montell
Technique as the true way to sing.

Moore, Gerald. Singer and Accompanist. New York: Macmillan Co., 1954.
The famed accompanist of many great singers
clearly and beautifully gives interpretation to 50 noted
songs. Invaluable to every singer and accompanist.

Moses, Paul J. The Voice of Neurosis. New York: Grune
and Stratton, 1954.
One of several books in the area of voice science
and therapy that will be of use to the singing teacher.

_____. "Pathology and Therapy of the Singing Voice. "
Archives of Otolaryngology, 69 (1959), 577-582.
    A respected laryngologist, known for his interest
in singing and the singer's throat, provides a comprehensive survey of the problems inherent in use and
misuse of the voice as it relates to medical needs.
Mowe, Homer G. "Voice Production Standards at High
Schools and Colleges. " National Music Council Bulletin, 11 (January, 1951), 5-6.
    The president of the National Association of
Teachers of Singing related the early efforts of the organization to establish standards for the teaching of solo
singing at high school, college and university levels.
_____. "Methodology and Terminology. " The NATS Bul-
letin, 9 (September-October, 1952), 14-15.
    Terminology is dealt with in its relation to the
methods, procedures and devices utilized in the studio.
_____. "The Complete Voice. " The NATS Bulletin, 11
(September, 1954), 3.
    Musicianship, languages, stage deportment, per-
sonality and all the supplementary items may receive
high rating, but it is the voice itself that is the keystone of the arch and no singer can be considered great
who fails in this area of accomplishment.
_____. "Quality in the Singing Voice. " Organ Institute
Quarterly, 5 (Summer, 1955), 8-10.
    A survey written for organists and helpful to
others as a descriptive article in the named area.
_____. "Terminology in the Field of Singing. " Organ
Institute Quarterly, 6 (Summer, 1956), 47-50.
    This article points out the vague and indefinite
terms commonly used in singing; it is particularly helpful to non-vocal musicians who need some knowledge in
this area.
Mudd, Charles Sumner. "The Effect of Chest Resonance
upon the Quality of the Voice. " Speech Monograph, 16
(September, 1949), 344-351.
    The experimenter placed his subjects in a sound-
proof box with their heads protruding. Microphone
readings were taken inside and outside the box. No
amplification of the voice inside the box was detected.
Munsel, Patrice. "Patrice Munsel Presents a Professional
Answer for Your Vocal Problem. " Etude, March, 1950,
p. 19.
Murtaugh, J. A. , and Campbell, E. J. Moran. "The Respiratory Function of the Larynx. " The Laryngoscope, 61
(1961), 581-590.

Music Educators National Conference. "Organization, Function and Technique of Voice Training Classes. " Music
Education Source Book. Chicago: Music Educators National Conference, 1947.
    A fundamental discussion which is principally con-
cerned with the increased emphasis on singing diction.

National Association of Teachers of Singing. Training the
Vocal Instrument. New York: National Association of
Teachers of Singing, 1957.
    A concise statement of principles related to the
training of the singing voice.
Needham, Lucien. "Vocal Technique: Some Observations. "
The NATS Bulletin, 26 (May-June, 1970), 28-29.
    Rambling, nebulous notions; few new ideas are
formulated.
Negus, V. E. The Comparative Anatomy and Physiology of
the Larynx. New York: Hafner Publishing Co. , 1962.
    An authoritative, highly respected work. Contains
well-written and easily understood information on the
physiology of the larynx.
Neilson, Vera Redgrove. "Practice Procedure for Students
of Voice. " The Southwestern Musician, 20 (January,
1954), 11.
    A brief account of usable and often repeated
practice guides.
Nelson, Howard D. "An Experimental Study of the Factors
That Contribute to Intelligibility of English in Singer's
High Register. " Unpublished D. M. A. dissertation,
University of Washington, 1967.
    The construction of a song articulation test was
made and seemed to be of value in indicating relative
abilities of the subjects to be understood. Consonants
were found to be more intelligible than vowels in the
high register.
_____, and Tiffany, William R. "The Intelligibility of
Song. " The NATS Bulletin, 25 (December, 1968), 22-
28.
    Using a newly devised intelligibility test, the
authors delved primarily into articulation problems at
high pitch levels.
Nelson, Russell C. "Liberating the Voice. " The Southwestern Musician, 18 (December, 1951), 14.
    Emphasis is given to a well-coordinated natural
production.
Nevina, Viola. Voice Production in Singing. London: Hutch-
inson's Scientific and Technical Publications, 1953.

           Succinct and pointed, this small volume is designed
primarily for the beginner.   The author attributes many
of her ideas to her teacher, Salvatore Cottone.
Newton, George.   "On Imaginative Singing. "   The NATS Bul-
      letin, 7 (November-December, 1950), 5.
           The singer must develop imagination in two direc-
tions: (1) He must first identify with the character to
be portrayed.   (2) He must understand the historical
period which produced the song.
      _____.   "Articulation--A Summary. "   The NATS Bulletin,
      11 (September, 1954), 8.
Newton, Grace.   "The First Singing Lesson. "   The NATS
      Bulletin, 13 (February, 1957), 20.
           A helpful procedural guide to the first lesson.
Newton, Ivor.   "Accompanying Lotte Lehmann's Classes. "
      Opera, 8 (December, 1957), 742-9.
           Personal insights into Miss Lehmann's career.
Only a few practical aspects of voice teaching are discussed.
Nicholas, Louis.   "Breathing for Singing. "   The Church
      Musician, 20 (March, 1969), 5-7.
           Technical explanations and work on breathing often
confuse the intuitive or natural singer.   A practical
statement of fundamentals of breathing for singing is
clearly presented.
Nikolaidi, Elena.   "Voices Aren't Made, They Grow. "   Etude,
      January, 1950, p. 14.
           Slow, careful effort with no forcing is urged. Often
repeated advice for singers provides the bulk of the
article.
      _____.   "The Language Problem in Singing. "   An interview
      by Rose Heylbut. Etude, October, 1952, p. 13.
           With sympathy for the American student's language
problems. Flena Nikolaidi relates her own struggle with
learni   _ relearning foreign languages.
      _____.   "Be Dissatisfied and Patient. "   Music Educators
      Journal, 49 (November-December, 1962), 130.
           Appealingly open impressions of a concert artist
after having taught for two years.
Normelli, Edith Bideau.   "Tone Coloring in Singing. "   Etude,
      August, 1955, p. 22.
Novotna, Jarmila.   "Good Voice Care Means Good Singing. "
      An interview by Benjamin Brooks.   Etude, July, 1945,
      p. 384.
           The art of singing is not a series of techniques
but a unified human expression.

O'Bannon, Chester T.   "A Study in Developing an Artistic
     Interpretation of the Song. "   Unpublished D. M. A. dis-
     sertation, University of Missouri at Kansas City, 1967.
          The author designed a step-by-step study aid to
     guide the singer's preparation in learning the mechanics
     of a song and then to work and blend in his personal
     creativity, in order to arrive at an artistic interpreta-
     tion of the song.
Oncley, Paul B.   "What Acoustics Means to the Teacher of
     Singing. "   The NATS Bulletin, 8 (September-October,
     1951), 8.
          As voice teachers, we have to deal with tone
     generation and with tone quality in a particularly basic
     and critical way, and we are compelled to use the
     terminology and to discuss the facts of acoustics.
O'Neal, Scott.   "Coaching and Conducting Singers. "   Music
     Journal, 19 (September, 1961), 78.
*Orton, James L.   Voice Culture Made Easy.   3d ed. Lon-
     don: Thorsons, 1945.
          Fundamental principles of voice culture are de-
     veloped from the instructor's viewpoint.
Osborne, Conrad L.   "Bernac and Lehmann: Pupils in
     Public. "   High Fidelity/Musical America, 15 (July,
     1965), 104-105.
          A critic's review of master classes.   Some helps
     in interpretation are given.
Otis, Arthur B. ; Feen, Wallace O. ; and Rahn, Herman.
     "Mechanics of Breathing in Man. "   Journal of Applied
     Physiology, 2 (1950), 592-607.
          The mechanical work done by the respiratory
     muscles in producing the movements of breathing were
     studied.   The researchers found their conclusions in-
     sufficiently precise.   Application to singing method is
     indirect.
Owen, B. J.   "Some Fundamentals of Better Diction. "   Choir
     Guide, 13 (March, 1960), 36.
          A brief article with the major emphasis on diction
     in children's voices.   The principles are, of course,
     applicable to all.

Paul, Ouida Fay.   "Working with Singing Problems of Adults."
     The Choral Journal, 7 (May-June, 1967), 13-15.
          An important addition to the literature on singing
     problems provides the pedagogue with needed methodol-
     ogy for working with particularly severe voice prob-
     lems.   Guidelines are listed for the application of those
     techniques.

Peerce, Jan. "Reaching Fame the Hard Way. " An interview
by Stephen West. Etude, April, 1944, p. 206.
Personal reflections from a celebrated American
tenor.
Perkins, William H. ; Sawyer, Granville; and Harrison,
Peggy. "Research on Vocal Efficiency. " The NATS
Bulletin, 15 (December, 1958), 4-7.
Time honored precepts of voice teachers are sup-
ported by objective research findings.
Pescia, Astolfo. "Singing Means Production. " An interview
by Myles Fellowes. Etude, December, 1948, p. 737.
Pescia outlines some of the sensations of correct
tonal production.
_____. "Mystery of the Voice. " Musical Courier, 152
(July, 1955), 10.
The author hopes to dispel the idea that there is
a general decadence of the singing art.
Peters, Roberta. "Opportunity Needs Preparation. " An in-
terview by Rose Heylbut. Etude, April, 1956, p. 27.
A few helpful suggestions for the coloratura voice
are presented amid personal reflections of Miss Peters'
career.
_____. "Problems of a Coloratura Soprano. " Music
Journal, 17 (September, 1959), 9.
The author expresses some worthwhile personal
concepts of vocal development. The title is a misnomer, however; no problems were related.
Peterson, Abel John. "The Scientific Rationale of Voice
Production Made Applicable in Principle and Method to
the Teaching of the College Voice Class. " Unpublished
Ed. D. dissertation, University of Oregon, 1959.
This study justifies the general conclusion that
scientific findings can be utilized in the development of
vocal principles and methods of applying them when
these refer to known facts which can be applied at the
level of conscious control.
Peterson, Paul W. Natural Singing and Expressive Conducting. Rev. ed. Winston-Salem: John F. Blair Publisher,
1966.
A well-ordered and easily understood textbook that
emphasizes the same vocal techniques for the soloist
and the choir singer, the voice teacher and the choir
director.
Phemister, Virgil. "A New Look into the Singer's Throat."
Music Journal, 16 (April-May, 1958), 34.
Provocative conclusions from experiments in vocal
physiology are presented. The vowel [ɑ] requires the

smallest opening of the pharynx; therefore, the feel of
a wide open throat is not the true action of the pharynx.
Pinza, Ezio. "What Is Your Vocal Problem?" Etude, January, 1950, p. 11.
        Questions asked by Etude readers are answered.
_____. "Ability and Training." An interview by Stephen
West. Etude, February, 1953, p. 9.
        In the last analysis, one's progress depends less
on outside influences than on one's inborn capabilities.
Pitts, Carol M. "In Search of Tone." Educational Music
Magazine, 23 (November, 1943), 12-13.
        The voice is an instrument and the ability to sing
well involves as definite a technique as learning to play
a violin.
_____. "Diction." Etude, September, 1944, p. 510.
        Some established principles of good diction are
reviewed by the author.
Potter, Ralph K.; Kopp, George A.; and Kopp, Harriet
Green. Visible Speech. New York: Dover Publications, 1966.
        The use of the sound spectrograph, particularly
in the area of phonetic research, is illustrated with
patterns of speech sounds. This important volume tells
of its development, explains its use and suggests its
employment in several areas. Implications for voice
pedagogy are strong.
Pressman, Joel J., and Kelemen, George. "Physiology of
the Larynx." Physiological Reviews, 35 (July, 1955),
506-554.
        The purpose of this review was to bring together
the literature of important studies and the highlights of
the results of these studies concerning the physiology
of the larynx.
Proctor, Donald F. "The Physiologic Basis of Voice Training." Annals of the New York Academy of Sciences,
155 (November, 1968), 208.
        Special emphasis is placed upon the use of the
vital capacity, the problem of proper attack and the
control of pitch and intensity.
Protheroe, F. A. "Vocal Interference." Music Teachers
National Association. Volume of Proceedings for 1945.
Pittsburgh, Pa., 1945.
        The author urges acquisition of the one thing that
almost no singers have--singing breathing.
_____. "The Art of Singing Expressively." The South-
western Musician, 17 (December, 1950), 6.
        Agile vocalization and clarity of diction are

necessary for expressive singing.

Punt, Norman A. <u>The Singer's and Actor's Throat.</u>   Rev.
ed. London: Wm. Heinemann, 1967.
The contents of this small volume are interesting,
assimilable, reading. Written by an English laryngologist, the technical material is factual and accurate.
The title belies the scope of the book.

Puritz, Elizabeth. "The Teaching of Elisabeth Schumann. "
<u>Score,</u> 10 (December, 1954), 20-32.
A method is suggested which is devoid of scientific accuracy and wholly dependent upon extended,
exaggerated use of imagery.

_____. <u>The Teaching of Elisabeth Schumann.</u>   London:
Methuen, 1956.
The material on vocal method is an expansion of
the <u>Score</u> article above.   There is additional biographical
information.

Radamsky, Sergei. "Beware of a Teacher's Method. " <u>Opera,</u>
19 (May, 1968), 358-360.
Avoid the teacher who teaches one method for all
students.   Each student must be guided according to his
individual needs.

Ragatz, Ruth Hammond. "The Physical Approach in the
Teaching of Singing. " <u>The Southwestern Musician,</u> 18
(May, 1952), 6.

*Randegger, Alberto. <u>Singing.</u> 1880. Reprint. New York:
H. W. Gray, 1951.
A primer of vocal training.   The larger portion
of the book includes a systematic introduction of graded
vocalises.

Rasely, George. "Role of the Words Is Important in Singing. " <u>Musical America,</u> 74 (August, 1954), 25.

Raskin, Judith. "American Bel Canto. " <u>Opera News,</u> 30
(January, 1966), 6.
The author urges the development of perfection in
American diction--an American <u>bel canto.</u>   Opera in
English will then be more acceptable.

Reid, Cornelius. <u>Bel Canto: Principles and Practices.</u> New
York: Coleman-Ross Co. , 1950.
An attempt to revitalize the basic principles of
tone production employed by teachers of the <u>bel canto</u>
style.

_____. <u>The Free Voice.</u>   New York: Coleman-Ross Co. ,
1965.
The author's second major work on vocal technique
continues to stress the precepts of the early singing

masters.   Significant contributions are made in the area
of registers and of aesthetic judgment.
Resnik, Regina.   "Rounding the Circle. "   An interview by
Myles Fellowes.   Etude, May, 1948, p. 281.
    The value of a complete education for the serious
voice student is examined.
Rice, Melanie Gutman.   "Interpretation. "   The NATS Bulle-
tin, 5 (November-December, 1948), 6.
    An effort is made to define the subtleties of in-
terpretation.
Rice, William.   Basic Principles of Singing.   Nashville,
Tenn. : Abingdon Press, 1961.
    A volume for the average singer written in under-
standable, nontechnical language.
Ringel, Harvey.   "Vowel Vanish--A Vocal Deterrent. "   The
NATS Bulletin, 4 (September-October, 1947), 3.
    An excellent discussion of vowel formation and
how the "vanish" should be properly treated.
_____.   "Consonantal Deterrence. "   The NATS Bulletin, 5
(November-December, 1948), 8.
    A worthwhile contribution to that part of articula-
tion which has to do with consonants.
Ririe, Edna C.   Voice through Vitality.   Salt Lake City,
Utah: By the Author, 35 East First North Street, 1960.
    Believing that the voice will find its highest
achievement in healthful living, the author fills twenty-
four lessons with dietary suggestions, physical exer-
cises and a potpourri of verse, scripture and appropriate axioms.   Though unorthodox in many aspects, this
approach is not to be entirely dismissed.
Rodman, Molly C.   "Find Your Song!"   Music Journal, 14
(December, 1956), 12.
    An account of a piano teacher's enjoyable time in
learning to sing.
_____.   "Singers Don't Grow Old. "   Music Journal, 16
(April, 1958), 59.
    With intelligent practice and sensible care, the
voice is able to continue into old age.
Rogers, Earl.   "To Belt or Not to Belt. "   The NATS Bulle-
tin, 26 (October, 1969), 19-21.
    Useful teaching aids are reviewed that pertain to
singing a song almost exclusively in the chest voice.
Rogers, Francis.   "Secrets of Vocal Color--Its Hold upon the
Interest of the Audience. "   Etude, May, 1943, p. 307.
    The training of the voice should be fundamentally
the study of tone color.
_____.   "What Is Bel Canto Anyhow?"   Etude, Part I,

March, 1944a, p. 147; Part II, April, 1944b, p. 207;
and Part III, May, 1944c, p. 267.

A history of singing in England and Italy is outlined in the first of two parts.   Part 3 examines the
qualifications of a good teacher and finally suggests that
the reward of a good teacher is long life.   The famous
voice teachers who lived more than 70 years are listed.
_____.   "The Value of Vocal Technique. "   Etude, January,
1945, p. 15.

Several examples are given to illustrate the
author's theory that many excellent voices are lost because of improper vocal technique.

Roma, Lisa.   The Science and Art of Singing.   New York:
G. Schirmer, 1956.

Recent researches into the physiology of the singing voice fail to give credence to the "scientific" claims
made in this book.   There is much repetition of text
and illustration.   The volume is not without merit,
however.

Roman, Stella.   "The Italian and German Approaches to
Singing. "   Music Journal, 7 (July-August, 1949), 22.

The Italian and German repertoire is discussed.
The various vocal approaches of the two national
schools are compared.

Rose Alice, Sister.   "The Voice: Tool or Vehicle. " Music
Journal, 21 (March, 1963), 66.

Sound suggestions for the voice teacher and for
the student who is working toward an undergraduate degree in music education.

Rose, Arnold.   "The Italian Method and the English Singer. "
Musical Times, 96 (December, 1955), 637-638.

Differences in personality and temperament between the Englishman and the Italian are discussed and
Englishmen are encouraged to attempt the Italian's
vigorous, robust production.

_____.   The Singer and the Voice.   London: Faber and
Faber, 1962.

A thorough and comprehensive volume containing
detailed descriptions of the anatomy of the larynx, the
accessory muscles of respiration and of the resonators.
Following the chapters on physiological function, practical application to the singing art is made.

Rosewall, Richard.   Handbook of Singing.   Evanston, Ill. :
Summy-Birchard Publishing Co. , 1961.

A guide for a year's study of basic vocal techniques in the voice class and, for the young teacher,
an extended discussion about the teaching of singing.

The latter is more valuable.

Ross, William E. "Voice Teaching." The NATS Bulletin, 2 (October, 1945), 3.

The author suggests that "the singer-teacher should have a basic scientific approach to work with his singing approach; the scientist-teacher should have some conception of a singer-teacher's ways and means of getting results to correlate with his scientific facts and truths."

_____. "Vocal Objectives Defined." Music Teachers National Association. Volume of Proceedings for 1947. Pittsburgh, Pa., 1947.

The vocal objectives of quality, diction, agility, range, power and good vocal condition are briefly stated.

_____. Sing High, Sing Low. Bloomington, Ind.: By the Author, Indiana University Bookstore, 1948.

Lesson plans, primarily prepared for class voice. Revised versions of these plans may be found in the author's Secrets of Singing.

_____. "Falsetto--The Key to the High Voice." The NATS Bulletin, 5 (January-February, 1949), 5.

A favorite topic of Dr. Ross, this article offers sensible advice to the male singer.

_____. "An Objective Study of Breathing for Singing." Unpublished Ed. D. dissertation, Indiana University, 1955.

On the basis of the experiment, the general conclusion is that intercostal high abdominal breathing is conducive to the best results in singing for both male and female singers.

_____. "The High-Voice Mechanism." The NATS Bulletin, 12 (May, 1956), 14.

The author's approach to the high voice through the falsetto.

_____. Secrets of Singing. Bloomington, Ind.: By the Author, Indiana University Bookstore, 1959.

A comprehensive synthesis of vocal pedagogy. This valuable book for the inexperienced teacher includes a review of research in voice science, twenty-four lesson plans for class voice, and a wealth of techniques, devices and suggestions for solving vocal problems.

_____. "Comparative Vocal Pedagogy Basic Teacher Requirement." Music of the West, 16 (February, 1961a),3.

An acquaintance with the several philosophies of vocal instruction is urged.

_____. "The Importance of Good Technique in Singing." Music Educators Journal, 48 (September-October, 1961b), 91-95.

_____. "The Singing Teacher. " American Music Teacher,
14 (September-October, 1964), 17.
        The author delineates the basic tenets of his
teaching philosophy.
Rothmüller, M. "Evaluating Vocal Performance. " Music
Journal, 18 (March, 1960), 50.
        Few really worthwhile articles are written on this
subject; this is one of the best.
Royak, Annette. "Leonardo da Vinci on the Voice. " Music
Journal, 16 (June-July, 1958), 36-37.
        More of the writer's opinions are found in this
than those of da Vinci. The few paragraphs from the
writings of da Vinci are concerned with physiology.
Rubin, H. J. "The Neurochronaxic Theory of Voice Produc-
tion--A Refutation. " Archives of Otolaryngology, 71
(1960), 913-921.
        By diverting the air stream through the external
neck opening of tracheotomized subjects, it was possible
to obtain research data which substantiated the aerodynamic theory of voice production and refuted the
neurochronaxic theory.
_____. "Experimental Studies on Vocal Pitch and Intensity
in Phonation. " The Laryngoscope, 73 (August, 1963),
973-1015.
        Within limitations imposed by artificially activating
the larynx of an experimental animal, several aspects
of the pitch-intensity problem were studied.
_____. "Role of the Laryngologist in Management of
Dysfunctions of the Singing Voice. " The NATS Bulletin,
22 (May, 1966), 22.
        Factual statements from a laryngologist give sup-
port to empirical beliefs regarding breath support, intensity, tessitura and other facets of singing. Dysfunctions of the voice are defined and an exchange of views
is urged among the professions concerned with the voice.
_____; LeCover, C. ; and Vennard, William. "Vocal In-
tensity, Subglottic Pressure and Air Flow Relationships
in Singers. " Folia Phoniatrica, 19 (1967), 393-413.
        Using the tracheal needle and pneumotachigraphy,
the effects of variations in fundamental frequencies and
sound intensities on transglottic air flow and subglottic
air pressure were studied in singers. Among several
conclusions, it was found that air flow is not the major
factor in supporting a tone of increasing loudness.
Runkel, Howard W. "On Stage Fright. " The NATS Bulletin,
12, (September, 1955), 16.
        Several hypotheses concerning the cause of stage

fright in public performance are advanced. This is a thoughtful analysis of the subject and well worth reading.

Rushmore, Robert. "The Singing Voice: First Sounds." Opera News, 31 (January 21, 1967a), 24.

An excellent series on various facets of singing includes this and the articles below by the same author. They are an important contribution to the literature on singing.

_____. "The Singing Voice: The Magic of the Singing Voice." Opera News, 31 (January 28, 1967b), 24.

_____. "The Singing Voice: Light and Soaring." Opera News, 31 (February 4, 1967c), 28.

_____. "The Singing Voice: Rarest of All." Opera News, 31 (February 11, 1967d), 28.

_____. "The Singing Voice: Lower and Darker." Opera News, 31 (February 18, 1967e), 24.

_____. "The Singing Voice: Heroes and Peach Fuzz." Opera News, 31 (February 25, 1967f), 26.

_____. "The Singing Voice: The Lower Depths." Opera News, 31 (March 11, 1967g), 28.

_____. "The Singing Voice: National Types." Opera News, 31 (March 18, 1967h), 22.

_____. "The Singing Voice: Indisposed." Opera News, 31 (March 25, 1967i), 28.

_____. "The Singing Voice: Ages of Man." Opera News, 31 (April 1, 1967j), 26.

_____. The Singing Voice. New York: Dodd, Mead, 1971.

An important, comprehensive storehouse of information about noted singers and the singing art.

*Russell, G. Oscar. The Vowel, Its Physiological Mechanism as Shown by X-Ray. 1928. Reprint. College Park, Md.: McGrath, 1970.

Ruth, Wilhelm. "The Registers of the Singing Voice." The NATS Bulletin, 19 (May, 1963), 2-5.

Important early research in X-ray tomography in Germany provides further substantiation of the actuality of registers in the voice.

_____. "The Cause of Individual Differences in the Sensation of Head Resonance in Singing." The NATS Bulletin, 23 (October, 1966), 20.

This research paper reports on recent efforts to explain the physiological causes of individual differences in the sensation of head resonance.

Sabin, Robert. "Werrenrath Urges Young Singers to Form
    Correct Habits at Beginning." Musical America, 72
    (November, 1952), 21.
        Sound advice on many subjects is given to the
    young student; personal reminiscenses are also in-
    cluded.
    _____. "Impulse Is Everything--An Interview with Samuel
    Margolis." Musical America, 73 (December, 1953), 19.
        A noted voice teacher relates the basic tenets of
    his teaching procedures.
Sacerdote, G. G. "Researches on the Singing Voice."
    Acustica, 7 (1957), 61-68.
        Some recent methods of electroacoustical analysis
    are employed to study some parameters characteristic
    of the singing voice. Particular attention is given the
    behaviour of the vibrato.
Samoiloff, Lazar. "The Singer's Intelligence." An interview
    by Juliette Laine. Etude, January, 1943, p. 61.
        The "singer's intelligence" is an ability to hear
    and see himself objectively.
Samuel, John Owen. "When Should the Study of Voice Be
    Started?" Music Teachers National Association.
    Volume of Proceedings for 1948. Pittsburgh, Pa., 1948.
        The author hopes to dispel the fear of training an
    immature voice.
    _____. Modern Voice Lessons. Rev. ed. Garfield
    Heights, Ohio: By the Author, 9421 Birchwood Road,
    1950.
        Thirty-six chapters on basic vocal technique are
    included in this revision of the author's 1938 publication
    Thirty-Six Modern Voice Lessons in How To Sing. A
    conventional approach is employed.
Sayão, Bidu. "Performer--or Artist?" An interview by
    Rose Heylbut. Etude, December, 1953, p. 12.
        Remarks concerning a genuine, unaffected inter-
    pretation.
Schiøtz, Aksel. The Singer and His Art. New York: Harper
    and Row, 1970.
        The heart of this book is the singer's approach to
    his music and its interpretation. The art song, the
    oratorio, and the opera must be approached in different
    ways. The volume is lucid, straight forward, and ex-
    tremely valuable in learning style and interpretation.
Schmalstieg, Emily B. "The Development and Evaluation of
    Programmed Instruction in Singing Correctly Produced,
    Uniform Vowels." Unpublished Ed. D. dissertation, Pa.
    State University, 1969.

Through the development and evaluation of an
aural-visual programmed course in the recognition and
production of correctly sung, uniform vowels, the author
sought to determine whether or not a relationship
existed between vowel production test scores of subjects
and musicality, and vowel production test scores of
subjects and scholastic aptitude.

Schmidt, Reinhold. "Diction in Singing." The Southwestern
Musician, 17 (October, 1950), 11.
Emphasis is given the role of consonants in artic
ulation.

_____. "Bricks Without Straw." The NATS Bulletin, 10
(January-February, 1954), 6.
An appeal for solid vocal foundations. The
"bricks" in the discussion are the messages which the
singer sends out through the instrumentality of his
voice, and the "straw" is his understanding of how his
vocal instrument is played.

Schnelker, J. "Some Musical Factors in Interpretation."
The NATS Bulletin, 13 (December, 1956), 14-15.
Learning the notes of a composition and performing them correctly mark only the initial stage in the
study of a musical work.

Schoep, Arthur. "The Singer and His Text." The NATS
Bulletin, 24 (February, 1968), 14.
A forceful plea for the increased use of English
translation in Lieder and in opera.

Schweisheimer, Waldemar. "Musicians and Digestion--
Physical Influences on the Efficiency of Composers,
Musicians, and Singers." Etude, May, 1946, p. 244.
The writer tells how the sensitive nature of active
musicians makes them prone to physical influences of
all sorts. He reveals various dietary concoctions of a
few musicians.

Scott, Anthony. "A Study of the Components of the Singing
Tone Utilizing the Audio Spectrum Analyzer." The
NATS Bulletin, 24 (May, 1968), 40-41.
The author urges electronic analysis of voices
once yearly to make sure the components are in the
right proportion.

Scott, Charles Kennedy. The Fundamentals of Singing.
London: Cassell and Co., 1954.
Comprehensive in scope, this book has much to
commend it, although its verbosity encourages only the
most inquisitive mind to draw from its wealth of ideas.
The first half of the book might be aptly entitled
"Essays on the Singing Art."

Scott, David W.   "A Study of the Effect of Changes in Vocal
    Intensity upon the Harmonic Structure of Selected Sing-
    ing Tones Produced by Female Singers. "   Unpublished
    Mus. D. dissertation, Indiana University, 1960.
        Within the limitations of the research, it was
    found that all harmonic partials, except the first, de-
    crease with the decrease in tone intensity.   The first
    partial remained constant.
Seltzer, Albert P.   "The Singer's Voice and the Sinuses of
    the Nose. "   Etude, May, 1951, p. 17.
        A physician writes that healthful sinus conditions
    are essential to a resonant, musical singing tone.
Seward, William.   "A Conversation with Amelita Galli-Curci."
    HiFi/Stereo Review, 13 (July, 1964), 50-55.
        Galli-Curci, in a rare interview, seeks to "help
    the vocal student to re-orient himself toward a saner
    outlook on the art of bel canto. "
Sharnova, Sonia.   "Diction. "   The NATS Bulletin, 3 (June-
    July, 1947), 4.
        Some random thoughts on singing diction stress
    how closely allied are diction and singing artistry.
_____.   "Breath Control--Foundation of Singing and Acting
    Technique. "   Music Journal, 7 (March-April, 1949), 36.
        The author reviews the "fads" of vocal approach
    and then directs the attention of the student to the
    proper foundation--breath control.
_____.   "The Free Throat for Singing. "   American Choral
    Review, 6 (July, 1964), 14-15.
        A personal approach to vocal production is ex-
    plained; particular emphasis is given vowel formation.
Shaw, George Bernard.   Shaw on Music.   Edited by Eric
    Bentley.   Garden City, N. Y. : Doubleday and Co. , 1955.
        This book is compiled from earlier publications
    of Shaw's musical criticism.   Provocative, entertaining
    and ever-current, these reviews reveal Shaw's intimate
    knowledge of the voice.
Shaw, Hollace.   "Important Secrets of Vocal Tone. "   An in-
    terview by Gunnar Asklund.   Etude, January, 1948,
    p. 15.
        Various concepts which were helpful to Miss Shaw
    and which she would suggest to students in their study.
Shearon, Wallace Ethan, Jr.   "A Rationale of the Teaching
    of Voice in the Liberal Arts College. "   Unpublished
    Ph. D. dissertation, Indiana University, 1966.
        Concepts of liberal arts study and voice study
    were compared.   Within the framework of the study, the
    investigator found distinct parallelism between the goals

and purpose of liberal arts and that of voice.

Shenk, Louis.   "We Must Find the Answer."   Etude, Part I,
January, 1950a, p. 20; Part II, February, 1950b,
p. 14; Part III, March, 1950c, p. 20; and Part IV,
April, 1950d, p. 26.

Vowel formation, general diction concepts and
breathing are discussed at length.

Siegle, Laurence W.   "An Investigation of Possible Correlation between the Chronaxy of a Branch of the Accessory
Nerve and Voice Classification."   Unpublished Mus. D.
dissertation, Indiana University, 1964.

The study revealed a correlation between chronaxy
and voice classification for the subjects tested.   The
correlation differed for trained and untrained singers.

Siepe, Cesare.   "Forget about Your Throat."   An interview
by Myles Fellowes.   Etude, June, 1952, p. 26.

The noted bass states that the essence of the
artist is the ability to forget self and serve the meaning of the music.

_____.   "Caring for the Voice."   An interview by Rose
Heylbut.   Etude, January, 1956, p. 14.

Diligent and careful practice, diction, breathing,
and registers are discussed.   The article is sensible
and worthwhile.

Simmons, Otis D.   "Neurophysiology and Muscular Function
of the Vocal Mechanism: Implications for Singers and
Teachers of Singing."   The NATS Bulletin, 22 (October,
1965), 22.

The study was made to provide the singer and the
teacher of singing a precise vocabulary and a body of
scientific knowledge pertinent to the neurophysiology and
muscular function of the voice under singing conditions.

_____.   "A Conceptual Approach to Singing."   The NATS
Bulletin, 26 (October, 1969), 15-17.

The conceptual approach to singing addresses itself to four fundamental principles: (1) a clear mental
image of all tones, (2) frequent demonstrations by the
teacher of correct vocal production, (3) the ability of
the singer to listen critically with his "inner ear," and
(4) systematic practice.

Simpson, James F.   "Principles for Teaching Young Voices."
The NATS Bulletin, 21 (May, 1965), 2-3.

A better title for this article would be "The Necessity of Establishing Singing Goals."   It offers little
specific help in approaching the young voice.

Skiles, Wilbur A.   "The Fundamentals of Good Voice Production."   Etude, Part I, June, 1943a, p. 375 and

Part II, July, 1943b, p. 441.

    Step-by-step vocalises are described and their use is encouraged in order to achieve freedom of vocal production.

Slater, Frank. "The Art of Singing and the Science of Teaching It. " The Southwestern Musician, 16 (February, 1950), 6.

    Personal reflections on teachers and teaching. Some worthy ideas are given in an unorganized manner.

Smith, Ethel C. "An Electromyographic Investigation of the Relationship between Abdominal Muscular Effort and the Rate of Vocal Vibrato. " The NATS Bulletin, 26 (May-June, 1970), 2.

    Conclusive findings revealed that when the subglottic air pressure within the trachea is directly or indirectly affected by expiratory muscles, controlled pressure applied to four expiratory muscles does result in an alteration of the ratio of the muscle action potential to the rate of vocal vibrato during the act of singing.

Smith, Kay. "Your Voice--It's the Only One You Have. " Musart, 24 (September-October, 1971), 14.

    Through an open letter to high school students, the author provides basic guidelines for sensible vocal habits.

Sonninen, Aatto A. "Is the Length of the Vocal Cords the Same at All Different Levels of Singing. " Acta Oto-Laryngologica, Suppl. 118 (1954), 219-231.

    The study revealed that the vocal cords lengthen with an increase in frequency. The maximal lengthening in going from lowest to highest pitch was four millimeters on an average. In none of the subjects studied did the vocal cords lengthen proportionally with the ascent in the scale.

_____. "The Role of the External Laryngeal Muscles in Length-Adjustment of the Vocal Cords in Singing. " Acta Oto-Laryngologica, Suppl. 130 (1956), 1-102.

    Studies of the mechanism of pitch change in the human voice with special reference to the function of the sternothyroid.

Stanley, Douglas. Your Voice: Applied Science of Vocal Art. Rev. ed. New York: Pitman Publishing Corp. , 1950.

    A controversial approach which suggests the use of a tongue instrument and external manipulation of the hyoid bone and larynx. Great emphasis is placed on the "purification" of the registers. The author does not

claim a method, but nevertheless condemns approaches
other than his own.

_____. The Science of Voice. 4th ed., rev. New York:
Carl Fischer, 1958.
    "The mother work" of a foremost advocate of
mechanistic voice building.

_____; Chadbourne, E. Thomas A.; and Chadbourne, Norma
J. Singer's Manual. Boston: Stanley Society, 1950.
    Part 1 is a biographical sketch of Stanley, a
critique of his philosophy, and reprints of articles
written by him. Parts 2, 3, 4 and 5 are concerned
with fundamentals, breath pressure, registers and how
to study and teach singing.

Stanton, Royal. Steps to Singing for Voice Class. Belmont,
Calif.: Wadsworth, 1971.
    A book for beginning singers and nonmusic majors
which incorporates numerous popular concepts of voice
training.

Steber, Eleanor. "Prepare for Good Luck." An interview
by Gunnar Asklund. Etude, July, 1946, p. 64.
    Helpful suggestions for daily practice habits are
given.

_____. "Let's Recognize American Singers." Music
Journal, 18 (April-May, 1960), 9.
    A pointed and convincing article which describes
the plight of the American singer in his own country.

Stevens, Rise. "Make the Right Start!" An interview by
Rose Heylbut. Etude, May, 1947, p. 245.
    Personal reflections on Miss Stevens' early years
of study. Some paragraphs about voice classifying are
especially worthwhile.

Stewart, Cecil. "Concomitant Learning for Teacher and
Pupil." The NATS Bulletin, 6 (February-March, 1950),
6.
    The teacher learns from the pupil and is en-
couraged to profit from the learning experience.

Stignani, Ebe. "The Elements of Bel Canto." An interview
by Stephen West. Etude, June, 1949, p. 350.
    Mme. Stignani writes what she conceives is nec-
essary to "make singing beautiful."

Stocker, Leonard. "The Singer as Actor." The NATS Bulletin, 21 (December, 1964), 8-9.
    The author convincingly explains why acting is
helpful to the student of singing.

Stout, Barrett. "Dynamics of the Human Voice." Music
Teachers National Association. Volume of Proceedings
for 1944. Pittsburgh, Pa., 1944.

An experiment to determine the functional singing
area of the voice by discovering its intensity range.

_____. "An Analysis of the Pupil's Problem in Learning
to Sing." American Music Teacher, 4 (January-February, 1955a), 10-11.

The author relates the acoustical phenomena which
produces sound and discusses to some length those processes which are subject to the will.

_____. "The Management of the Resonating System in
Singing." American Music Teacher, 4 (March-April,
1955b), 6.

Interesting and helpful physical actions, which are
correlated to vocal goals, are performed sometime by
the teacher and sometime by the students. They are
convincingly stated.

Strickling, George F. "Ship or Sheep?" Educational Music
Magazine, 31 (September-October, 1951), 25.

A careful approach to singing diction is urged.

Strongin, Lillian. "What Is Bel Canto?" The NATS Bulletin, 22 (December, 1965), 14.

Quotations from Lamperti and William Earl Brown
provide the substance of this article. The author contributes no original thoughts.

Stults, Walter A. "Master Teachers of Singing." The
Southwestern Musician, 16 (June, 1950), 4.

After an introductory essay on the controversies
of the profession in the formulation of pedagogical principles, the three master teachers of nature, common
sense, and experience are discussed at length. A
roster of great singing teachers of the past is included.

_____. "Polarity ... Secret of Great Singing." The
Southwestern Musician, 17 (May, 1951), 15.

The physical law of polarity is applied to the
vocal situation. The process of phonation must be
counterbalanced by a properly resisting force.

_____. "Polarity, Its Relation to, and Influence upon the
Singing Voice." The NATS Bulletin, 12 (September,
1955), 3.

_____. "Expressive Singing Technique Based on Law of
Polarity." Music of the West, 16 (October, 1960), 22.

Suckling, Norman. "The Neglected Art of Singing." Monthly
Musical Record, 86 (July-August, 1956), 143-145.

In a radical article, the author suggests that the
singers of today give emphasis to the wrong qualities;
the chief culprits are "warm, emotional tone" and the
vibrato. The purity of the boy soprano voice is suggested as ideal.

Sullivan, Ernest G.   "An Experimental Study of the Relationships between Physical Characteristics and Subjective
Evaluation of Male Voice Quality in Singing. "   Unpublished Ph. D. dissertation, Indiana University, 1956.
An attempt to determine the physical attributes of
vocal tone which contribute to subjective judgments of
excellence of voice quality.
Sunderman, Lloyd Frederick.   Basic Vocal Instructor.   Rock-
ville Centre, N. Y. :   Belwin, 1958.
A useful, well-devised volume for beginning study.
The author stresses resonance sensation and examines
register development more precisely than is usually
found in books on singing fundamentals.
_____. Artistic Singing: Its Tone Production and Basic
Understandings.   Metuchen, N. J. :   Scarecrow Press,
1970.
Designed primarily for choral directors as well
as the soloist.   In addition to 22 specific lessons on
vowel, consonant and diphthongal action, there are
principal chapters on tone register development, resonance development and diction.
Svanholm, Set.   "Imitation,   Its Use and Abuse. "   An interview by Gunnar Asklund.   Etude, September, 1948,
p. 540.
An important advance a singer can make is to
hear his own recorded voice and "imitate himself. "
The Swedish tenor comments on both the advantages
and disadvantages of imitation in singing.
Swarthout, Gladys.   "Your Vocal Problem. "   Etude, February, 1950, p. 16.
The author answers questions asked of her by
readers of Etude.
Swing, Dolf.   "Your Pupil and His Artistic Development. "
The NATS Bulletin, 9 (May-June, 1953), 6.
The author gives his attention to the "middle
years" of vocal study that are devoted to building interpretative powers.

Taff, Merle E.   "An Acoustic Study of Vowel Modification
and Register Transition in the Male Singing Voice. "
The NATS Bulletin, 22 (December, 1965), 8.
Spectrographic analysis was made of octave scales
as sung by trained singers on certain vowel tones.
Analysis revealed that the subjects made significant
changes in the formant frequencies of all vowels at or
near the point of register transition as determined by
jury evaluation.

Tagliavini, Ferrucio. "Let Your Ear Be Your Master. " An
    interview by Rose Heylbut. Etude, October, 1948,
    p. 581.
            Tagliavini tells of his work and his views on sing-
    ing. An interesting portion of the article relates his
    early opposition to music study and a performing career.
Tarneaud, Jean. "A Psychological and Clinical Study of the
    Pneumophonic Synergy. " The NATS Bulletin, 14 (Feb-
    ruary, 1958), 12-15.
            The coordination of breathing and phonation,
    pneumophonic synergy, is an essential factor of voice
    production.
Tarnóczy, Thomas A. "The Opening Time and Open Quotient
    of the Vocal Folds During Phonation. " Journal of the
    Acoustical Society of America,   23 (January, 1951),
    42-44.
            Two factors play a part in the final shaping of a
    sound picture: the cord-tones and the resonators. This
    paper deals with the cord-tones and with the peculiari-
    ties of vibrations of the vocal cords.
Taylor, Bernard U.   Group Voice--A Systematic Course in
    Singing for Use in Group Instruction.   Rev. ed. New
    York: G. Schirmer, 1950.
            A series of 20 lessons designed to cover a period
    of study 30 to 40 weeks long.   Local effort devices are
    prevalent.
_____.   "Good Voice Teachers Don't Like It Either. "
    Music Journal, 9 (January, 1951a), 15.
            Efforts to raise the ethical standards of the pro-
    fession and to foster a commonly understood terminol-
    ogy are discussed.
_____.   "Teaching Objectives. "   The NATS Bulletin, 8
    (September-October, 1951b), 6.
            The author explains why he believes that the
    "Psychological-technical" approach to the teaching of
    singing is the most desirable.
Taylor, Robert M.   "Acoustics as an Aid to Ease of Sing-
    ing. " The NATS Bulletin, 12 (November, 1955), 19-20.
            An article designed to discuss and correct some
    of the misconceptions which quite often are found to be
    the basis of more or less unconscious tensions when
    the student is subject to misapprehensions regarding the
    physical basis of singing.
_____.   Acoustics for the Singer.   Emporia, Kansas:
    Kansas State Teachers College, 1958.
            This informative research study provides scientific
    explanations of acoustical phenomena in language

assimilable for the beginning college student and is helpful concerning the application and investigation of acoustical principles in studio procedures. This annotator is not aware of another contribution to the above need.

Tebaldi, Renata. "Good Vocal Habits. " An interview by Rose Heylbut. Etude, May-June, 1957, p. 13.

Tebaldi comments on an operatic career and some personal history. Practice habits and admonitions to young singers against a forced voice production are given.

Teyte, Maggie. "A Philosophy of Vocal Study. " An interview by Rose Heylbut. Etude, January, 1946, p. 5.

Breathing, daily practice and interpretation are emphasized.

Thain, Howard. "Gigli's Advice for Young Singers. " Music Journal, 27 (October, 1969), 48.

An assessment of a few qualities which Gigli felt were indispensable in order that the singer might reach full artistic maturity.

Thayer, Lilian Aldrich. "Emphasizing Overtones in Voice Study. " Etude, April, 1946, p. 195.

The author uses physiological terms somewhat at variance with common usage. She presents an interesting theory which, in its presentation, lacks scientific stature.

Thebom, Blanche. "Conquering Tensions. " An interview by Allison Paget. Etude, July, 1948, p. 411.

Helpful hints on how to avoid undue tensions in performance. Emphasis is given to thorough preparation.

_____. "The Amazing Versatility of American Singers. " An interview by Leroy V. Brant. Etude, June, 1953, p. 11.

Miss Thebom expresses her belief in the initiative of the would-be artists of America and asks that teachers properly challenge their pupils.

Theman, Karl. "A Musical Approach to Singing. " The NATS Bulletin, 4 (February-March, 1948), 5.

The author feels that the messa di voce is the most valuable tone and voice builder. He explains the value of its application to such matters as "stage fright" and diction as well as tonal progress.

Thibault, Conrad. "The Secret of Song Speech. " An interview by Gunnar Asklund. Etude, December, 1946, p. 669.

The interrelation between tone production and

enunciation is emphasized.

Thomas, John Charles. "Color in Singing. " An interview
by Rose Heylbut. Etude, November, 1943, p. 701.
     Vital points of basic production concerning reso-
nance and singing diction.

Thomson, Virgil. "Too Many Languages. " The NATS Bulletin, 6 (April-May, 1950), 2.
     A noted composer and critic regrets that tradition
forces young vocalists to sing four languages and all of
them badly.   This article later became a portion of his
book Music Right and Left (New York: Henry Holt and
Co. , 1951).

Thornfield, Emil A.   Singing Diction, from Thornfield's
"Tongue and Lip Training. "   Revised and edited by
Ralph Jusko.   Toledo, Ohio: Gregorian Institute of
America, 1954.
     A technique of "accurate and distinct word-pro-
duction. " First published in 1915.

Thorpe, Clarence R.   Teach Yourself to Sing.   London:
English Universities Press, 1954.
     Written in extremely plain language and planned
for the student who chooses to learn independently.

Tkach, Peter.   Vocal Technic.   Park Ridge, Ill. : Neil A.
Kjos Music Co. , 1948.
     The first half of this book presents vocal funda-
mentals through a series of progressive vocalises and
songs; the latter portion of the book is devoted to sight
singing.   A teacher's manual and a student's book are
published separately.

_____.   Vocal Artistry.   Park Ridge, Ill. : Neil A. Kjos
Music Co. , 1950.
     Vocal Artistry is a continuation of the author's
first book, Vocal Technic.   The subject is covered in
depth and worthwhile material is found here.

Tomlins, William L.   Song and Life.   Boston: C. C.
Birchard and Co. , 1945.
     A compilation of Tomlins' writings and lectures,
in which he sought the awakening and expression of the
inner life through rhythm, the song voice and a good
attitude.   Particular emphasis is placed on breathing
as the essence of life.

Topping, Clorinda.   "How to Study a Song. " The NATS Bulletin, 14 (December, 1957), 28.
     This approach to song study is primarily speech
centered.

Toren, E. Clifford.   "The Student-Teacher Partnership in
the Study of Singing. " The NATS Bulletin, 12 (Novem-

ber, 1955), 16.

Emphasis is upon the student's obligations and responsibilities as he comes to the studio for voice lessons.

*Tosi, Pietro Francesco. Observations on the Florid Song. Translated by J. E. Galliard. 2d ed., with a new preface by Paul Henry Lang. New York: Johnson Reprint Corp., 1968.

An important 1720 essay on vocal techniques continues to be significant to our reading and usage.

Tourel, Jennie. "A Basis for Good Singing." An interview by Allison Paget. Etude, March, 1943, p. 154.

The secret of good vocal production lies in a complete mastery of breath support.

Traubel, Helen. "Make Haste Slowly." An interview by Rose Heylbut. Etude, January, 1943, p. 5-6.

The responsibility of successful work rests upon the individual singer.

Treash, Leonard. "The Importance of Vowel Sounds and Their Modification in Producing Good Tone." The NATS Bulletin, 4 (November-December, 1947), 3.

A singer should strive for an evenly produced scale of pure vowel sound with no modification whatsoever.

_____. "Vocal Workmanship." The NATS Bulletin, 5 (November-December, 1948), 4.

The author seeks to encourage that seldom encountered ability to drill vocal, musical and interpretive features into the reflexes of a singer in such a way that, in his performance, he may sing the way he intended to sing with reasonable consistency.

Triplett, W. M. "An Investigation Concerning Vowel Sounds of High Pitches." The NATS Bulletin, 23 (March, 1967), 6.

Easily understood and well-written, this technical research gives insight into the singing of certain vowel sounds on high pitches.

Truby, H. M. "Contribution of the Pharyngeal Cavity to Vowel Resonance and in General." Journal of the Acoustical Society of America, 34 (December, 1962), 1978.

The researcher found that the pharyngeal cavities vary in shapes and sizes predictably and characteristically for any given sound.

Trusler, Ivan and Ehret, Walter. Functional Lessons in Singing. Englewood Cliffs, N. J.: Prentice-Hall, 1960.

A series of 18 lessons, designed primarily for

class voice, are structured around specific vowels,
diphthongs or consonants. Fundamentals of singing are
included in the first 12 lessons. The physiological
descriptions concerning breathing are misleading. Eight-
een songs, usable for study, are included.

Tucker, Richard. "The First Step Is Honesty." An interview by Rose Heylbut. Etude, November, 1954, p. 13.
       This is one of the most helpful of the Etude
articles by noted singers. The areas discussed are
resonance (bel canto with masque), patience (Mozart
before Verdi) and interesting personal philosophies.

_____. "Proceed with Caution." Music Journal, 20
(April, 1962), 24-25.
       The famed tenor writes convincingly on the
dangers of approaching difficult dramatic arias before
sufficient maturity and training are achieved. The
folly of imitation of great artists is also stressed.

*Ulrich, Bernhard. Concerning the Principles of Vocal
Training in the A Capella Period, 1474-1640. Translated by John Seale. Milwaukee: Pro Musica Press,
1968.
       First English translation of a 1910 Leipzig publi-
cation. A comprehensive treatment of Renaissance
vocal teachings.

Uris, Dorothy. "English Can Be Sung." Musical Courier,
154 (December, 1956), 7.
       A defense of English as a singing language.

_____. To Sing in English. New York: Boosey and
Hawkes, 1971.
       A comprehensive guide to intelligible delivery of
American English. The contents will prove useful to
singers, voice teachers, coaches, choral directors,
and others.

Vail, James S. "Dicshun." Educational Music Magazine,
32 (March, 1953), 22-24.
       A basic approach to good diction.

van den Berg, Janwillem. "On the Air Resistance and the
Bernoulli Effect of the Human Larynx." Journal of the
Acoustical Society of America, 29 (May, 1957), 626-
631.
       The research is implicational to the teaching of
singing in respect to the falsetto and the chest register.

_____. "On the Myoelastic-aerodynamic Theory of Voice

Production. " The NATS Bulletin, 14 (May, 1958), 6-12.
_____. "Vocal Ligaments versus Registers. " The NATS
Bulletin, 20 (December, 1963), 16-21.
     A technical article in which the author reports on
a new concept of the origin of the main registers.
Practical application to the singing pedagogue is difficult to discern.
_____. "Register Problems. " Annals of the New York
Academy of Sciences, 155 (November, 1968), 129-134.
     The author provides physiological explanations in-
volved in singing as it relates to vocal registers.
_____, and Vennard, William. "Toward an Objective Vo-
cabulary for Voice Pedagogy. " The NATS Bulletin, 15
(February, 1959), 10.
     The writers suggest that, through recorded
samples and acoustical analysis of singing tones, a
beginning could be made for a more objective vocabulary. The process is extensively explained by a study
of selected vague concepts.
Van der Veer, Nevada. "What Are We Doing With the Individual Voice?" Music Teachers National Association.
Volume of Proceedings for 1944. Pittsburgh, Pa. , 1944.
     A personal plea for high standards in singing.
Van Grove, Isaac. "The Vocal Studio: Idols and Ideals. "
The NATS Bulletin, 25 (February, 1969), 3.
     Speaking from a very wide experience, the author
urges a continued striving for high ideals in the voice
studio.
Varkonyi, Louise. "The Singer's Lie Detector. " American
Record Guide, 26 (February, 1960), 414-415.
     A voice teacher explains why the tape recorder is
the "singer's lie detector. "
Varnay, Astrid. "Opportunity and the Ability to Grasp It. "
An interview by Myles Fellowes. Etude, October, 1943,
p. 643.
     It is a mistake to sing sustained and difficult music
before the voice is ready to support it technically. But
once it is ready, it is an equal mistake to postpone the
approach to full serious study.
_____. "Hear Yourself As Others Hear You. " An inter-
view by Annabel Comfort. Etude, May, 1952, p. 10.
     An article, pointed and purposeful, about the need
for accurate self-analysis.
Veld, Henry. "The Effects of Choral Singing on the Solo
Voice. " Music Teachers National Association. Volume
of Proceedings for 1948. Pittsburgh, Pa. , 1948.
     A discussion of the advantages and disadvantages

of the young singer's participation in vocal ensembles.
Vennard, William.   "'Natural Singing' Termed a Fallacy."
     Musical Courier, 147 (February, 1953a), 13.
          A brief article fostering the concept that singing
     artistry is a developed skill, not a natural phenomenon.
_____.   "How to Sing High Tones."   Music of the West,
     8 (August, 1953b), 5.
_____.   "More Than Teaching."   American Music Teach-
     er, 3 (November-December, 1953c), 6.
          The voice teacher must do "more than teach"; he
     must inspire each student to his full potential.
_____.   "Three Ways to Sing Softly."   The NATS Bulle-
     tin, 11 (February, 1955), 5.
          Selective use of various colorings of the falsetto
     is suggested; used as illustration are some suitable ex-
     amples from vocal literature.
_____.   "Pitch Difficulties."   The NATS Bulletin, 12
     (May, 1956), 4-5.
          A practical analysis of pitch problems in singing
     and some general suggestions for improving intonation.
_____.   "Some Implications of the Husson Research."
     The NATS Bulletin, 13 (February, 1957), 4.
          Husson believes that the vibration of the vocal
     cords is an active process controlled by the brain via
     the recurrent nerve.   Vennard suggests that the Husson
     theory throws light on the controversial subject of re-
     gistration.
_____.   "Philosophies of Vocal Pedagogy."   American
     Music Teacher, 7 (May-June, 1958), 4-5.
          An important survey of various theories of vocal
     pedagogy.   The author includes a valuable analysis of
     each approach.
_____.   "Registration."   Music Journal, 17 (March,
     1959a), 45.
          The idealistic, realistic and hypothetical concepts
     of registration are clearly and interestingly outlined.
_____.   "Some Implications of the Sonninen Research."
     The NATS Bulletin, 15 (May, 1959b), 8-12.
          An objective study of the external musculature of
     the larynx is examined in the light of useful pedagogical
     implications.
_____.   "Tricks of the Trade."   Music of the West, 14
     (July, 1959c), 5.
          In a two-page article, the author lists many
     teaching devices which he finds useful.
_____.   "The Bernoulli Effect in Singing."   The NATS
     Bulletin, 17 (February, 1961a), 8.

The glottis can be vibrated by breath alone under the influence of the Bernoulli principle.

_____. "Singers and Science. " Showcase, 41 (Winter, 1961b-1962), 8-9.
A fundamental defense of the position of science and voice physiology in singing.

_____. "Building Correct Singing Habits. " Voice and Speech Disorders. Edited by Nathaniel M. Levin. Springfield, Ill. : Charles C Thomas, Publisher, 1962.

_____. "An Experiment to Evaluate the Importance of Nasal Resonance. " Folia Phoniatrica, 16 (1964a), 146-153.

_____. "The Psychology of the Pupil-Teacher Relationship. " American Music Teacher, 13 (May-June, 1964b), 8-9.
A significant statement by a foremost advocate of the "mechanistic approach" on the more subtle aspects of vocal pedagogy.

_____. Singing: The Mechanism and the Technic. 4th ed. New York: Carl Fischer, 1967.
An important and exhaustive treatment of voice instruction from a mechanistic viewpoint. A book which should be studied by every serious student of the singing art.

_____. "Singers and Their Emotions. " American Music Teacher, 20 (April-May, 1971), 24.
A concise discussion of a variety of emotions that are helpful or detrimental to the mental health of the singer. Comments on stage fright are particularly helpful.

_____; Hirano, Minoru; and Ohala, John. "Laryngeal Synergy in Singing. " The NATS Bulletin, 27 (October, 1970), 16-21.
Electromyography is an important tool in the study of physiology. When a muscle is active a minute electrical charge is present. If a needle is inserted in the tissues it can transmit this to a sensitive recorder that will register its voltage, and hence the degree to which the muscle is exerting itself. By this means, it is now possible to state definitely how the most important muscles of the voicebox behave in the performance of many tasks.

_____. "Chest, Head, and Falsetto. " The NATS Bulletin, 27 (December, 1970), 30-37.
Using electromyographic investigation, certain intrinsic musculature was identified as to function in the chest, head and falsetto registers.

_____, and Hirano, Minoru. "Varieties of Voice Produc-
tion. " The NATS Bulletin, 27 (February-March, 1971),
26-32.

      Figurative expressions (normal, breathy, pinched,
etc.) more or less used by teachers of singing to describe right and wrong ways to sing, are discussed in
the light of this electromyographic investigation.

_____; Hirano, Minoru; and Fritzell, Björn. "The Ex-
trinsic Laryngeal Muscles. " The NATS Bulletin, 27
(May-June, 1971), 22-30.

_____, and Irwin, James W. "Speech and Song Compared
in Sonagrams. " The NATS Bulletin, 23 (December,
1966), 18-23.

      This comparison strongly suggests that "the
slogan, 'sing as you speak' or at least, 'sing as you
should speak' holds good in most vowels and almost
all consonants. "

_____, and Isshiki, Nobuhiko. "Coup de Glotte. " The
NATS Bulletin, 20 (February, 1964), 15.

      A review of the literature both erroneous and
accurate concerning the coup de glotte. A defense is
made of Garcia's original concept. In conclusion, the
authors suggest avoidance of the term because of the
prevalent misunderstanding of it.

_____, and von Leden, Hans. "The Importance of In-
tensity Modulation in the Perception of a Trill. " Folia
Phoniatrica, 19 (1967), 19-26.

      The authors have conducted an experiment which
extends somewhat the vibrato research of the Seashore
group at the University of Iowa.

"Vocal Success Factors Told by Coast Teacher. " Musical
Courier, 145 (June, 1952), 31.

      The greatest factors in becoming a singer are
wish, desire, urge, want.

von Leden, Hans. "The Mechanism of Phonation. " Archives
of Otolaryngology, 74 (1961), 660-676.

      On the basis of his personal investigation, the
author reached the conclusion that the Husson neuro-
muscular theory of vocal production does not meet the
test of scientific analysis.

Voorhees, Irving W. "Oh Doctor, My Throat!" Etude,
January, 1953a, p. 18.

      A physician, who has been a counselor to singers
for many years, has advice concerning the care which
should be given the singer's voice.

_____. "Do You Know the Symptoms of Vocal Strain?
What Causes Hoarseness? Will a Tonsillectomy Hurt

My Voice?" <u>Music Clubs Magazine,</u> 33 (November, 1953b), 5-6.

_____. "The Voice Physician. " <u>Music Journal,</u> 8 (April, 1955), 40-41.

> Cooperation of physician and singing teacher is urged in the treatment of vocal disturbances.

_____. "A Singer's Contribution to Science (Garcia's Invention of the Laryngoscope). " <u>Music Journal,</u> 14 (January, 1956), 34.

> A tribute to Manuel Garcia, who helped the laryngologist more than he helped the teacher of singing.

_____. "The Vocal Cords. " <u>Choral and Organ Guide,</u> 18 (May, 1965), 28.

> A concise explanation of the vocal cords.

Vrbanich, Lav. "On the Teaching of Voice. " <u>The NATS Bulletin,</u> 17 (October, 1960), 4.

> A condensed report of lectures on the subject "Practical Pedagogy of Singing. " These lectures were part of the program of the First Yugoslav Seminar for teachers of music, which was held in Dubrovnik during September, 1959.

Waengler, Hans-Heinrich. "Some Remarks and Observations on the Function of the Soft Palate. " <u>The NATS Bulletin,</u> 25 (October, 1968), 24.

> A comprehensive review of research relevant to the use of the soft palate in speech and song. The summary points to the need for more conclusive findings.

Waight, J. M. "Theory of Adjustable Resonators. " <u>Choral and Organ Guide,</u> 15 (January, 1962), 17-18.

> Tone is always produced under the same conditions. It is the resonance areas that change.

Walls, Robert B. "Tremolo. " <u>The NATS Bulletin,</u> 4 (June-July, 1948), 1.

> A definition, cause and remedy of the tremolo.

Walsh, Gertrude. "Speech and Singing. " <u>Etude,</u> October, 1947, p. 555.

> The correlation of diction in speech and in singing is advocated.

Waring, Fred. "What Voice Auditions Reveal. " <u>Music Journal,</u> 10 (March, 1952), 17.

> A noted choral conductor laments the inadequate preparation given young singers.

Warren, Leonard. "How to Build Confidence. " An interview by Rose Heylbut. <u>Etude,</u> March, 1949, p. 149.

Singing should be taught as an integral and natural act instead of as a series of separate and disassociated problems.

Waters, Crystal. "Singing Centers Everywhere." Etude, February, 1943a, p. 91.

Some self-help aids for those who want to learn to sing but do not have the opportunity to seek a teacher.

_____. "Communicating the Song's Real Message." Etude, October, 1943b, p. 571.

The very purpose of a song is to communicate a message.

_____. "Do You Want to Sing for Money?" Etude, December, 1946, p. 679.

Professional singers utilize all the technical skill they have developed to make the message clear and beautiful.

_____. "Is There a Break in Your Voice?" An interview by Annabel Comfort. Etude, April, 1949a, p. 221.

The writer has a novel approach to the management of the "break."

_____. "Singing before the Microphone." An interview by Annabel Comfort. Etude, June, 1949b, p. 351.

Radio singing is nothing more or less than good singing.

_____. "Steps to Artistic Vocal Success." An interview by Annabel Comfort. Etude, March, 1953, p. 11.

Conditions are given which allow the voice to fulfill itself in vocal performance.

_____. "How to Sing More Fluently." Etude, August, 1954, p. 17.

If the mind knows where it is going, and thoughts flow in that direction, so will the voice flow that same way.

Weede, Robert. "Intelligent Care of the Singing Voice." An interview by Rupert Holdern. Etude, December, 1947, p. 679.

Sensible advice, which includes comments on "covering" a tone.

Weer, Robert Lawrence. Your Voice. Los Angeles: By the Author, n. p., 1948.

Many generally accepted vocal concepts are present. The author's objections to a raised soft palate are extended and dogmatic.

Wehr, David A. "A Few Conductor 'Tips' to Singers." Choral and Organ Guide, 14 (January, 1961), 14.

A brief discussion primarily concerned with

posture and breathing.

Weiss, Deso A. "Discussion of the Neurochronaxic Theory
(Husson). " Archives of Otolaryngology, 70 (1959),
607-618.

    The basic experiments and assumptions of Husson's hypothesis are examined as to their scientific
validity; they are found unacceptable.

Welitsch, Ljuba. "Breathing Is Everything. " An interview
by Rose Heylbut. Etude, October, 1950, p. 18.

    Resonance, breathing and some principles of
practice are discussed.

Werrenrath, Reinald. "Singing Can Be Simple. " Etude,
February, 1951, p. 16.

    Having to master too many rules and theories
often confuses the vocal student instead of helping him.

Westerman, Carol F. "Research for Singers. " Music
Journal, 17 (March, 1959), 53.

    Personal teaching methods developed from scientific research are explained.

Westerman, Kenneth N. "Resonation. " Music Teachers
National Association. Volume of Proceedings for 1949.
Pittsburgh, Pa. , 1949.

    A comprehensive review of various theories on
resonance and a discussion of research which relates
to this acoustical phenomenon.

_____. "The Framework for Developing the Coordinated
Muscle Actions of Singing. " The NATS Bulletin, 6
(April-May, 1950), 2.

    A brief explanation of a principle expounded by
the author.

_____. "The Physiology of Vibrato. " The NATS Bulletin,
9 (January-February, 1953), 14.

    A review of research concerning the vibrato.
This is a notable addition to the literature.

_____. Emergent Voice. 2d ed. Ann Arbor, Mich. :
Carol F. Westerman, 1955.

    Emergent Voice is written on the working hypothesis that the study of skills in singing is not primarily the study of tone, but the study of the effect
upon tone of the muscle movements used in posture,
respiration, phonation, resonation, and articulation as
the tone emerges from the human body. The student
who wishes to make intelligent and rapid development in
the beauty and flexibility of his voice needs a knowledge
of how that voice emerges.

Wheeler, William. "The Problem of Pressures. " The
NATS Bulletin, 3 (September-October, 1946), 1.

The author uses the word "pressures" as synonymous with breath control. The ideas expressed are
conventional.

_____. "Voice Classification. " The NATS Bulletin, 6
(December, 1949-January, 1950), 10.

Often repeated, though sound, bases for voice
classification are given.

_____. "Diction--What It Is. " The NATS Bulletin, 7
(April-May, 1951), 7.

Pronunciation, articulation and enunciation are
defined with some brief comments.

_____. "Controlled Spontaneity in Singing. " The NATS
Bulletin, 10 (May, 1954), 8.

Singing is best when it is spontaneous, or seems
to be.   Devices and suggestions to achieve this goal
are listed.

*White, Ernest.   Science and Singing.   5th ed. , rev. Boston:
Crescendo Publishing Co. , 1969.

An exposition of the author's theory that the voice
is generated in the sinuses and not in the larynx.
The second to the fourth editions of this 1909 book
were published as The Light on the Voice Beautiful.

*_____. Sinus Tone Production.   1938.   Reprint. Boston:
Crescendo, 1970.

Whitlock, Weldon.   "The Importance of Personality. " The
NATS Bulletin, 17 (December, 1960), 24.

_____. "Voice Classification. " The NATS Bulletin, 19
(October, 1962), 4.

_____. "Stage Deportment. " The NATS Bulletin, 21
(December, 1964), 20.

_____. "Practical Use of Bel Canto. " The NATS Bulle-
tin, 22 (May, 1966a), 28.

_____. "The Responsibilities of Musical Talent. " Ameri-
can Music Teacher, 15 (May-June, 1966b), 40.

_____. "Singing--Yesterday and Today, A Comparison. "
The NATS Bulletin, 23 (December, 1966c), 4.

_____. Facets of the Singer's Art.   Champaign, Ill. :
Pro Musica Press, 1967.

The preceding five articles form a portion of this
valuable addition to the literature of vocal pedagogy.
With a flair for writing interesting material, the author
sets forth his views of the singing art which have been
drawn from a long experience of performing and teaching.

_____. Bel Canto for the Twentieth Century.   Champaign,
Ill. :   Pro Musica Press, 1968a.

Practical application of the principles of the bel

canto era is made. The writing is precise, lucid and
persuasive. Pure vowels, legato, the long unbroken
phrase, ornamentation, recitative and the problem of
the passaggio are discussed.
_____. "The Problem of the Passaggio. " The NATS
Bulletin, 24 (February, 1968b), 10.
        An informative article related to the "break" in
the voice. It is perhaps more helpful to the tenor than
to other voice classifications. A condensation of
chapter six in Bel Canto for the Twentieth Century.
_____. "Modern Vocal Pedagogy. " The NATS Bulletin,
26 (December, 1969), 11-13.
        Basic pedagogical principles for the discerning
voice instructor and a number of teaching problems
are discussed.
Whitworth, James R. "A Cinefluorographic Investigation of
the Supralaryngeal Adjustments in the Male Voice Accompanying the Singing of Low Tones and High Tones."
Unpublished Ph. D. dissertation, State University of
Iowa, 1961.
        A study was made of the changes which occurred
in the supralaryngeal structures of five tenors and five
baritones when moving from low pitches to high pitches.
Widoe, Russell. "A Big Lie?" Music Journal, 10 (September, 1952), 31.
        The "Big Lie" is the prevalence of double-talk,
meaningless phraseology and erroneous concepts used
by teachers of singing.
_____. "Science, Singers, and Sense. " Educational
Music Magazine, 34 (March-April, 1955), 12-13.
        When we teach singing we are working with the
human body as it is controlled by the human mind.
Wilcox, John C. "Time for Pedagogic Inventory. " Music
Teachers National Association. Volume of Proceedings
for 1944. Pittsburgh, Pa. , 1944a.
        Singing teachers are urged to measure carefully
the worth of traditional terminologies and avoid those
which are misleading and nebulous.
_____. "Fatuous Philosophy of the Famous. " Educa-
tional Music Magazine, 23 (March, 1944b), 29.
        The author wisely cautions against blindly follow-
ing the advice of a famous singer; his methods were
good for him, but not necessarily for others.
_____. "About Tone Placing. " Etude, June, 1944c,
p. 327.
_____. The Living Voice. Rev. ed. New York: Carl
Fischer, 1945.

The author's most important procedure is the de-
velopment and extended use by all voices of the lower
mechanism in progressively higher pitches.
Williams, Richard F.   "Bel Canto Reviewed. "   Music
    Journal, 25 (March, 1967), 44.
        The nebulous concepts of focusing and placement
    are stated as bel canto principles.
Williams, Tudor.   "Must You Sing. "   Etude, October, 1953,
    p. 17.
        Advice is given to the beginning singer regarding
    practice habits, selection of a teacher and possibilities
    for a career.
Williamson, John Finley.   "How to Classify Voices. "   Etude,
    June, 1950, p. 23.
_____.   "Correct Breathing for Singers. "   Etude, Part I,
    February, 1951a, p. 18 and Part II, March, 1951b,
    p. 22.
        Despite the elaborate theories advanced by many
    people, no thinking and no muscular control are re-
    quired for breathing.   The secret of correct normal
    breathing lies in good posture.
_____.   "Good Singing Requires Good Diction. "   Etude,
    September, 1951c, p. 23.
_____.   "The Importance of Vowel Coloring. "   Etude,
    October, 1951d, p. 23.
        Correct pronunciation of vowels helps to create
    the mood which the composer intended.
Wilson, Harry Robert.   "What! Another Voice Book?"
    Choir Guide, 4 (December, 1951), 21.
        In a series of articles, the author points to a
    number of basic faults of singing and offers excellent
    suggestions for their correction.
_____.   "Establishing the Resonance. "   Choir Guide,
    Part I, 5 (February, 1952a), 17-18 and Part II, 5
    (March, 1952b), 13-16.
_____.   "The Formation of Vowels. "   Choir Guide, 5
    (October, 1952c), 20.
_____.   "The Connection of Vowels. "   Choir Guide, 5
    (November, 1952d), 18.
Winsel, Regnier.   The Anatomy of Voice.   New York: Expo-
    sition Press, 1966.
        A book for teachers of singing written by a pupil
    of Douglas Stanley.   He continues the encouragement of
    external manipulation of the vocal mechanism.   The
    proper use of the registers is the central prevailing
    thought.   Recordings of prescribed "great singers of
    the past" are to be thoroughly studied.   Most of the

techniques suggested are not conventional.

Wise, Claude. _Applied Phonetics._   Englewood Cliffs, N. J. :
Prentice-Hall, 1957.

A standard work in the area of speech and
phonetics will be most useful to the voice teacher in a
better understanding of the International Phonetic Alphabet as a tool applied to singing diction.   A more
condensed approach may be found in the author's _Intro-
duction to Applied Phonetics._

Withers, A. M.   "Language and Song Symposium. "   _Modern
Language Journal,_ 29 (October, 1945), 461.

A statement of the possible contribution of modern
language study to music.   Helen Traubel, Richard
Crooks and Lauritz Melchior discuss the subject.

Wollmann, Anna M.   "Empirical Method versus the Scientific. "   _The NATS Bulletin,_ 9 (March-April, 1953), 20.

Both methods have merit and the author feels it
would seem unwise to say either approach is wrong.

Wooldridge, Warren B.   "Is There Nasal Resonance?"   _The
NATS Bulletin,_ 13 (October, 1956), 28-29.

Through experimental processes (packing cotton
into nasal passages up to the edge of the soft palate)
the author proves to his satisfaction that the term
"nasal resonance" is without validity in describing voice
quality.

Wragg, Gerald.   "The Singer's Language. "   _Musical Opinion,_
79 (June, 1956), 529-560.

The key to artistic singing is a true concept of
vowel formation.

Wright, Charles W.   "A Study of Concept Formation, Concept Learning and Vocal Pedagogy. "   Unpublished Ed. D.
dissertation, North Texas State University, 1969.

It is theorized in this study that certain vocal
techniques and their subordinate factors can be reduced
to a minimum number of inclusive vocal concepts.

Wyckoff, Olive.   _Why Do You Want to Sing._   New York: Exposition Press, 1955.

The writer strongly advocates directing the stream
of tone through an open throat, and decisively into the
nose and upon the hard palate, above the teeth.   "In
the masque" is a prevalent vocal concept.

York, Wynn.   "The F. M. Alexander Technique in Singing. "
The NATS Bulletin, 13 (May, 1957), 28-29.

A distinctive, all-encompassing technique of vocal
instruction is explained.

_____. "Stress and Vowel Values. " The NATS Bulletin,
16 (October, 1959), 10-12.
    The author stresses the importance of a singing
pronunciation which is free from artificiality, clear to
the listener and which retains as much as possible the
nuances of the spoken text.
_____. "The Use of Imagery in Posture Training. " The
NATS Bulletin, 19 (May, 1963), 6.
    A convincing rationale of the use of imagery in
singing instruction.
Young, Gerald Mackworth. What Happens in Singing. New
    York: Pitman Publishing Corp. , 1956.
    The author describes in simple language the main
physiological and acoustical facts of singing and how
these are related to the singer's own sensations and to
the principles of orthodox teaching.

Zemlin, W. R. ; Mason, Robert M. ; and Holstead, Lisa.
    "Notes on the Mechanics of Vocal Vibrato. " The NATS
    Bulletin, 28 (December, 1971), 22-26.
    The number of pitch and intensity modulations
used by four subjects ranged from five to five and one-
half per second.   The activity of the cricothyroid
muscle for all subjects appeared to be the single most
important factor relating to the production of vibrato.
Cricothyroid activity was seen to occur in phase with
the crests of the vibrato modulations.
Zerffi, William A.   "The Laryngologist's Place in Advising
    Vocalists. "   Musical America, 72 (January, 1952), 25.
    Many singers would sound better and last longer
if vocal teachers would seek the advice of competent
physiologists in helping them to eliminate methods of
tone emission injurious to the larynx.
_____. "Mail Pouch: Care of Vocal Cords. "   The New
York Times, 105 (January 1, 1956), Section 2, 7.
    The shortage of tenors is due to the fact they
misuse the voice more often.   Vocal problems are
discussed.
_____. "The Physiology of the Human Voice. " Music
Journal, 15 (January, 1957), 23.
    The writer emphasizes that the vocal organ is
not subject to conscious control.
_____. "Male and Female Voices. " Archives of Oto-
laryngology, 65 (1957), 7-10.
    The only difference between the male and female
larynx is one of size.   The author's principal concern

and emphasis is that the voice be sensibly used within the confines of the singer's best range.

SUBJECT INDEX TO THE BIBLIOGRAPHY

Under the appropriate subject headings, authors' names are given which refer to the complete listing in the bibliography. The year of publication is also provided when more than one item by the same author appears in the bibliography. Books from the bibliography were indexed only when the subject matter was generally confined to one topic or theme.

Acoustics for the Singer.   Borchers 1951; Culver; Daghlian; Fry and Manèn; Husson 1962; Long; Oncley; Stout 1955a; Taylor, Robert 1955, 1958

Basic Vocal Instruction Texts.   Granville; Haywood; Liebling 1956; Samuel 1950; Sunderman 1958; Tkach 1948. See also Class Voice Texts.

Beginning Vocal Instruction/First Lessons.   Franca 1951b; Fuchs 1952; McDonald; McLean 1951b; Mallett 1962; Newton, Grace; Randegger; Rice, William; Rosewall; Ross 1948; Sabin 1952; Samuel 1948

Bel Canto.   Alberti; Casselman 1950; Duey 1951; El Tour; Franca 1959; Kay; Reed 1950; Rogers, Francis 1944; Seward; Stignani; Strongin; Whitlock 1966a, 1968a; Williams, Richard

Bernoulli Principle.   Vennard 1961 a

Breath Control.   Bollew 1952a; Sharnova 1949; Tourel

Breathiness.   Borchers 1950b

Breathing.   Armstrong 1945b; Bouhuys, Proctor, and Mead; Bullard; Campbell; Casselman 1951; Dwyer; Garlinghouse 1951; Gigli; Gunnison; Hardy; Jones, Arthur; Jones, William E. ; Kelsey 1951a; Korst; Large 1971; Lester 1957; Li; MacRae; Murtaugh and Campbell; Nicholas; Otis, Feen, and Rahn; Protheroe 1945; Ross 1955; Schenk; Tarneaud; Welitsch; Williamson 1951a, 1951b

Career in Singing.   Cecil; Eddy; Elmo; Fields 1957; Liebling
    1950

Chest Tones.   Fuchs 1954

Choosing a Teacher.   Buckingham; Harvey; Radamsky; Wil-
    liams, Tudor

Choral-Vocal Conflicts.   Beachy; Casselman 1952; Crawford
    1967; Veld

Class Voice.   Angell 1950, 1956, 1957, 1959; Huntley;
    MENC; Peterson, Abel; Ross 1948

Class Voice Texts.   Bowen and Mook; Cates; Christy 1965,
    1967; Stanton; Taylor, Bernard 1950; Trusler and Ehret

Classification.   AATS 1956; Armstrong 1944a; Bagley 1947;
    Banks; Craig, Mary 1951b; Husson 1957a; Landeau;
    Large 1968; Large, Iwata, and von Leden; Maurice-
    Jacquet 1943; Siegle; Wheeler 1950; Whitlock 1962;
    Williamson 1950

Comparative Approach to Vocal Pedagogy.   Collins; Farley;
    Fields 1947; Ross 1961a

Coordination.   Crawford 1951; Lester 1951; Novotna

Coup de Glotte.   Kelsey 1950; Vennard and Isshiki

Covering.   Bollew 1956; Fuchs 1951b; Weede

Diction.   Adler 1965, 1967; Belisle; Bollew 1956; Camburn;
    Cashmore; Coffin; Craig, Don; Downes; Eberhart;
    Fields and Bender; Fonticoli; Green; Hemus; Lee; Mac-
    Collin; Marshall 1953, 1956; Nelson, Howard; Nelson
    and Tiffany; Newton, George 1954; Owen; Pitts; Rasely;
    Ringel 1947, 1948; Schenk; Schmidt 1950; Sharnova
    1947; Strickling; Thornfield; Vail; Wheeler 1951; Wil-
    liamson 1951c; York 1959

Dissertations, Unpublished Doctoral.   Appelman 1953; Arant;
    Arment; Davis; Dickson; Farley; Govich; Gunn; Harper,
    Andrew; Hohn; Johnson, Donald; Johnson, Merion;
    Jones, Arthur; Lyon; Manley; Nelson, Howard; O'Ban-
    non; Peterson, Abel; Ross 1955; Schmalstieg; Scott,
    David; Shearon; Siegle; Sullivan; Whitworth; Wright

Dramatic Training.   Hensellek; Stocker

Dynamics.   Angell 1952; Ekstrom; Isshiki; Manley; Rubin
    1963; Rubin, LeCover, and Vennard; Scott, David;
    Stout 1944

Electromyographic Research.   Vennard and Hirano 1971;
    Vennard, Hirano, and Fritzell 1971; Vennard, Hirano,
    and Ohala 1970

Emotion.   Freer 1959b; Garns; Vennard 1971

Empirical-Scientific Conflict.   See Scientific-versus-Em-
    pirical.

Exercises.   See Vocalises.

Falsetto.   Bollew 1954b; Frisell 1954; Fuchs 1954, 1956;
    Ross 1949, 1956; Vennard 1955

Foreign Language Singing.   Adler 1965, 1967; Nikolaidi 1952;
    Thomson; Withers

Head Voice.   Herbert-Caesari 1950, 1951b; Hisey 1971

High Tones.   Freemantel; Fuchs 1950b; Ross 1956; Rushmore
    1967c; Vennard 1953b

Historical Treatises.   "Anatomy of Voice"; Bacilly; Bacon;
    Bérard; Foreman; Mancini; Tosi; Ulrich

History of Singing/Vocal Instruction.   Baker 1965; Cassel-
    man 1950; Duey 1958; Freud; London, S. J.; Stults
    1950; Whitlock 1966c

Imitation.   Hines; Svanholm; Tucker 1962

Instrumental Training/Performance by the Singer.   Charles
    1946; Duschak 1962; Miller, Rosalie 1957

Interpretation.   Barrett; Buchanan; Djanel; Drew; Ewing;
    Freer 1959a; Frijsh; Gilliland 1967; Greene, Harry P.;
    Holler; Holst; Jacobi 1961a; Kelsey 1951c; LaForge;
    Lehmann, Lotte 1946a, 1946b; Lewando, Olga; Mann-
    ing; Miller, Richard; Moore; Newton, George 1950;
    O'Bannon; Protheroe 1950; Rice, Melanie; Sayão;
    Schiøtz; Schnelker; Waters 1943b

Intonation.   Coleman; Madsen 1966; Vennard 1956

Judging Vocal Performance.   Rothmüller

Laryngoscope.   Gange; Voorhees 1956

Lesson Plans.   Haywood; Ross 1948, 1959; Sunderman 1970

Longevity.   DeLuca 1946; Hempel

Low Tones.   Armstrong 1944b; Berglund; Rushmore 1967e, 1967g

Messa di Voce.   Theman

Methods, Vocal.   Beckett; Bellows 1963; Brody and Wester-
man; DeLuca 1950; DeYoung; Gilliland 1955; Lehman,
E.; Matthen; Ragatz; Rose, Arnold 1955; Ross 1945;
Taylor, Bernard 1951b; Vennard 1958; Westerman,
Carol

Mezza-voce.   Kipnis

Musical Style.   Duschak 1969

Musicianship for the Singer.   Best; Charles 1953; Fuchs
1950a; Judd 1957; Kockritz

Nasality.   Dickson; Hisey 1971

Natural Singing.   Albanese; Cornwall; de los Angeles; Farrell 1947; Litante; Nelson, Russell; Vennard 1953a;
Werrenrath

Neurochronaxic Theory.   Husson 1956; Rubin 1960; Siegle;
Vennard 1957; von Leden; Weiss

Objectives in Singing Instruction.   Appelman 1968; Ewing;
Foote; Fox; Garlinghouse 1955; Gilliland 1954, 1965;
Griffith; Moe; Ross 1947; Taylor, Bernard 1951b

Open Throat.   Borchers 1950a; Sharnova 1964

Passaggio.   Whitlock 1968a, 1968b

Pathology, Vocal.   Bolstad; Ferguson; Greene, Margaret;
Moses 1959; Rubin 1966

Phonation. Bollew 1953; Golde; Gould 1949; Herbert-Caesari
    1951c; Husson 1956, 1960; Rubin 1960; Tarnóczy; van
    den Berg 1957, 1958; Vennard 1959b; von Leden

Phonetics. Adler 1965, 1967; Aikin; Appelman 1959, 1967;
    Conley 1954; Kantner and West; Wise

Physiology. Campbell; Carp; Horowitz; Husson 1957b, 1960;
    Jones, Arthur; McClosky; Meano; Proctor; Simmons
    1965; Zerffi 1957

Physiology--Larynx. Hollien 1960; Hollien and Curtis; Hus-
    son 1956; Negus; Phemister; Pressman and Kelemen;
    Punt; Sonninen 1954, 1956

Planigraphic Studies. Appelman 1953; Griesman

Professional Cooperation. DeYoung 1946; Huls; Madsen 1965

Quality. Mowe 1955

Range. Gardini 1947; Johnson, Donald; Madeira

Recordings, Use of. Arant; Corelli; Ehret; Hoffelt; Mc-
    Collum; Varkonyi

Registers. Appelman 1953; Austin; Berglund; Fields 1970;
    Large, Iwata, and von Leden; Nelson, Howard; Reid
    1965; Ruth 1963; Taff; van den Berg 1963, 1968; Ven-
    nard 1959a; Waters 1949a

Research, Review of Vocal. Brodnitz 1961, 1962; Fields
    1947, 1970; Heaton and Hargens; Hisey 1971; Perkins,
    Sawyer, and Harrison

Resonance. Appelman 1959; Armstrong 1947, 1945c; Banks;
    Davis; DeBruyn; Fuchs 1965; Golde; Hinman; Jones,
    William E.; Mudd; Ruth 1966; Stout; Vennard 1964a;
    Waengler; Waight; Westerman, Kenneth 1949; Wilson
    1952a; Wooldridge

Rhythm. Freer 1961

Scientific Approach Not Desirable. Briggs; Gardini 1950;
    Kelsey 1952

Scientific Knowledge Desirable. Borchers 1947; Brodnitz 1954;

Madsen 1965; Peterson, Abel; Vennard 1961b

Scientific-versus-Empirical.   Craig, Mary 1954; De Bidoli;
    Duey 1958; Garlinghouse 1970; Hisey 1970; Kelsey 1952;
    Widoe 1955; Wollmann

Self-Instruction.   See Teach Yourself.

Sing as You Speak.   Bollew 1951; Middleton

Singing in English.   Akmajian; Easton; Freer 1956; Miller, J.
    Oscar; Schoep; Uris 1956, 1971

Sinus Tone Production.   White 1969, 1970

Soft Palate.   Armstrong 1945a, 1945c

Song, Technical Aid.   Carson

Song-versus-Technique.   Gerry 1949

Sopranos.   Bjørklund; Flechtner; Frisell 1966

Spectrographic Studies.   Appelman 1953; Arment; Fry and
    Manén; Luchsinger and Arnold; Potter, Kopp, and Kopp;
    Taff; Vennard and Irwin

Speech and Singing.   Bairstow and Greene; Bakkegard;
    Miller, H. Thomas; Thibault; Walsh

Stage Fright.   Bagley 1949; Martin, Anna Y. ; Runkel

Standards, Vocal.   Bellows 1960; Mowe 1951; Van der Veer

Straight-Tone.   Christiansen

Studio Practices.   Bassett; Van Grove

Teach Yourself.   Granville; Thorpe

Teacher Personality Traits.   Coladarci; Fuchs 1953

Teacher-Pupil Relationship.   Cady; Clark; DeYoung 1953,
    1957; Duey 1959; Hill; Stewart; Toren; Vennard 1964b

Tenors.   Frisell 1964; Gafni; Jagel

Tensions.   Thebom 1948

Terminology, Vocal.   AATS 1969; Cox, George; Ehrhart;
     Fields 1952; Lukken 1945; Mowe 1952, 1956; Taylor,
     Bernard 1951a; van den Berg and Vennard; Wilcox 1944a

Tone (color).   Normelli; Pitts 1943; Rogers, Francis 1943;
     Shaw, Hollace; Thomas

Tonsillectomy.   Douty; Voorhees 1953b

Trill.   Franca 1951a

Vibrato.   Bjørklund; Deutsch and Clarkson; Field-Hyde 1946;
     Kelsey 1951b; Lukken 1956; Mason and Zemlin; Sacer-
     dote; Smith, Ethel; Vennard and von Leden; Walls;
     Westerman, Kenneth 1953; Zemlin, Mason, and Holstead

Vocal Hygiene.   Bollew 1954a; Brodnitz 1953; Cooper;
     Felderman; Lester 1950; Rodman 1958; Rubin 1966;
     Schweisheimer; Seltzer; Voorhees 1953a, 1955; Zerffi
     1952, 1956

Vocalises.   Bori; Hopkins; Lukken 1946; Skiles

Voice Pedagogy, an Overview.   Foote; Kelsey (Grove's);
     Leonard; Mowe 1954; NATS

Voice Strain.   Brown, Oren 1958

Voice Therapy.   Brown, Oren 1953

Vowel Formants.   Flechtner; McGinnis, Elnick, and Kraich-
     man

Vowel Modification.   Hohn; Taff; Treash 1947

Vowels.   Cohen; Delattre; Gigli; Gunn; Gunnison; Harper,
     Andrew; Howie and Delattre; Johnson, Merion; Mac-
     Collin; Margolis; Russell; Schmalstieg; Shenk; Triplett;
     Truby; Williamson 1951d; Wilson 1952c, 1952d; Wragg

Why Study Singing.   Ettinger; Kagen

Young Voices.   Crawford 1948; Dickenson; Simpson

SUMMARY OF BOOKS LISTED IN THE BIBLIOGRAPHY

Adler, Kurt.   The Art of Accompanying and Coaching

_____ .   Phonetics and Diction in Singing

Aiken, W. A.   The Voice: An Introduction to Practical
Phonology

American Academy of Teachers of Singing.   Terminology in
the Field of Singing

Angell, Warren M.   The Advanced Vocalist

_____ .   The Beginning Vocalist

_____ .   The Progressing Vocalist

_____ .   Vocal Approach

Apel, Willi.   Harvard Dictionary of Music

Appelman, D. Ralph.   The Science of Vocal Pedagogy

Bachner, Louis.   Dynamic Singing

Bacilly, Bénigne de.   A Commentary upon the Art of Proper
Singing

Bacon, Richard Mackenzie.   Elements of Vocal Science

Bagley, Silvia R.   Viewpoint for Singers

Bairstow, Edward C., and Greene, Harry Plunket.   Singing
Learned from Speech

Baker, George.   The Common Sense of Singing

_____ .   This Singing Business

Banks, Louis.   Voice Culture

Barbareux-Parry, Mame. Education from Within

Beckman, Gertrude W. Tools for Speaking and Singing

Behnke, Kate Emil. The Technique of Singing

Bérard, Jean-Baptiste. L'Art du chant

Bergman, Adolph. Creating and Developing a Singing Voice

Berkman, Al. Singing Takes More than a Voice

Bowen, George O., and Mook, Kenneth C. Song and Speech

Brodnitz, Friedrich S. Keep Your Voice Healthy

_____. Vocal Rehabilitation

Brown, Ralph Morse. The Singing Voice

Brown, Sarle. Super-Pronunciation in Singing

Brown, William Earl. Vocal Wisdom--Maxims of Giovanni
    Battista Lamperti

Bryant, Chauncey Earle. Scientific Singing versus Individu-
    alized Guessing

Campbell, E. J. Moran. The Respiratory Muscles and the
    Mechanics of Breathing

Cates, Millard. Guide for Young Singers

Christy, Van A. Expressive Singing, Vol. I

_____. Expressive Singing, Vol. II

_____. Foundations in Singing

Cor, August, E. The Magic of Voice

Cranmer, Arthur. The Art of Singing

Culver, Charles. Musical Acoustics

Davies, David Ffrangcon. The Singing of the Future

Dengler, Clyde R.   Read This and Sing

DeYoung, Richard.   The Singer's Art

Duey, Philip A.   Bel Canto in Its Golden Age

Duval, John H.   Svengali's Secrets and Memoirs of the
        Golden Age

Field-Hyde, Frederick C.   The Art and Science of Voice
        Training

_____.   Vocal Vibrato, Tremolo and Judder

Fields, Victor A.   The Singer's Glossary

_____.   Training the Singing Voice

_____, and Bender, James F.   Voice and Diction

Flack, Nannette, and Sherman, Leila.   Singing Can Be
        Ecstasy

Foreman, Edward, ed.   The Porpora Tradition

Fracht, J. Albert, and Robinson, Emmett.   Sing Well,
        Speak Well

_____.   _____.   You, Too, Can Sing

Franca, Ida.   Manual of Bel Canto

Freemantel, Frederic.   High Tones and How to Sing Them

Frisell, Anthony.   The Soprano Voice

_____.   The Tenor Voice

Fuchs, Viktor.   The Art of Singing and Voice Technique

Gamber, Eugene.   Your Guide to Successful Singing

Garcia, Manuel.   Hints on Singing

Gardiner, Julian.   A Guide to Good Singing and Speech

Gilliland, Dale V.   Guidance in Voice Education

Gould, Herbert.   Handbook for Voice Students

Granville, Charles N.   The Granville Vocal Study Plan

Graves, Richard M.   Singing for Amateurs

Greene, Harry Plunket.   Interpretation in Song

Greene, Margaret C. L.   The Voice and Its Disorders

Harper, Ralph M.   G-Suiting the Body

Haywood, F. H.   Universal Song

Heaton, Wallace, and Hargens, C. W., eds.   An Interdis-
   ciplinary Index of Studies in Physics, Medicine and
   Music Related to the Human Voice

Henderson, William James.   The Art of Singing

Herbert-Caesari, Edgar F.   The Alchemy of Voice

_____ .   The Science and Sensations of Vocal Tone

_____ .   Vocal Truth

_____ .   The Voice of the Mind

Howe, Albert P.   Practical Principles of Voice Production

Husler, Frederick, and Rodd-Marling, Yvonne.   Singing, the
   Physical Nature of the Vocal Organ

Judd, Percy.   Musicianship for Singers

_____ .   Vocal Technique

Judson, Lyman, and Weaver, A. T.   Voice Science

Kagen, Sergius.   On Studying Singing

Kantner, Claude E., and West, Robert.   Phonetics

Kay, Elster.   Bel Canto and the Sixth Sense

Kelsey, Franklyn.   The Foundations of Singing

Kester, George. Your Singing Potential

Klein, Joseph J., and Schjeide, Ole A. Singing Technique:
      How to Avoid Vocal Trouble

Kwartin, Bernard. New Frontiers in Vocal Art

_____. Vocal Pedagogy

Lagourge, Charles. The Secret

Lamberti, Carlo. Improving Your Voice

Lamson, Martha, ed. Duval's Svengali on Singing

Lawson, Franklin D. The Human Voice

Lawson, James Terry. Full-Throated Ease

Lehmann, Lilli. How to Sing

Lehmann, Lotte. More Than Singing

Levinson, Grace. The Singing Artist

Liebling, Estelle. The Estelle Liebling Vocal Course

Litante, Judith. A Natural Approach to Singing

Longo, Teodosio. Fundamentals of Singing and Speaking

Luchsinger, Richard, and Arnold, Godfrey. Voice-Speech-
      Language

McClosky, David Blair. Your Voice at Its Best

MacDonald, Florence. Think Intelligently--Sing Convincingly

Mancini, Giambattista. Practical Reflections on Figured
      Singing

Mansion, Madeleine. How to Sing

Marafioti, P. Mario. Caruso's Method of Voice Production

Marshall, Madeleine. The Singer's Manual of English Diction

Martino, Alfredo. Today's Singing

Mary Rosemarie, Sister. See and Sing

_____. Vocal High Fidelity

Maurice-Jacquet, H. The Road to Successful Singing

Meano, Carlo. The Human Voice in Speech and Song

Metzger, Zerline Muhlman. Individual Voice Patterns

Montell, Marjorie. Montell Vocal Technique

Moore, Gerald. Singer and Accompanist

Moses, Paul J. The Voice of Neurosis

Negus, V. E. The Comparative Anatomy and Physiology of the Larynx

Nevina, Viola. Voice Production in Singing

Orton, James L. Voice Culture Made Easy

Peterson, Paul W. Natural Singing and Expressive Conducting

Potter, Ralph K.; Kopp, George A.; and Kopp, Harriet Green. Visible Speech

Punt, Norman A. The Singer's and Actor's Throat

Puritz, Elizabeth. The Teaching of Elisabeth Schumann

Randegger, Alberto. Singing

Reid, Cornelius. Bel Canto: Principles and Practices

_____. The Free Voice

Rice, William. Basic Principles of Singing

Ririe, Edna C. Voice through Vitality

Roma, Lisa. The Science and Art of Singing

Rose, Arnold. The Singer and the Voice

Rosewall, Richard. Handbook of Singing

Ross, William E. Secrets of Singing

_____. Sing High, Sing Low

Rushmore, Robert. The Singing Voice

Russell, G. Oscar. The Vowel, Its Physiological Mechanism
    as Shown by X-Ray

Samuel, John Owen. Modern Voice Lessons

Schiøtz, Aksel. The Singer and His Art

Scott, Charles Kennedy. The Fundamentals of Singing

Shaw, George Bernard. Shaw on Music

Stanley, Douglas. The Science of Voice

_____. Your Voice: Applied Science of Vocal Art

_____; Chadbourne, E. Thomas A.; and Chadbourne,
    Norma J. Singer's Manual

Stanton, Royal. Steps to Singing for Voice Class

Sunderman, Lloyd F. Artistic Singing: Its Tone Production
    and Basic Understandings

_____. Basic Vocal Instructor

Taylor, Bernard U. Group Voice--A Systematic Course in
    Singing for Use in Group Instruction

Taylor, Robert M. Acoustics for the Singer

Thornfield, Emil A. Singing Diction, from Thornfield's
    "Tongue and Lip Training"

Thorpe, Clarence R. Teach Yourself to Sing

Tkach, Peter. Vocal Artistry

_____. Vocal Technic

Tomlins, William L.   Song and Life

Tosi, Pietro Francesco.   Observations on the Florid Song

Trusler, Ivan, and Ehret, Walter.   Functional Lessons in
    Singing

Ulrich, Bernhard.   Concerning the Principles of Vocal Train-
    ing in the A Capella Period, 1474-1640

Uris, Dorothy.   To Sing in English

Vennard, William.   Singing: The Mechanism and the Technic

Weer, Robert Lawrence.   Your Voice

Westerman, Kenneth N.   Emergent Voice

White, Ernest.   Science and Singing

_____.   Sinus Tone Production

Whitlock, Weldon.   Bel Canto for the Twentieth Century

_____.   Facets of the Singer's Art

Wilcox, John C.   The Living Voice

Winsel, Regnier.   The Anatomy of Voice

Wise, Claude.   Applied Phonetics

Wyckoff, Olive.   Why Do You Want to Sing

Young, Gerald Mackworth.   What Happens in Singing

INDEX

Abdominal breathing, 44
Accompaniment, dependency
  upon, 37
Acoustics, 82, 96
Adult vocal range, 97
Aerodynamic principle, 64
Aesthetics, 138
Ah vowel, 149
Articulation, defined, 140
Artistic performance,
  criteria of, 169
Arytenoid cartilages, 63
Attack, defined 74; high
  tone, 112; improvement
  of, 74
Auditory sense, 131
Aural concepts, 131

Bass, 97
Beginners, first lessons,
  33; handling, 30
Bibliography, annotated 11,
  179
Bone conduction, 134
Breath, capacity, 55, 57;
  economy of, 54; renewal,
  56; support, 58
Breath control, by phrasing,
  48; interpretational, 48;
  intuitive, 55; natural, 46,
  57; psychological approach,
  46; technical approach, 47
Breath pressure, 55; con-
  trols dynamics, 56, 123
Breathing, defined, 41;
  mouth and nose, 52, 57;
  physiological factors, 44;
  postural controls, 49, 57;

pre-vocal training, 44,
  57; primary, 41; respiratory function described,
  41; voluntary, 50, 57
Breathing action, abdominal,
  44; coordinations, 83;
  costal, 44, 58; diaphragmatic, 44, 51, 57; mus-
  cles, 45; quantitative factors, 54; speed of, 56
Bucco-pharyngeal, 73

Categories, total number of,
  7
Chanting, 149
Chest, cavity, 89; expan-
  sion, 45; position, 54;
  register, 102, 104; re-
  sonance, 89
Citations, mode of, 11
Classifying voices, criteria
  for, 30
Compass (vocal), 97
Concepts, correlations of,
  10; defined, 9
Consonants, as antivocal elements, 143; defined, 145;
  exaggeration of, 154; importance of, 146, 156;
  production of, 153; tone
  interrupters, 154
Contralto, 99
Coordination, 64; its im-
  portance, 21; total, 67, 82
Coup de glotte, 76
Covering, 116
Crico-arytenoid muscles, 63

Declamation in singing, 147
Diaphragm, action of, 44
Diction, defined, 140; gen-
    eral considerations, 142;
    lingual controls, 70, 150;
    psychological approach,
    146; technical approach,
    149
Diminishing and swelling,
    125
Dynamics, defined, 120;
    governed by hearing, 122;
    gradation of vocal volume,
    121; indirect approach,
    122; methods of control-
    ling, 122; physiological
    controls, 126; psycholog-
    ical approach, 122; related
    to breathing, 123; related
    to resonance, 123; theo-
    retical considerations, 120

Ear training, defined, 129;
    general considerations,
    129; importance of, 129;
    methodological consider-
    ations, 132; psychological
    approach, 132; technical
    approach, 135
Economy of effort prin-
    ciple, 25
Emotional emphasis, 161
Empirical knowledge, 16,
    39
Enunciation, defined, 140
Epiglottis, 145
European languages, 165
Exaggeration as a device,
    154
Expression, defined, 158
Expressional intent, 90

Facial expressions, 168
Falsetto, 96, 99; defined,
    102; female, 104; mech-
    anism, 100; register, 102

Falsetto tones, 108; legiti-
    macy of, 108
First lessons, 33
Focus, defined, 92
Focusing the voice, 95
Foreign language study, 165
Formant, low and high, 92
Freedom in singing, 24

Glottal muscles, 122
Glottis, 60, 123; stroke of,
    75

Habit formation, 22
Half-voice, 126
Head cavities, 84
Head register, 102
Head resonance, 84, 94
Head voice, 96, 104
Hearing, 131, 133
High tones, 112; fallacy of,
    110, 119
Hoarseness, 148
Humming, value of, 94

Ideas, exchange of, 8
Imagery, defined, 132; role
    of, 132
Imitation, defined, 136, 139
Individual differences, 160
Individuality of voices, 7,
    137
Information, sources of, 177
Inhibitions, overcoming, 26
Intensity, defined, 120; de-
    grees of, 122
Interferences, muscular, 29
International Phonetic Alpha-
    bet, 155
Interpretation, defined, 158;
    elements of, 166; im-
    portance of, 158; individ-
    ual differences, 160;
    methods of cultivating, 161;

performance aspects, 168;
psychological approach,
101; technical approach,
163; theoretical considerations, 158
Intoning, 149
Italian language as a
medium, 145, 149

Jaw, 69; position, 150

Language study, foreign,
165
Laryngeal, action, 64;
muscles, 74
Larynx, position of, 73;
research, 74
Legato, 167
Lessons, vocal, 33
Letting versus striving, 25
Lingual movement, 70, 150
Lips, 151
Loud versus soft practice,
124
Loudness, defined, 120
Lungs, capacity, 55, 57

Male, compass, 97;
falsetto, 96
Mask, 85
Mechanism, heavy-light, 90
Mechanists, 16, 40
Memorizing songs, 166
Mental control of vocal
tone, 22, 68, 109, 122,
132, 147
Messa di voce, 125
Mezza voce, 126
Mezzo-soprano, 97
Mouth, as resonator, 88,
95; breathing, 52; roof
of, 71, 77
Muscle action, 80
Muscles, laryngeal, 74;
coordinations, 83
Muscular interferences, 29
Musical, scale, 113,
phrase, 167
Myoelastic theory, 62

Nasal cavities, 86
Nasality, 72
Natural breathing, 46, 57
Natural voice, defined, 23
Nose, 53
Note connection, 166

Objectives, educational, 20
Objectives, Teaching Sing-
ing, 9
Open throat, 72
Oral, 69
Oral pharynx, 58
Organization, Teaching Sing-
ing, 10
Orificial controls, 52, 78
Overtones, 95, 145

Palate, 71, 77
Passaggio, 115
Pedagogy, vocal, 13; defined,
13; methodological considerations, 16; physiological
approach, 16; problems, 7;
psychological approach, 22;
schools of thought, 7;
technical approach, 28;
theoretical considerations,
13; two-fold approach, 16
Performance aspects, 168
Personality, 169; and singing voice, 162; defined,
162
Pharynx, 58, 88
Phonation, 60; and breathing,
64; defined, 60; experi-
mental findings, 62, 74;
open throat concept, 72;

physiological factors, 63; psychological approach, 67; theories of, 62

Phonetics, defined, 142; International Phonetic Alphabet, 155

Phrasing, 167

Piano accompaniment, 37

Pitch, deviations, 76; high and low, 110, 119; range, 97

Placement, vocal, 93

Pneumophonic synergy, 65

Posture, 49

Practice, defined, 36; hints for, 37; piano accompaniment, 37; principles, of, 36, 111; silent, 37; soft versus loud, 124; supervision of, 36

Professional singers, 173

Professional standards, 12

Pronunciation, 140

Psychological approach, in breath control, 46; in diction, 146; in dynamics, 122; in ear training, 132; in interpretation, 161; in phonation, 67; in range, 109; in resonance, 90; in vocal pedagogy, 19

Published data, reliability of, 7

Quality, vocal, 92

Range, defined, 97; main divisions, 97; methods of cultivating, 109; psychological approach, 109; technical approach, 110

Recordings, use of, 136

Registers, blending, 114; causes and action of, 99, 105; coordination of, 114;

fallacy of, 101; number of, 106; theory of, 99; whistle, 118

Relaxation, a factor in voice training, 24, 39

Research, aims, purposes and incentives, 9; area defined, 10; plan of, 10; problems for, 7

Resonance, acoustical factors, 82, 96; defined, 80, 82; experimental findings, 82; in vowel sounds, 95; methodological considerations, 90; nasal, 86; physiological factors, 84; psychological approach, 90; quality as a guide, 92; technical approach, 92; theories of, 80

Resonators, vocal, 87, 89, 94

Ribs, action of, 45

Roentgenograms, 105

Scale, defined, 113

Scale practice, importance of, 113

Scientific and pedagogical viewpoints reconciled, 40

Scientific research, modern, 9

Score, deviations from, 170

Self-expression in singing, 26

Self-listening, importance of, 133

Sensation, a guide to singing, 134

Silent practice, 37

Sing-as-you-speak approach, 27

Singing, benefits of, 17; can everyone sing, 18; components of, 7; defined, 13; guiding principles, 20

Singing art, its complexity, 7

Singing compared to speaking, 27

Singing profession, causes of confusion, 7; exchange of ideas, 8

Singing voice, characteristics of, 13; training defined, 15; pedagogical aspects, 19

Sinus, function of, 85; vibration in, 86

Self-listening, 133

Soft singing as a technique, 124

Song analysis, various factors, 168

Song approach, 34, 57

Song literature, choice of, 164

Soprano, 97

Sostenuto, 167

Sources of information, 177

Speaking as a teaching device, 147, 156

Speaking the song, 164

Spectrographs, 118, 153

Speech analogy, 147

Spontaneous singing, 24, 39

Staccato, 167

Standardization in vocal teaching, 21, 38

Striving versus letting, 25

Subject matter covered, 11

Summary and interpretation sections, pedagogy, 38; breathing, 57; phonation, 78; resonance, 95; range, 117; dynamics, 126; ear training, 138; diction, 156; interpretation, 170

Support, vocal, 58

Swelling and diminishing, 125

Tape recorders, 134

Teaching, lack of standards, 8; use of songs, 34, 57

Teaching methods, appraisal of, 40; defined, 16, 17; inconsistency of, 8; standardization of, 21, 38

Technical approach, defined, 28; breath control, 49; cultivating range, 110; diction, 149; dynamics, 123; ear training, 135; interpretation, 163; phonation, 69; resonance, 92

Tenor, 97

Tensions, 29

Terminologies, conflicting, 7

Text, comes before tone, 163; mastery of, 163

Thorax, 59

Throat, 72, 73

Thyro-arytenoid muscles, 63, 106

Thyroid cartilage, 103

Timbre, 92

Tonal imagery, 83, 132, 139

Tone, and word interrelated, 164; characteristics of, 83, 92; mental concepts, 68, 83, 90; quality, 83, 84, 92

Tone color, 167

Tongue, 145; positions, 71, 88, 150

Trachea, 59

Tremolo, 76

Uvula, 71

Velum, 71

Vibrato, 92; action, 76; and tremolo, compared, 76; defined, 76; experimental findings, 76

Visualization, 68, 83, 90

Vocal act, constituent elements, 23

Vocal action, involuntary,
    23, 39
Vocal cavities, 87
Vocal cords, action of, 62,
    78; defined, 62; elasticity
    of, 63, 66; energy applied
    to, 78; excitability, 33;
    segmental vibration, 62;
    synonyms for, 60
Vocal functions, its com-
    plexity, 62, 95
Vocal models, use of, 135
Vocal study, benefits of, 17,
    38; prerequisites of, 18;
    when to begin, 19
Vocal tract, 95, 109; ab-
    sorption of tone in, 82
Vocal training period, 19
Voice, analogies, 65;
    characteristics, 62, 137;
    controlled by ear, 133;
    placement, 93
Voice culture, 15
Voice production, 65
Voice teachers classified, 16
Voix mixte, 105, 118
Vowel, factors in diction,
    143; formant, 144; mould,
    151; purity, 143; reson-
    ance, 95; shaping, 143, 150
Vowels, ah, 149; altered,
    152, 156; attack, 152;
    characteristics, 143; im-
    portance of, 143; the
    vehicle of voice, 142

Whisper as a device, 148
"Whole" concept of singing,
    66
Whole methods of instruc-
    tion, 66
Whole versus part methods,
    66

Yawning as a device, 73